The
PRACTICE *of* CLASSICAL
PALMISTRY

HAND OF A SUCCESSFUL PROMINENT BUSINESSMAN

FAIRLY SHORT FINGERS - IMPATIENT - AN EXECUTIVE PLANNER - LEAVES DETAILS TO OTHERS. WIDELY SPREAD FINGERS GENEROUS, A CURIOUS MIND.

LARGE JUPITER FINGER (BROAD)
AMBITIOUS, PUSHY,
ISLAND IN EARLY
LIFE LINE - A
SERIOUS CHILDHOOD
ILLNESS APX. AGE 7-8
ACCOMPANIED BY A DOT -
PROBABLY HIGH FEVER.
JUPITER (1) BENDING
A COLLECTOR

DEVELOPED 2/3RD DIGIT
A GOURMET -
CROSSLINES ON LIFE LINE -
STRESS AFFECTING HIS HEALTH -
(DUE TO WOMEN)

HEAD LINE ATTACHED TO
LIFELINE - ATTACHED TO HIS
FAMILY - CLOSE-KNIT FAMILY

LONG HEAD LINE - GOOD MEMORY
GOOD MATH APTITUDE
STRONG DEEP CLEAR HEAD LINE -
A MAN WHO FOLLOWS THRU

WHORLS ON SATURD TIPS
ON JUP TOO

CONSTANTLY
ON THE
GO
ORIGINAL
IDEAS

PRONOUNCED
APOLLO LINE
SUCCESSFUL
IN BUSINESS
GOOD AT
GAMBLING

POINTED
PINKY
GOOD TALKER
SALES APTITUDE

HEART ON
BEGINNING
UNDER
SATURN
FINGER -
LOYAL IN
LOVE. SERIOUS
SEXUALLY
CONSERVATIVE

POWERFUL
LUNA -
IMAGINATIVE

A BROAD THUMB -
COURAGEOUS
OUTSPOKEN

BROAD
2ND PHALANGE
BLUNT

SHORT THUMB
HASTY - AGGRESSIVE
INCLINED TO JUMP TO
CONCLUSIONS
LIKES A GOOD FIGHT

LONG DEEP LIFE LINE
STRONG STAMINA
ATHLETIC, GOOD RECOVERY
POWER FROM ILLNESSES
AGGRESSIVE, RELIABLE

The hand of a successful businessman.

The
PRACTICE *of* CLASSICAL PALMISTRY

Madame La Roux

SAMUEL WEISER, INC.

York Beach, Maine

First published in 1993 by
Samuel Weiser, Inc.
Box 612
York Beach, Maine 03910-0612

02 01 00 99 98 97 96 95
11 10 9 8 7 6 5 4 3 2

Library of Congress Cataloging-in-Publication Data
La Roux, Madame.
    The practice of classical palmistry / Madame La Roux.
        p.   cm.
    1. Palmistry.   I. Title.
    BF921.L34 1993
    133.6--dc20   92-5951
                                                      CIP
ISBN 0-87728-503-9
BJ

Typeset in 11 point Times Roman

Hand illustrations by Madame La Roux.

Printed in the United States of America

The paper used in this publication meets the minimum requirements
of the American National Standard for Permanence of Paper for Printed
Library Materials Z39.48-1984.

The author welcomes correspondence. Please write to her c/o Samuel
Weiser, Inc., P. O. Box 612, York Beach, ME 03910-0612.

Table of Contents

Introduction vii

CHAPTER 1. Basics of Hand Reading 1
CHAPTER 2. Reading Fingers 23
CHAPTER 3. The Mounts 65
CHAPTER 4. The Mount of Jupiter 73
CHAPTER 5. The Mount of Saturn 83
CHAPTER 6. The Mount of Apollo 93
CHAPTER 7. The Mount of Mercury 105
CHAPTER 8. The Mount of Venus 115
CHAPTER 9. The Mounts of Mars 125
CHAPTER 10. The Mount of Luna 129
CHAPTER 11. The Lines of the Hand 141
CHAPTER 12. How to Read Palms 231

Appendix A—How to Make a Palm Print 237
Appendix B—Reading the Palm Prints 239
Appendix C—Worksheets for Readings 253
Index 268
About the Author 276

This book is dedicated to my late father Anthony,
a detective whose patience and perserverance inspired me
to write everything down — Thanks Da.

Special thanks to Phyllis Patterson
and also to my beloved colleagues Darleen, Tobi,
Coran, Rowan, Alwyn, Ramond, Bob, Maureen, Barton,
Theresa, Katie Heflin, and Scott Martin.
Extra special thanks to Dr. Anne Vercoutre and
Dr. Terry Hand for saving my life in 1991.
Thank you all for your inspiration and encouragement.

Introduction

Long ago, when the world was still young, the story of palmistry was only beginning. People in those days were simple, but the imperative for survival forced them to be alert to their surroundings. No matter how primitive were the tools of these ancients, and no matter how simple their minds, they constantly had their eyes on the heavens, carefully noting the movement of the Moon, the planets, and the patterns of the stars. As we became more civilized, we began to look within as well. That moment, so long ago, was when palmistry began.

In the early quest for cosmic understanding, people elevated the planets to a state of godhood. Each planet had a character, a behavior pattern, certain human attributes, and strengths or weaknesses commensurable to the planet's size, color, and brightness. These godlike features later became a standardized alphabet for the many occultists who followed. Early palmists applied these planetary attributes to their observations of the human hand and fingers. These ancient references to the gods and goddesses are still applied in the practice of palmistry today. To properly understand palmistry, it is important to familiarize yourself with the attributes of these gods and goddesses. These archetypical descriptions are the keys to the seven basic types of personality which we will discuss in depth later in this book.

Gods and Goddesses

The seven human attributes that assume godlike proportions are: Aggression (Mars), Receptivity (Venus), Ambition (Jupiter), Wisdom (Saturn), Artistry (Apollo), Communication (Mercury), and Imagination (Luna). The two most fundamental features of human nature are the masculine (Mars) and the feminine (Venus). These two deities represent the polar opposites within everyone.

Readers need to understand that Gypsies mix metaphors. Apollo is the Greek name for the Sun God. The rest of the names used for the mounts are Roman. Luna is not the name for the moon Goddess, but is a popular name used for her instead of Diana. These names have been used by traditional readers regardless of any historical differences. Gypsies and other practitioners kept the practice of palmistry alive despite persecution, revolutions, wars, and the continual reshaping of homelands in Romania, Hungary, Bavaria, etc. The Gypsies were kept moving and were not generally lucky enough to be educated in the classics of Greek and Roman history. I have traveled with Gypsies who speak a language called *Rom*, an ancient language resplendent with slang and swear words from every country imaginable. It is very much in character for traditional practitioners of palmistry to intermingle the Greek and Roman pantheon, as well as using the Romany name Luna to represent the Moon. In the interest of preserving tradition, the gypsy names have been maintained.

Mars

In the Roman pantheon, Mars (δ) was the god of war and aggression. Known to the Greeks as Ares, he represented determination, courage, and mighty resistance. He can manifest in two ways. On the positive side, Mars is zealous, resolute, and capable of command. On the negative side, he can be overly forceful, prone to fights and very stubborn. On the hand, Mars is located in three areas as shown in the Mars chapter on p. 125ff. Prominence in these areas of the palm would show an emphasis on aggression, strong vitality, and a courageous attitude.

Venus

Venus ($\female$), to the Romans, was the goddess of love. Her attributes were receptivity, sexuality, and fertility. Known to the Greeks as Aphrodite, she was the patroness of courtesans, and seen as healthy, beautiful, agreeable, enthusiastic, cheerful, and affectionate. She has two sides of her nature—warm and pleasurable, or fiery and passionate. On the hand, Venus is found ruling the ball of the thumb. Emphasis on this part of the hand indicates an abundance of the aforementioned qualities.

Jupiter

The Roman god, Jupiter ($\jupiter$), was known to the Greeks as Zeus. He was the god of the skies and keeper of the thunderbolts. He commanded the rain and was looked on as a beneficent god. To this day, he represents financial ambition, desire for authority, and religious leadership. Other qualities associated with Jupiter were justice, loyalty, integrity, sociability, and pride. The Jupiter finger is known in the world of palmistry as the index finger and, when Jupiter is strongly pronounced in the hand, it represents a strong-willed individual who can lead, and sometimes dominate others. Jupiter, also known as Jove, is famed for his sensuous appetite, his protection and guidance of small children and animals, his love of learning, and his sense of fair play. The concepts of Law and Order are also associated with the great and just spirit of Jupiter. The areas of the hand that represent Jupiter are both the index finger and the mount or pad of flesh just below the finger.

Saturn

Saturn ($\saturn$) was known to the Greeks as Chronos or Father Time. His task was to measure and regulate time. For this reason he is depicted as a brooding, serious, introspective god with severe and specific ideas of right and wrong. His attributes are skepticism, prudence and serious study. He is also known for his cautious, reserved, reclusive, self-reliant, and independent spirit. On the positive side, he is an ardent student, and represents the search for truth through scientific or metaphysical investigation. On the hand, Saturn rules the middle finger and the mount of flesh just below it.

Apollo

Apollo ($\odot$), God of the Sun, was one of the most important of the Greek Olympian gods. He was the patron of art, music, archery and medicine. Known as the god of prophesy, his most famous oracle was at Delphi. He rules the fine arts, the creative impulses, and is associated with beauty in all its forms. He was seen as attractive and pleasing, and particularly talented in literature and art. Apollo possessed a quick, fierce temper and a love of gambling. Lively and genial, Apollo was known as a great traveler, with a keen appreciation for aesthetics. On the hand, Apollo rules the ring finger and the mount of flesh just below it. He was called Helios by the Romans, but the Greek name Apollo is still used to represent these attributes in palmistry today.

Mercury

The Roman god, Mercury (☿), was called the messenger of the gods. He was known to the Greeks as Hermes, and was the patron of wayfarers and travelers. Famed for his skills at gaming, commerce and language, he excelled in mathematics and science. He was quick, shrewd, intuitive and eloquent. He was also highly versatile and dexterous, moving around Mount Olympus with wings on his feet. Successful commerce and diplomacy are natural to Mercury, and his quick wit enhanced his power of self-expression. On the hand, Mercury rules the little finger and the mount of flesh just below it.

Luna

Diana was the Roman goddess of the Moon (☽). Called Artemis by the Greeks, she was the twin sister of Apollo. Diana was the patroness of seafarers, poets, and madmen—lunatics, following the Latin name for the Moon, Luna. Luna represents the imagination, the unconscious mind, the powers of reflection and intuition. Luna is mutable and restless, and her affects fluctuate with the tides and the phases of the Moon. Luna rules the emotions, and all things invisible or below the surface. On the hand, Luna is located on the outer edge of the palm, directly opposite the ball of the thumb.

Palmistry—A Practical Science

When palmists examine a hand, their eyes are searching for specific features. Although intuition may play an important part in our deductions, we do not rely on intuition alone. Palmists are looking for *visible* clues and will sometimes need to make certain tests of the client's hand to find them. These clues are markings which can be seen by anyone who takes the time to examine the hand with the tenants of palmistry in mind. Palmists are investigators and technicians who observe, test, and ask lots of questions!

Modern palmists are a far cry from the prophesying Gypsies of the past. The Gypsies, however, passed on the subject of palmistry orally, using an elaborate system of signs and symbols as a kind of hieroglyphic alphabet. It was not until the 16th and 17th centuries that books on the subject of palmistry became available to the public at large. These books were written by European scholars who transcribed what they were taught orally by the Gypsies.

C H A P T E R   1

Basics of Hand Reading

There are several basic methods that a good palmist uses in order to read a set of palms. In the following pages, a variety of techniques have been arranged for both beginners and advanced palm readers. Good palmists keep their eyes on many things simultaneously when looking at a pair of hands. Shape, color, skin texture, the depth of the lines, the length of the fingers and their accompanying fingertip shapes are all valuable clues to the person's character and professional inclinations. I will outline my basic overall methods and give explanations as to why these clues are of value. In later chapters we will take a more in-depth look at these clues, and what they reveal.

Spotting the Clues

The first of many clues we look for when searching a hand is its *color*. This will describe the circulation and the dietary habits of the person in question. The color also indicates enthusiasm — a direct result of the circulation or lack of it. The next clue is found by assessing the *muscle tone* in the various areas of the hand. The muscle tone provides information regarding talents and special interests. *Flexibility* of the hand will reveal the amount of agility the person has, as well as the amount of mental flexibility he or she possesses. Another important factor when considering the palm is the overall *depth* and *clarity* of the lines themselves. Stamina as well as the ability to recover from illness is revealed by the depth and clarity of the lines. The *texture* of the skin (fine, medium or coarse) reveals the person's taste and sense of style. The *length of the fingers* provides still more information regarding patience, reasoning ability and power of analysis.

After considering all these areas of the hand, we are ready to examine the lines. First, examine the Life Line to discern the vitality and the enthusiasm of the person in question. The Heart Line is then examined to assess the strength of the heart organ itself. The Heart Line also gives information about the depth of the emotions as it is the blood circulation which considerably influences the individual's emotions. We then look to the Head Line to see what kind of mental concentration power the person possesses. Next, we look at the Fate Line to examine the career. We use the Health Line to verify any health problems found in other areas of the hand. Finally, a glance at the Girdle of Venus will give a clue to the person's sexual nature.

As you can see, modern palmists are not soothsayers. They look for specific information, and know exactly *where* to look for it. Palmistry is an applied method of physiological analysis. It examines the nerves, the skeleton, the vital organs and the disposition that clothes them all.

———————————————— Summary ————————————————

1) Check color
2) Check muscle tone
3) Check flexibility
4) Check depth and clarity of lines
5) Check texture of skin
6) Check length of fingers
7) Check Life Line
8) Check Heart Line
9) Check Head Line
10) Check Fate Line
11) Check Health Line

Right and Left Hand Comparison

Palmists need to compare one hand with the other to get the most accurate interpretation possible. No two hands are alike, not even two hands belonging to the same person. A proper comparison can provide a great deal of information regarding past occurrences and future trends for the client. To begin a comparison of the two hands, ask your client which hand he or she writes with. Many people are ambidextrous when it comes to sports or other hobbies, but very few are able to write with both hands. The hand the person writes with represents present and future trends. The reason for this is quite simple. The hand a person writes with is the hand which is used to send messages from the present into the future. We will refer to this hand as the *sending hand*. The other hand will be referred to as the *receiving hand*, and, to the palmist, it represents past influences regarding the person's conditioning and circumstances as a child. This hand also reveals the kind of health or temperament that resulted from the childhood environment.

Assuming for a moment that the client is right-handed, the left hand will show what was inherited from the parents in terms of health and conditioning, while the right hand will tell what was actually done with these qualities. Sometimes, we will find a left hand that indicates talent, and a right hand that is a mishmash of snarled lines, flabby muscle tone, and other unfavorable markings. A minute's glance will be enough to disclose that the client came into this world with talent that might have led to many opportunities. However, as the right hand—the message-sending hand—was so unfavorably marked, it would lead us to believe that these talents and opportunities have not been utilized. We then return to the left hand to discern the age at which the person began to misuse or squander his or her energy. There will always be at least one telltale spot on this otherwise marvelous hand that provides the clue to unraveling the mess that later ensued. If there is no clue to indicate where the trouble began, look closely at the thumbs. It is not unusual for the thumb of one hand to differ slightly from that of the other, but if the thumbs differ radically, the person's willpower and reasoning—or lack of it—was the culprit in creating this chaos. Read more about the thumbs in the subsequent chapters for more specific information.

Flexibility

Another thing to look for when comparing the two hands is the flexibility of one hand as compared to that of the other. If the receiving hand is stiff and the sending hand is flexible, we can deduce that the person was brought up rather rigidly and had a somewhat conservative approach to life as a result of early conditioning. This rigidity lessened as the person matured, and the future is likely to loosen up the personality even more. In this case, the person's present attitude has outdistanced an uncompromising past. If the reverse is found (the receiving hand flexible and the sending hand stiff), it will not be as pleasurable a discovery. The receiving hand—the past—shows us a very flexible upbringing, while the sending hand—the present—tells of unyielding formality. The future trend of this hand, therefore, may not look as happy.

The Mounts

The next thing to look for when examining the hands for comparison is the raised pads of flesh known as the mounts. If the mounts of the receiving hand (the past) are firm and pink in color, and the other hand has mounts that are flabby and white, a serious health depletion and laziness is indicated for the present, and is likely to continue into the future. The same comparison technique applies if only one mount shows this kind of deficiency and is modified in some way by the same mount in the other hand.

An example of this would be a right-handed person with a pink cast to the Mount of Venus in the left hand and a pale, flabby Mount of Venus in the right hand. The pink mount—that of the past—shows a healthy capacity for love, and a warm, outgoing disposition. This person loved heartily as a child and was not inclined to hold back love in any way. However, laziness, lack of openness and a reluctance to express a loving nature became the habit as the person grew older. Undoubtedly, the person's love relationships suffered accordingly.

Depth of Lines

The overall depth of the lines should be compared from hand to hand. If the lines are shallow in one hand and deep in the other, the hand with the deeper lines will indicate the period of better health. The same is true for the overall color of the skin. If the color shows a pink cast on one hand, and is pale in the other, apply this factor to interpretation.

When examining the lines, it is essential to compare each line to its counterpart found in the other hand. When a break, or some other unfavorable marking is found in a line, check the line in the other hand at the exact same spot. If the break occurred in the hand that represents the past, and the other hand shows a healthy, unbroken line, we can assure the person that the health debility indicated by the break will be overcome. If the reverse is seen, prepare the person for a possible health difficulty concerning that line. Explain that his or her constitution has been healthier in the past than it appears to be now. Show the person this particular marking, and advise how he or she can strengthen health in that area.

Be sure to leave your client feeling hopeful and encouraged. Palmists can convey concern for a client's health without intimidating the person. If a client's health appears to be in serious jeopardy, we cannot in good conscience gloss over what we see. Palmists never know what is to be found in someone's hand until they look and compare specific features from the left hand to those of the right. Whether we find tremendous good or tremendous danger in a person's hand, we are obliged to aid and encourage this person in whatever way we possibly can.

Always check the Life Line to ascertain what kind of vitality the client possesses. This is one of the major keys to understanding the temperament and recovery power the person has inherited from the collective gene pool. Look at the nails to see if any other debility would offset recovery. Always give the person whose health is in danger undivided attention, no matter how long it may take, and have alternatives ready to augment any present methods of health care. Encourage clients to care for themselves, rather than leaving health solely in the hands of others.

Skin Texture

Conclusions cannot be drawn from skin texture alone when practicing proper palmistry. However, skin texture will provide a valuable clue to the nature of a person's taste, and how he or she is likely to respond to the physical senses. We will not discuss the medium texture of the skin, as there is nothing extreme or conclusive about it. But we will discuss very fine texture, as well as coarse texture to help understand the kind of role skin texture plays in a person's attitude.

Fine Skin

Fine skin tells of refined taste and a sensitive disposition. These people are likely to have expensive possessions and are attracted to the world of luxury and fine arts. People with very fine skin often come from wealthy homes where they are pampered and protected by a somewhat sheltered environment. These people are appalled by crassness in any form, and will seek beautiful surroundings wherever they find themselves, adding a sense of refinement to whatever they touch. On the bad side, these people can be hypersensitive and squeamish. They are intolerant of any coarseness they might find in more down to earth people, and they can be suspicious and easily offended. In addition to this, fine-skinned people can be selfish, luxury-seeking, and highly unsympathetic to the needs of those less fortunate than themselves.

Coarse Skin

Coarse-skinned people are the complete opposite of the fine-skinned type. They can be crass and aggressive in their mannerisms. They do not abide by social customs, and are more at home with animals and pets than they are with people. Loud and brash, coarse-skinned people have unmatched stamina, and are more likely to keep their heads in a crisis than their fine-skinned counterparts. These people are anything but squeamish, and will fight vigorously to maintain independence and an uncompromising style. On the bad side, coarse-skinned people can be pigheaded, argumentative, brash, belligerent, and violent. Much depends on the thumb (the willpower) and the shape of the hand. These will disclose whether the aggressions have sufficient powers of self-control to keep the coarseness of the type from being too forceful and assertive.

Hand Gestures

The physical posture and the hand gestures of a person can be instrumental in telling us who they are. Always note these factors silently for a better understanding of what is shown by the shape of the hand and its lines.

Hand gestures will tell the person's current mood, and his or her attitude toward palmistry in general. Always take special care to note the way a person delivers the hand to you for examination. If the hand is extended to you in a tightly closed position when you ask for it, the client's mind is also likely to be tightly closed. This gesture reveals that the person is reluctant to open up. He or she may have secrets we are not supposed to know, or this person may just be closed-minded to the subject of palmistry. This person is also likely to be tightfisted with money and, if the thumb is tucked tightly in toward the palm, this will be especially true. A person with a tightly closed hand and thumb will press us to prove everything we say when reading.

When a hand is presented with fingers open and widely spread, this is an indication of broad-mindedness. These people will be open to the subject of palmistry, and their openness will help us to understand their hands. These people are curious and outgoing, and are usually delighted with whatever information we provide for them. They are usually quite healthy in their attitude toward the opposite sex and will be warm and demonstrative in most everything they do.

If clients are wringing their hands, they are obviously worried about something. Do not press them to tell what it is because by making them more nervous than they already are, they are likely to freeze up and become very introverted. This will hamper our hand-reading ability considerably! Look at these people and tell them to relax. We already know that something is bothering them, so make it easy for them to talk. Aside from curiosity, most people come to palm readers seeking advice for a problem in one of four areas — love matters, health problems, financial problems, or mental problems.

When I say mental problems, I am referring to those people who may be having difficulty applying their minds to jobs or home life, who feel unable to fit in with the environment. With regard to love problems — these people may have difficulty getting along with a spouse or loved one, and may need to make some adjustments in attitude before abandoning an otherwise good relationship. Sometimes the temperament is not suited for the work environment. Palmists can spot these things from the hand and counsel accordingly.

Clients must first be made aware of who they, themselves, are in the present, in order to assess where to apply their talents in the future. For example, people who long for the applause of the theater may not be happy or successful in a less glamorous environment, such as banking or medicine. These professions may be contrary to the basic temperament, and no matter how long they work in these areas, they will always be at odds with their surroundings. It is also important for palmists to realize that people may be talented in one area, but may content themselves with pursuing an area wherein this talent is not required.

Good and Bad Hands

It is no easy task to separate the good hands from the bad hands in life, but palmistry can help to guide us in selecting friends who will be easiest for us to get along with. No matter how repulsive a hand may look at first glance, there are always good qualities to be found in it somewhere. It is our duty to comb this bad-looking hand for the most promising qualities we can find. Every human being is good at something, or good *for* something, and palmists never discuss the negative qualities people possess unless asked about them directly. The best policy is to foster good and encourage positive traits. *Remember*, people strain to listen to every word we say, and any opinion may be remembered for a lifetime. So, when we look at a hand, we should try to begin reading on a favorable note. Announce the most positive qualities first. For example, suppose we are looking at an overly red, thick, flabby hand with short fingers, a short thumb, and very coarse skin. By the standards of classical palmistry, these features tell us that the person is hot-headed, lazy, impatient and crass, but do we say this? *No!* A person of this nature will surely be outraged. Instead, keep in mind that this person (no matter how disagreeable) is allowing us the opportunity to continue our study of palmistry — and at his or her expense. Try not to frown because we know he is watching. If we look up at this fellow and smile wryly, saying, "My good man, your idea of a good time is to lounge away the day without a care in the world," we have addressed his laziness without offending him. Now he will be laughing at his problem. One of the best ways to get someone to look at a shortcoming objectively is to introduce it with humor. Now the person is ready to receive whatever observations we make, and will do so with humor and open-mindedness. We can see from the redness in his hand that he is irritable and does not like to be kept waiting (short thumb), so we take special care to be as brief as possible. This short-fingered fellow is not going to want to labor over details and cross-references. Details are abhorrent to people with short fingers, especially those with a red tone to the skin. Therefore we will do our best to spare him this discomfort. Rather than confronting him on the subject of his irritability, encourage him to relax, and slip him this information in a way that is more palatable for him. He is likely to meet this kind of reading with enthusiasm, and will always remember the advice that was given with fondness. If we blurt out observations, the results of this reading could have quite a different effect. Therefore, it is very important to refrain from making judgments, and to take the nature of the person into consideration before saying anything. Palmistry is a tool for observing the nature of human beings, and if we use it well, we can work wonders.

Not all hands that palmists like are beautiful to look at. Often, the most beautiful-looking hands are slender in appearance, with pointed fingers, and lily-white skin. These hands, however, are not so beautiful in temperament, as any palmist will tell you. Hands with these features belong to people with poor stamina, hypersensitivity, hysterical tendencies, and a proclivity for anemia. Do not be dazzled by how pretty a hand may look.

Good Hands

What makes a hand beautiful to a palmist is an entirely different set of features than one may expect. In my opinion, these qualities are features that illustrate strength of character, originality, and good health. So, when we speak of good hands in this book, we are talking about those features. First we will define the terms, and then see how they surface in the features of the hand.

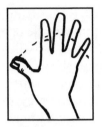 Strength of character indicates people who have taken the time to define and to cultivate the natural talents they possess, and are willing to take risks in order to do so. These people are not afraid to assert individuality, they are dedicated to improvement, and they are not discouraged by the opinions of others. Physical features that signify strength of character are as follows:

□ A long thumb with square or spatulate tip, good flexibility, and a waist-shaped second phalange.

□ A pink cast to the skin color, and firm muscle tone.

□ Smooth skin which is not overly glossy.

□ Flexibility in all the fingers.

□ Deep, well-marked lines, and clarity of lines.

□ A strong Heart and Head Line, free from unfavorable markings, and a Life Line free of breaks or other interruptions.

□ Well-developed mounts that are firm and pronounced— especially the Mount of Venus.

□ A straight Finger of Saturn.

□ A well-developed Mount of Apollo and/or Line of Apollo.

Originality is another factor that contributes to a good hand. Originality is possessed by people who use creativity in unique ways, and who are not bound by social custom when it comes to expressing special talents. People do not have to be painters or poets to be original. They merely have to be alert, curious, and energetic. Physical features which bespeak these qualities are:

□ Spatulate fingertips.

□ Flexible thumb and fingers.

□ A Head Line that is well-defined and deeper than the rest of the lines in the hand.

□ Good muscle tone, with a pink cast to the hand.

□ Well-developed mounts, especially Luna and Jupiter.

□ Long, well-formed thumbs, especially the spatulate thumb.

We have already touched upon good health as seen in the hand, and the following points will show what a healthy hand looks like:

□ Pink cast to the skin.

□ Flexible joints with good muscle tone.

□ Deep lines with no unfavorable line markings.

□ Well-developed, firm mounts.

□ Medium to fine skin texture.

Bad Hands

Criminal hands come in all shapes and sizes, but certain features remain prevalent regardless. Just as there are many different types of crimes, it is hard to pinpoint one specific hand as being criminal. The first and most noteworthy feature is the pinky. Most likely *both* pinkies will appear twisted or otherwise noticeably misshapen. The pinky tells how we relate to the parent of the opposite sex. A bad relationship between a man and his mother, for example, may cause him to carry resentment and a lack of honesty into all relationships with women thereafter. With this feature being the most prominent in both hands, the person is likely to lie his or her way out of every unpleasant situation. With long fingers, the lie will be painstakingly detailed. With all fingers appearing twisted and gnarled, be sure to ask the person if he or she has arthritis, if not, the individual is not likely to know the difference between the truth and a lie. Hands with all fingers twisted are found on the hands of pickpockets and kleptomaniacs. Short, stubby fingers and a red cast to the color of the hand will produce a hard-headed, aggressive, demanding individual. This person can easily be roused to violence and will impatiently push his or her way through all obstacles. The following is a checklist of features a bad hand is likely to possess. Remember that no one single feature alone is enough to render an entirely bad hand, but if these features are found in combination on either or especially on *both* hands, they will detract from the better qualities possessed by that person. A bad hand would contain the features mentioned below:

□ Shallow lines, very coarse skin, or skin which is too glossy and overly fine.

□ Fingers that are extremely stiff, or overly flexible (with no spring in them when pressed backward).

□ Pale hands; yellow, blue, or overly red cast to the hands.

□ Twisted or gnarled fingers.

□ An abundance of grills or other unfavorable markings such as dots, dents, X's, or breaks in the major lines, especially if found in both hands.

□ Flabby hands with poor muscle tone.

□ A Head or Heart Line which droops severely.

□ Chained lines, blueness on the lines, lines which zig-zag in appearance, an abundance of crosslines which mar the major lines, lines that waver drastically.

□ Very narrow nails, brittle nails.

□ Flat mounts, especially the flat Mount of Venus.

No one feature on this checklist is enough to qualify a hand as a bad hand, but if these features are found in combination on either one or especially on both hands, they will detract from the better qualities possessed by that person. If these features are found in abundance, and we are hard-pressed to find a good feature to offset these findings, we have what I would call a bad hand, indeed. It is difficult to read these hands. That's why Gypsies get paid *before* they read, and God knows I have sweated through readings where people have had hands that tell some rough stories.

Fingernails

The nails provide several valuable clues to the health and character. They should not be overlooked when assessing the hand. Their shapes will disclose the way people use their mental energy. If they have very long, or otherwise accentuated fingertips, the nails will show how this energy is put to use. A good example of this would be people with long fingertips and very narrow nails. The long fingertips will show people who rely on the mind rather than the emotions to make decisions. With broad nails, this reasoning ability will be firm and practical. With a frail-looking, narrow nail, they are more likely to be delicate and excitable, regardless of how long the fingertips may be.

Narrow nails show people who are very specific in their tastes. They will be likely to have specialized professions. They are the opposite of the broad nails that show broad-minded, more outgoing types. Square nails, like square fingertips, show practicality and precision, while conic or round nails show quick inspiration and amiability.

Another valuable clue the nails have to offer is their *color*. This tells what the stamina, enthusiasm, and blood circulation is like, and will indicate whether these people have the perseverance to finish what they start. With white or pale-looking nails, they tire easily. With red nails, they will not only finish what they start, but they will have plenty of energy left over to argue about the way it was done. Redness of the nails is a sure sign of argumentative people, but they also have stamina, and recover very quickly from illnesses. However, when black people have very pink nails, it usually indicates wonderful circulation.

Consider nails as windows into the bloodstream. The more red they appear, the more vigorous is the blood circulation. Good circulation is one of the best indications of a healthy body, and a healthy, active, energetic mind usually follows suit. White nails are nearly the opposite of red nails, indicating poor circulation and a tendency for low blood pressure and anemia. These people have poor recovery power from illnesses. There is a certain lack of enthusiasm which affects not only their resistance to illnesses, but their willingness to assert themselves as well. White nails that are tinged with blue are an indication of a heart condition. They can indicate the possibility of constricted arteries. Constrictions caused by colitis, varicose veins, or pinched nerves in the spine would make this blue color quite likely. Always ask what their health condition is before pronouncing people afflicted with a terrible thing such as a heart problem. Certainly blueness of the nails is a serious problem not to be overlooked by both palmists and medical doctors, but there is no need to alarm clients and fill their already delicate hearts with fear.

The yellow nail was traditionally read as an indication of bile in the blood. This would indicate gastric problems, and afflict the disposition with irritability. This problem is not so difficult to correct, but counseling must be handled with care. It is very likely that this condition was brought about by negligent eating habits. When counseling, remember that nutrition is one area of their lives that people are very reluctant to alter. Poor food combining is usually the culprit that accompanies yellow nails as well as excessive amounts of nicotine.

When counseling people with yellow nails keep in mind that they are likely to be cranky and irritable. Encourage them to eat simple foods that will aid the digestion. There are two other diseases which will cause yellowing of the nails. The first is hepatitis, and the second is jaundice. Always ask about these two problems, and ask, too, if your client is a heavy smoker before suggesting the restructure of his or her eating habits.

Brittle nails are often the result of respiratory problems such as emphysema and bronchitis. In their early stages, these ailments may not leave serious markings such as a grill on the Mount of Jupiter or fraying on the Heart Line, but will show evidence in the nail first. An exotic virus or high fever will also render the nails brittle and may cause vertical ribbing.

The Four Quadrants of the Hand

To make hand analysis easier, palmists divide the hand into four areas. The first division is made by drawing an imaginary line down the middle of the hand, beginning at the tip of the middle finger and extending to the wrist. It is important to divide the middle finger with this imaginary line to distinguish whether the finger leans more toward the index finger or more toward the ring finger. This will be discussed in more detail later. For now, beginning palmists should accustom their eyes to note which side of the hand is more emphasized.

The part of the hand containing the thumb and index finger represents the externalized part of the personality — the active, extroverted part. This side of the hand also refers to the ambitions, willpower, and dominance over others.

The second half of this division includes the other half of the middle finger, the ring finger and the pinky. It also includes the side of the hand below these fingers (known as the percussion). This half of the hand represents the inner world, namely, the imagination, dreams, and intuition.

Another division can be made by dividing the hand horizontally. This dividing line falls just below the pads of flesh beneath each finger, separating the hand into upper and lower areas. The upper area includes the fingers and the pads or mounts just below them. The lower area includes the palm area, the percussion and the thumb. The top half of the hand relates to the mind and the way the intellect functions. The second half, the lower part, represents the instincts and those features which we have in common with animals.

Dividing the hand in this fashion will provide information at a glance. If one part of the hand is more developed than the others, the palmist can deduce which area of the hand is most emphasized.

The Three Worlds of Palmistry

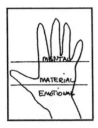

Another simple division of the hand is made by separating the palm into thirds. This is one of the oldest methods used in palmistry and is still very useful today. These three divisions give distinctions to three important areas of expression—the physical, the material and the mental. Emphasis in one of these areas will give a clue as to which method of expression is favored.

The fingers and pads of flesh below them, known as mounts, comprise the mental world. Fingers actively carry out the person's thoughts and methodologies and these busy appendages are responsible for sending messages and sorting them. Emphasis here shows a sensitive idealist with a love of detail—a person who favors the mental world and is at home among intellectuals.

The middle zone of the hand represents the material world and social behavior. This area also reveals how important money and prestige are and also indicates concern for the business side of life. If this area is well-developed, the person is likely to be active in the business world and its accompanying social whirl. For this person, the excitement of making deals and the challenge of conducting big business play an important role. This zone also shows the capacity for dealing with large groups of people. Emphasis here shows an adaptability and a keenness for observing human nature. This person will need to stay active and dedicated to business. Good power of projection, strong ambition, and a heightened awareness in the world of commerce and industry are indicated.

The lower third of the hand represents the physical side of the person. It shows the deeper biological drives, the animal nature and physical zest. This area is a valuable key to assessing stamina and physical strength. Excessive bulges in this area should be regarded with caution, as this person will be very strong, physically, and prefers to dominate others. This kind of person will be tireless in sports and a courageous, outgoing soldier on the battlefield. He or she will also be very demonstrative in affairs of the heart.

Palm Shapes

The next form of distinction the palmist makes is to identify the shape of the palm itself. This is done by measuring the palm with the eye, comparing its length against its width to assess whether it is longer than it is wide or vice versa. For an idea of the many different types of palm shapes see fig. 1 on p. 18. If the palm is the same in width as it is in length, it is referred to as square. The square hand usually has a broad appearance with firm muscle tone. These kind of palms belong to active, decisive people. Their thinking is down-to-earth and organized. They are formal and traditional and greatly value things which are useful. This kind of hand is often found on architects, sculptors, bricklayers and engineers. It tells of an appreciation for the classics and a level-headed ability to cope. These people are conventional and hard working, their energy is distributed in a balanced fashion, and they are possessed of an honest, enduring sense of affection.

The spatulate hand is distinguished by a noticeable difference of width between the top and bottom half of the hand. When the hand is narrow at the top and wide at the base, it shows good powers of concentration. The narrowing of the hand shows that the energy sent out through the fingers is being channeled in a concentrated fashion.

If the hand is narrow at the bottom and wide at the top it shows the opposite. This person is very active and original but lacks concentration. These are restless hands with a need for vicarious excitement. This person is easily distracted and is often scatter-brained. A high degree of physical energy is present in a hand that is wide at the top, but this person must be given a more formalized profession to channel the energy more effectively. This type of hand is adventurous and unpredictable. With a noticeably broad base, this is the hand of an explorer who is determined to make the most out of every opportunity. He or she would have strong physical stamina and a desire to be constantly on the move.

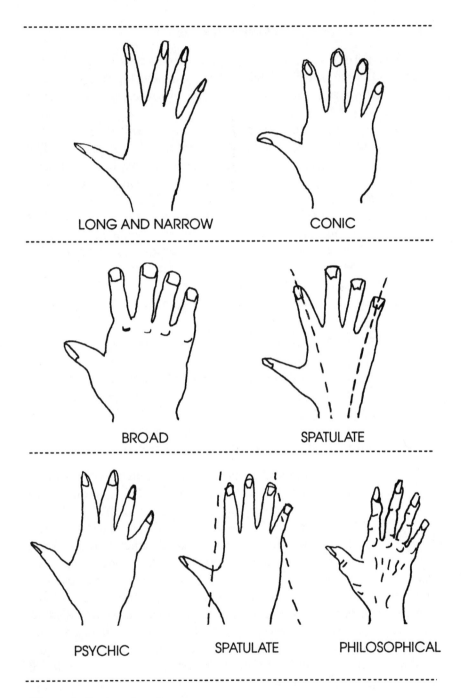

Figure 1. Basic palm shapes.

The oval or round-looking hand is referred to by palmists as conic. These palms are often accompanied by a small thumb. Here we have a person of whim and fancy to whom beauty in all its forms is an inspiration. This person is a good companion, but is inclined to be flighty and unrealistic. Versatile and artistic, this type usually does his or her best to make things as attractive as possible. These hands may lack persistence, but are nonetheless fun-loving and lively. The conic hand is highly sociable, with a love of music and the performing arts. This person communicates well and is more emotional than other types.

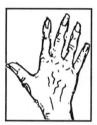

The philosophical hand is identified by its long bony shape and long knotty fingers. The owner of such a hand is inclined to ponder deeply, delving into the sciences such as mathematics, geology, or other professions where digging for the facts is a necessity. The owner of a philosophical hand has a good eye for facts and procedures, with a curious mind and a need for solitude. He or she is cautious and methodical, and is happiest when engrossed in a complex subject. Painstaking and thorough, the owner of these hands will deliberate for a long time before making up his or her mind on any subject. There may be a tendency to criticize anything that can't be tangibly proven as well.

The psychic hand is characterized by its long, narrow bone structure, pointed fingertips and fine, glossy skin. Those with psychic hands are quickly inspired and very sensitive. They depend heavily on their intuition and are greatly influenced by first impressions and vibrations. They live in the visionary world of the imagination and have to really make an effort to get along on the material plane. These are spiritual people who are often too sensitive to be practical. Highly idealistic and quickly inspired, they will suffer greatly in coarse surroundings where there is a shortage of natural beauty. They are easily hurt and will go to great lengths to insulate themselves from the world of the commonplace.

The broad hand is very distinctive in appearance. It resembles the square palm in that it is equal in width to its length. What distinguishes it from the square hand is its muscles — which are very firm and pronounced. The fingers are of equal proportion to the rest of the hand, and the color is usually very pink or red. The owner of this hand is inclined to be practical, steady and true in regard to convictions. This type possesses the necessary drive to finish what he or she starts. Robust health inclines the person to work hard to obtain a life of comfort and luxury. The broad hand is level-headed about accomplishments and not given to egocentricities.

Long and narrow hands, with fingers longer than the length of the palm indicate a thoughtful, inward turn of mind. Shy, sensitive, and inquiring, with a reflective nature and good powers of abstract reasoning, the owner of long and narrow hands is often introverted and very likely to remember an offense. This person is easily hurt, fastidious, and detail oriented. He or she is most at home in genteel surroundings, and tires easily. Hysteria is not uncommon, and loud noises are highly offensive to this type.

Hands that are large by comparison to the rest of the body show a person who is patient with small details, and who is fond of intricate work. This person likes to tinker for hours and is frequently found among jewelers and lacemakers. If the hand appears excessively large, it indicates a moody disposition, and a rather temperamental personality.

Hey, There's Color on the Mount!

There are color variations in the palms of all people—Blacks, Indians, Asians, as well as Caucasians. Pink, yellow, red, and blue pallor to the skin is distinguishable regardless of race. It is true, however, that color is easier to detect in a Caucasian hand, but good palmists adapt their eyes to the overall pallor of the skin and make their notations from experience.

Color variations are not as important as the lines and mounts are, but I have included them as a backup resource to help discern important features, such as high and low blood pressure. The yellow color present in a person with jaundice or hepatitus is noticeable in any race if the eye is accustomed to looking at hands that are normal to the race. Blue color, which is rarely seen, will appear in dark-skinned people as a darkening with a bluish cast to it.

CHAPTER 2

Reading Fingers

After looking at the hand as a whole, and then separating it into sections according to the Three Worlds of Palmistry, the next observation should be the fingers. This will lead the palmist to various classifications of finger lengths, fingertip shapes, nails and flexibility.

Consider each finger separately at first, noting if any one finger is dissimilar to the rest of the fingers on either hand. Always view the fingers in context with the hand to which they belong.

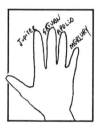

Palmists call the index finger the Finger of Jupiter. The middle finger is called the Finger of Saturn, the ring finger is known as the Finger of Apollo, and the little finger is the Finger of Mercury. Each of these gods has certain attributes to which the finger is related. If one finger is more prominent than the others, it is believed that the attributes of that god are likely to dominate that person's character.

When examining the fingers, note their length or shortness in relation to the length of the palm itself. Next, observe the finger joints to see if they are knotty or smooth. See fig. 2 on p. 24 for examples of each. Judge the degree of the knots' development carefully and check to see which joint is most prominent in length

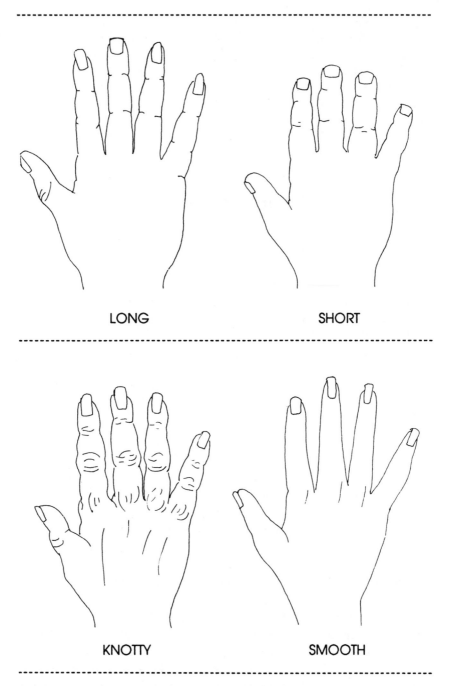

Figure 2. Examples of finger length and joints.

or width. Examine the flexibility of each finger by pressing them gently and bending them backward. If one finger is more flexible than the others, the qualities of the mount to which it is attached will be more pronounced. Next, note whether the fingers are bent in any way, or twisted on their axes, or just plain straight.

Fingers that are bent laterally show a certain shrewdness which will operate in a style particular to the mount on which they are found. Fingers that are twisted on their axes show a liability to the more negative attributes of the mount on which they are found. We will discuss mounts in greater detail later.

Note whether any one finger seems to stand more erect than the others, especially if one or more fingers lean toward it. This will show you the most dominant finger on the hand. One finger leaning toward another will contribute some of its strength to the finger toward which it leans.

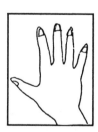

For fingers to be well balanced with their energy well distributed, they should be evenly set on the palm, with a relatively equal distance between each one. This rule does not include the thumb.

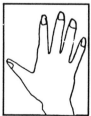

One finger should not be placed lower down or higher up than any other. Any finger which is set lower than the others reduces the strength of the mount beneath it, depleting the mount of its more positive qualities.

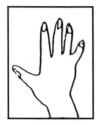

One finger set higher than the rest increases the strength of the mount beneath it.

Finger Separation

Certain facts can be revealed by the separation of one finger from the next. Try to observe the fingers casually at first, before telling the person what you are looking for specifically. It is best to look at a hand as it is held naturally. Be sure to give special attention to the position of the hand as the person outstretches his or her hand to have it read by you. If the fingers are held tightly together at this time, be aware that the person is skeptical about palmistry, and may have secrets that he or she does not want you to discuss. If the person tucks the thumb underneath the palm, or holds the thumb tightly against the side of the palm, he or she is tightfisted with money and may be concealing a measure of hidden anger. If the thumb is folded over the middle of the palm when the person extends a hand to you, he or she is downright stingy and is probably stewing about the price of your reading. If the hand is open wide when outstretched, this shows a curious mind and an open-minded disposition.

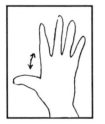

If the space between the thumb and the side of the palm is fairly wide, with the thumb bending outward widely, this is a sure sign of generosity. This person is independent and loves freedom, and is also intolerant of any kind of restraint.

If the index finger and middle finger separate widely, the person is independent in thought and is not bound by the views of others.

If the middle finger separates widely from the ring finger the person is a carefree and Bohemian type. This person will shun the stiffness and constraints of formality.

If the ring finger and the little finger are separating widely, the person will be independent. He or she will have a unique approach to most everything, and prefers to work without supervision. The person is also apt to be highly communicative and inclined for a profession in the communication field. These people are also excellent in sales.

———————————— Finger Checklist ————————————

□ Observe the knuckles. Are they knotty or smooth? Is any one knuckle more prominent than the others? Which one? Which hand?

□ Bend the fingers backward. Is one more flexible than the others? Which one? Is this true on both hands?

□ Are any of the fingers bent? Which one(s)? In which direction is it leaning? Do any of the fingers twist on its axis? Which one? Which hand? Is any finger more erect than the others? Which one? Which hand?

□ Are the index finger and the ring finger equal in length? If not, which one is longer? Which one of these two fingers is more dominant? Why? Is this true in both hands?

Phalanges

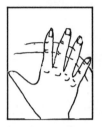

The fingers are divided into three joints by their knuckles. Each division is called a *phalange* by palmists. Apply the Three Worlds of Palmistry to each of these phalanges. The first phalanges are the fingertips and represent the mental world. The middle zone represents the practical world, and the lower, or third represents the instinctual world.

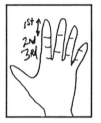

If the first phalange of any finger is noticeably longer than the other two, the qualities of that finger will be expressed in a mental fashion. If the second phalange is longest, the material world will rule, and the energies of that finger will be expended on practical concerns, such as the business world. If the lower third of the finger is the most pronounced, the physical qualities of the finger type (Jupiterian, Saturnian, or otherwise) will be the most emphasized. Chapters that follow on the individual fingers will explain how the attributes of the gods (that rule each finger) manifest themselves in their characteristic fashion. Emphasis on the lower phalange will disclose sensuousness, and a person who is more devoted to the world of physical gratification than to the intellectual or business worlds.

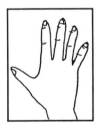

If the first phalange of any finger is noticeably short, it detracts from the better qualities of the mount and finger to which it belongs. The mental side of the person will be deficient in relation to the attributes of that particular finger.

With the middle phalange thick or otherwise emphasized, the person will be absorbed in the business world and will find real gratification in making money and cutting deals. The more pronounced the thickness is, the more pronounced this trait will be. This area also emphasizes the sociability of the person. The owner of a hand with emphasis here will have many friends and associates.

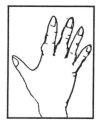

If the lower phalanges are noticeably thick on one or all of the fingers, it shows that the person has a great love for eating and drinking. Also note that luxury and the pleasure of the senses will absorb the greater part of his or her attention.

Length of the phalanges shows an emphasis of the good qualities of that finger. Thickness of the phalange shows coarseness and a liability to excess.

When the third phalange is narrow and waist-shaped it indicates a person who is not a creature of excess. He or she would be more likely to devote time to the intellectual or business world than to the world of the senses. This person is not dazzled by luxury and is not inclined to want money for the comforts it can buy. Money will slip through these hands like water, as the person considers money a vulgarity to be disposed of for the sake of whimsy, rather than something to be saved or hoarded. Examine and classify the fingertips according to the categories of square, conic, spatulate, or pointed. The shape of the cuticle will give a clue if the classification is a difficult one. Since the fingertip itself describes the mind, the tip shape will provide additional information about how the mind operates.

When the fingers separate widely, it discloses free thought, eccentricity, and independence in action. This is one person who won't be pinned down by convention, especially in art, literature and business. This person will be easy to meet, but will not be confined by the rules of etiquette.

The opposite is true for the person with fingers held tightly together. This rigid person is lacking in independence and is a virtual slave to formality. To make his or her acquaintance, one must use a respectful approach. This type is also stingy, self-centered, and constantly looking out for the future.

Compare the length of the fingers to each other. The middle finger should be longest. If it leans drastically favoring one side of the hand or the other, it will describe a personality which is off-balance. The index finger and the ring finger should be somewhat equal in length for a nice even temperament. *Remember*: if one finger is dominant in length, the qualities of that finger will also dominate.

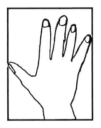

If the index finger and the ring finger are of equal lengths, the fingertips will give a clue as to which one has the greater influence upon the person. The square or spatulate tip will always be more dominant than a conic or pointed tip.

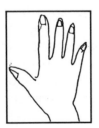

If the index finger is excessive in length, so too are the qualities attributed to that finger and its accompanying mount. If it is deficient in length, the finger *and* the mount will both suffer from this deficiency.

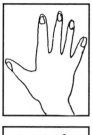

Conic and pointed fingertips show idealism, sensitivity, and artistic ability. Square tips show precision and practicality while spatulate tips show originality and restlessness.

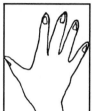

Because the long second phalange shows an emphasis toward business acumen when combined with conic or pointed tips, the person will likely be found in the world of commercial art. The artistic sensitivity of the conic and pointed tip, coupled with the strong business instincts of the long second phalange, would incline the person to market sensitivity in a practical fashion.

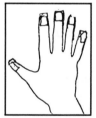

Square tips with this long second phalange would incline the person toward a different kind of profession. The precision and meticulousness of someone with the square tip, combined with the business drive of the long second phalange would make this individual most at home as a draftsman, mapmaker, sculptor, to name just a few professions. The profession will be scrupulously executed and will have commercial value.

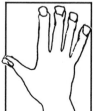

The spatulate tip combined with this long middle zone will render the person a human dynamo in the business world. This person can sell you the Brooklyn Bridge. This is the high-powered salesman, or the high-volume ad person who can't sit still unless a deal of some kind is being made.

With an emphasis on the third phalanges the liability for excess is very strong. The conic tips (whimsy and idealism) will increase the liability for excess when coupled with overly developed third phalanges. Square tips will tone down this liability by adding a note of practicality to the individual.

Those with spatulate tips will find an original way to utilize the physical abundance and sensuality of the excessive third phalange. They are likely to be found in the food service industry.

The previous pages considered only a few examples of how the fingertips combine with other attributes to give us clues to professional talents. If the client has yet to choose a profession, these combinations can help the client select a profession appropriate to his or her talents.

—————————— Phalanges Checklist ——————————

Test your own fingers and list the characteristics you find. Using the Three Worlds of Palmistry, find the area most emphasized in your left hand. How about your right hand?

□ Is any one phalange longest? Which one? Left hand or right hand?

□ Is any one phalange fattest? Which one? Left hand or right hand?

□ Of the first phalanges, which finger possesses the longest one? Left or right hand?

□ Of the second phalanges, which finger possesses the longest one? Left or right hand?

□ Of the third phalanges, which finger possesses the longest one? Left or right hand?

□ Are any of the phalanges noticeably narrower than the others? Which ones?

□ Take the most pronounced phalange and list its tip shape. What does the combination of tip, phalange, and finger tell you?

Finger Length

The proper way to measure the length of the fingers is to measure them against the palm to which they belong. Using the middle finger as a gauge, its length can be compared in inches or centimeters against the length of the palm itself. The average length of the fingers is approximately three-fourths the length of the palm. If the fingers are only half the length of the palm they are considered short. If they are longer than three-quarters the length of the palm they are considered long. Ask the person to stretch his or her fingertips toward the wrist as far as he or she can. Then their length will be quite evident.

Long Fingers

Once it has been established that the fingers are long by measuring their length against the length of the palm, you are ready to consider what effects these long fingers exert. It makes a great deal of difference whether these fingers are thick or thin.

The long-fingered person is peculiar in a number of ways. This individual separates things into parts rather than accepting them as a whole. The mind is detail oriented. This person is likely to engage in small particulars and let the large overview of things escape. He or she has a somewhat suspicious tendency and does not trust others easily, even friends. In dealing with the long-fingered person, it is important to be careful of what you say as this person is easily offended. Things which may seem inconsequential to others may be construed as an intended insult. The long-fingered person is a careful type who dresses neatly and tries to project a tidy image. Exceedingly sensitive, easily wounded, and capable of carrying a grudge for a long period of time, this person is also fussy, fastidious, and has a keen eye for the small details. The long-fingered type is inclined to have good memory, and makes a good bookkeeper or office worker where detailed work and accuracy are required.

If the fingers are long and have square fingertips, the person will have a strong sense of practicality, and is likely to be very punctual. This person makes a superb accountant. He or she is patient, diligent, and will not forsake a love of accuracy for the sake of haste.

If the fingers are long and smooth, with an absence of conspicuous knuckles, the person is inclined to grasp ideas more quickly.

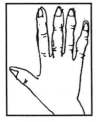

Long, knotty fingers show a love of detail in the form of analysis. This person will be very slow and will plod along, fussing over everything. Slow and careful labor is the method he or she applies to achieve success. As musicians, long and knotty fingers achieve success from careful and close observation to detail. These musicians are not likely to depart from the composer's conceptions and are likely to adhere strictly to every original detail. In telling a story, this person is apt to be tiresome, presenting details with wearisome accuracy. To say the long, knotty-fingered person is long-winded would be an understatement! However, the enquiring mind is very useful. This person is thoughtful, watchful, careful and patient. In the home, this person would be inclined to look after all of the little things. On the bad side, he or she may be tedious, boring, slow, frequently selfish, suspicious, introverted, and uncomfortable socializing. Thin fingers, and/or very short nails will accentuate these shortcomings.

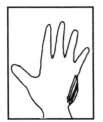

If the person with long fingers lacks a good Mount of Venus, the ball of the thumb, or a good Mount of Apollo, the area just beneath the ring finger, selfishness is likely. Selfishness is also a trait if you see an excessive Mount of Luna with long fingers. This person is inclined to exhibit generosity for appearances and also lacks sympathy. He or she does not grant favors readily and is often stingy except in matters which give personal pleasure. This applies particularly to lean-looking, long fingers, unless accompanied by spatulate fingertips and good strong thumbs to grant them greater willpower and generosity. The long, lean-fingered person is always ready to receive a favor, but never go out of his or her way to grant one. The long-fingered friend is not always steadfast, and may be suspicious, often nursing feelings of resentment. Thick, long fingers will be more steady as friends.

• • •

In considering long fingers, give careful attention to the fingertips to see in which direction the long finger's love of investigation and details will expend itself. If the long fingers have square tips, a love of investigation and precision will direct the person into research because precise methodology is important. He or she can also be a technician, a watchmaker, or a repairperson. With spatulate tips and long fingers, the desire for activity and originality will make a remarkable inventor, or a careful explorer. With conic tips, long fingers will find the patience to express a love for beauty. Here is the painter, beautician, dancer and artist. Attention to detail is important. With pointed tips, the long-fingered person will be a lot quicker, and may possess psychic abilities. This combination is often found in the healing arts.

Short Fingers

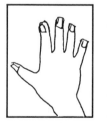

Short fingers will barely reach the ball of the thumb when the hand is closed. Short-fingered qualities are the reverse of long-fingered qualities. Instead of wishing to go into detail, short-fingered people despise it. Instead of tarrying with trifles, these people want everything considered as a whole. If the fingers are not overly short these people think quickly. If the fingers are very short, they think as quick as a flash, and act as quickly as they think. In stating a proposition, these people come right to the point. Unlike the slow and tedious pace of their long-fingered counterparts, these people are brief and quickly snap into action. They are highly intuitive and adept at spotting an untruth. With their rapidly working minds, these people are forming their opinions before the proposal has even been completed. They do not take time to analyze and fuss over details. They desire to get to the heart of the matter without delay, and their main concern is with results, leaving the details to someone else.

Short-fingered people are often hard to handle. They act impulsively, on the spur of the moment, and are inclined to do things hastily for which they are later sorry. While they possess very brilliant qualities, they often risk them by being impetuous. They run the risk of error by jumping to conclusions, and they can be very hot-headed. People with short fingers are pushy and diligent in any enterprise they undertake. They are not satisfied unless they are doing *big* things. They prefer to do things that are of consequence to society. They cast detail aside as they build enormous buildings, set policies, and lead armies, leaving the details of how it is to be done to the people with long fingers. While people with long fingers are plodding, careful, even stingy, those with short fingers are dashing, extravagant, full of big plans and look down on small matters.

Short-fingered people are not always careful of appearance since the grand scale of their plans inclines them to overlook the little details of tidiness in dress. They are too occupied with large matters to attend to the details of etiquette and society. They do not notice a slight which would drive their long-fingered counterparts to despair. They are quick to comprehend everything said, and are usually lively and happy companions. People with short fingers are swift, dynamic, quick-witted, and very concise in their method of expression. The writing style is brief, and they are capable of saying a great deal with the fewest words possible. These people are excellent newspaper reporters or short story writers. Short-fingered people need discipline and strength of character to carry out their plans. Check the thumb to see if they have determination and tact, and check the fingertips to see if they are an asset to this already quick and versatile temperament.

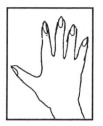

Short fingers with pointed fingertips are a bad combination. The pointed tip shows the idealist, the dreamer who lives in a world of inspiration and fantasy. This kind of impracticality will lead the short-fingered person to be even more impulsive and hasty, with the added liability of social detachment and a preoccupation with the world of vision and dreams. Conic tips will also lead the person toward these pursuits, but not as dangerously as the pointed tips would. Both conic and pointed tips are quickly inspired and idealistic, but the pointed fingertip is the more impractical of the two.

Square fingertips, when found on the short-fingered person, will direct impetuosity into more practical channels and make the person less impressionable. This person will be a more careful planner, and allow his or her genius to surface in a precise and useful fashion. Square fingertips add more calmness and common sense than the other tips and are a real asset to the short-fingered person.

A flexible hand with short fingers will add flexibility of mind to the short-fingered person, and render this person adaptable to a large variety of subjects. Flexibility adds keenness. A combination of short fingers, pointed tips, and flexibility would not be a good one. This person would be too assertive, quick-witted and hasty. Flabby consistency will detract from a person's better qualities and will indicate laziness. The flexible hand will enhance the force of the short fingers more fully. Hard hands show the energy of a pigheaded mind, and will be likely to make the short-fingered person too headstrong.

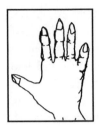

Knotty joints reduce the short-fingered qualities of quick thought and are an excellent combination for short fingers. The knotty qualities of reason and analysis keep the impulsiveness of the short fingers in check. If only the first knots of the hand are developed, the person with short fingers will be well organized.

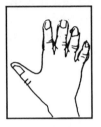

If only the second knots are developed the short-fingered person will not be as careless in dress and surroundings. The thumb plays a very important part with short fingers as it adds determination and will power if it is a strong thumb.

The clubbed thumb with short fingers will add a fearsome obstinacy and will drive the short-fingered qualities to temperamental extremes.

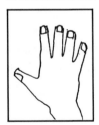

The flat, nervous thumb will add excitability to a set of forces already too quick.

A thumb with a short tip combined with short fingers will show that reason is lacking in this already unreasoning nature. This combination indicates intolerance and impatience. The strong thumb tip may bestow added reasoning abilities to the short-fingered person.

According to traditional palmistry, each finger is ruled by a planet. This planetary emphasis influences the behavior in a way that reflects the planet's characteristics. The following is a list of planetary traits which are enhanced or otherwise affected by the presence of short fingers. The dominant finger will determine which planet is most emphasized in the personality.

The ambition, pride, honor and religiousness of the Jupiterian will be more impulsive and spontaneous with short fingers. The Saturnian will be less slow, less introspective, and less stingy with short fingers. With Apollo prominent, the person will be more brilliant, since quick wit is already a strong quality of the Apollonian. The Mercury-ruled person will be quick as a flash whether an orator, businessperson, scientist, or thief.

The person ruled by Mars will be in need of help to keep short-fingered impetuosity from running away and causing him or her to undertake hazardous ventures. The Lunar person will be less dreamy, less selfish, and quicker with short fingers. The Venusian will have added passion and spontaneity.

Note the Three Worlds of Palmistry when examining the short fingers to see if there is an emphasis on any one zone — mental, material, or physical. It is very important to note the Head Line to see if it is strong, clear and straight rather than drooping or otherwise defective. A good clear Head Line showing sound, healthy judgment will add more to the perfection of short fingers than any other feature.

Short fingers are a fine possession. These people are not small-minded in their views, but possess a disdain for details and a tendency to be hasty; thus, they are in constant danger of making mistakes resulting from a lack of careful thought. Even with quick wit and big plans, the short-fingered people need square tips, flexible skin consistency, thumbs which bespeak discipline, and a fine, straight Head Line to keep their nasty nature in check.

———————————— Finger Length Checklist ————————————

☐ Are the fingers longer than the length of the palm, about equal to the length of the palm, or shorter than the length of the palm?

☐ Are the fingers considered long, short, or average by the standards mentioned in the previous pages?

☐ Is this true for both hands?

□ If they are long, are they also knotty, or smooth?

□ If they are short, are they also knotty, or smooth?

□ Does any one finger differ noticeably in length from the rest? Which one? Is this true for both hands?

□ Note the fingertip shapes in combination with the long-fingered characteristics.

□ Note the fingertip shapes in combination with short-fingered characteristics.

Knots on Fingers

People with knotty fingers are philosophical and analytical. They search for truth; they are hard to change, slow to arrive at conclusions; they are patient and systematic; they are down-to-earth workers.

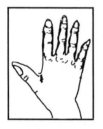 When examining the hand for knots on the fingers, a simple test can reveal a great deal. Hold the finger in question between your thumb and index finger and run these fingers down the sides of the finger you are testing. You will immediately feel which joint has the knot and which knot is greatest. Test your own fingers in this fashion and jot down what your findings are.

The smooth and knotty development indicates opposite types of people. Smooth fingers are most often found on young people while knotty ones are found on those who are more mature in years.

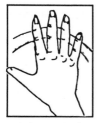

The first joint is located close to the fingertips and is called the Knot of Mental Order. It refers to the symmetrical qualities of the mind. The second joint is called The Knot of Material Order. Knots of the Material Order indicate a love of order which manifests itself through tidiness and accuracy in the business and social worlds. A combination of both knots on all fingers will describe a person who acts slowly, thinks carefully, and deliberates. Thoughts and actions are painstaking and methodical. Reason and analysis are apparent in all that he or she does. The person will trace a problem back to its most fundamental elements, and consider every detail before coming to a conclusion. Thus, we find that analysis, reasoning, investigation, and thoughtfulness are the most prominent qualities of knotty joints.

People with both knots in evidence are not carried away by sentiment, enthusiasm or impulse. They are philosophical and hunt for truth. They do not analyze with frivolous motives; they are searching for facts and dig deeply to get to the bottom of things. They do not respond as quickly as people with smooth fingers. Facts and results are their two best friends, reason is their guide and they are seldom emotional or impulsive. These people are studious and do not rely on inspiration to carry them through life. They usually convey an impression of diligence and common sense. Knotty fingers make careful deductions, and they never swerve once they are convinced that they are right. They also require much proof before they believe anything.

If only the first knots are prominent on the hand, it will indicate an intelligent mind and a systematic way of thinking. The mental processes are organized and analytical.

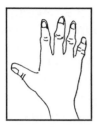

If only the second knots are evident, it indicates being methodic in material affairs. This person wants everything neat, clean and orderly. He or she will be neat in appearance, and inclined to have daily or weekly routines. This person is systematic and conservative.

Square tips with knotty fingers show a hard taskmaster and a severe disciplinarian. These people thrive on red tape, and can appear to be quite fanatical. They make excellent sculptors, masons, dentists, mechanics, and technicians where precision, and attention to detail or procedure are necessary.

Spatulate tips with knotty fingers show very obstinate people who are cranky in the extreme. This indicates realists who will be very contrary and challenging to people who are idealistic and intuitive by nature. Spatulate and square tips are so skeptical when combined with knotty fingers that they will not believe what can't be seen or touched. These people, however, are very inventive and will show patience when developing unique and unusual creations.

Conic and pointed tips will lighten the intensity of the knotty fingers and will be a real compliment to them. The severity of the philosophical disposition will be softened by the idealism of the conic or pointed tips. Conic fingertips with knotty fingers are found in all types of professions. The hand with pointed fingertips and knotty fingers is much more unusual and is apt to be in an equally unusual career. Methodical work combined with spirituality and idealism is a combination that may be found as lay people in the clergy or in other kinds of charity work. These are religious hands that use the power of analysis for understanding theology and esoteric matters.

Be sure to examine the consistency of the knotty hand as softness or flabbiness will detract from analytical powers. Flexibility is not often found with knotty fingers. The knotty-fingered type of mind is not usually flexible by nature. Results are achieved from labor and study, rather than from quick bursts of inspiration. If the knots are very pronounced on the fingers, so too will be the qualities of the person. If an excessive development of knotty fingers is apparent, be sure to ask if the person has arthritis. This disease thickens and stiffens the joints, and should not be mistaken for knotty qualities.

When finding a hand with only one or two fingers possessing knots, apply the knotty qualities to the qualities of that finger alone. See the chapter on individual fingers to get an idea of how a knot affects the finger in question. The same is true if the finger only has one knot rather than two. Apply the Knot of Mental Order or the Knot of Material Order to the character of the finger in particular.

Smooth Fingers

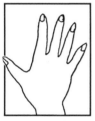

The next personality that we will look into is that possessed by someone with smooth fingers. These are fingers that appear to have no discernable bulge at the finger joints. Smooth-fingered people are activated by inspiration and impulse. They are intuitive and quick-thinking. Palmists usually consider this lack of knots an indication of an artistic temperament, especially when accompanied by conic fingertips. Reason and logic are foreign concepts to these people. Decisions are propelled by quick flashes of thought, which often carry them away with the sentiment of the moment. People with smooth fingers rely on impressions without stopping to reason out all the whys and wherefores. Such intuitive deductions seem to serve smooth-fingered people infallibly. These people are not inclined to tarry over details: they think quickly and dispose of a subject just as quickly. Consequently, they may cover more ground in a day than most people, but they are not as thorough as they could be. They are inclined to take things for granted. Being less engrossed in the mental world than the average person, they think more of decoration in dress and in decor. Their love of beauty will be their most prevalent characteristic, but with a coarse hand, this love of beauty can degenerate into a love of showiness.

In dealing with smooth fingers, always bear in mind what they represent. Remember, these people do not rely on reason and analysis, but on inspiration, impulse and intuition. They are lovers of beauty who generally act on the spur of the moment. They are emotional and sentimental. They play their hunches, and thus, are often successful in business. Smooth-fingered people are inclined to choose a business where they can put their intuition to use. These types move very fast and will need a good Head Line to make them more thoughtful and rational. They are successful as actors, as they lack stiffness and conventionality, and can use their inspiration to instantly create a character.

People with short and smooth fingers are inclined to be opportunists, seizing the moment and applying ingenuity if the combination is operating favorably. They are easily flustered. They are inclined to spend money too freely, relying on what they make rather than on what they save. They are sociable and personable, and are inclined to have more leisure hours than those with knotty fingers.

Examine the hand's consistency and color when there are smooth fingers present. Too much energy, signified by a hard hand, and too much enthusiasm, signified by a red cast to the hand, will cause the person to be overly impetuous. Also examine the fingertips. If they are pointed, the more artistic features are emphasized, as well as a strong propensity for religious inspiration. If the smooth fingers are square at the fingertips, their quickness and inspiration will be guided by more practical sentiments. The person will also be less idealistic, and more successful in the business world. With spatulate fingertips, the person will be original and very active. This combination will make a dynamic and unusual person indeed, but it is a combination which is rarely found.

No matter the combination found with smooth fingers, those qualities will be heightened by a quick wit, impulsiveness and swiftness in action. Remember this, and apply these qualities to the person in question. Remember also, that most people have knots on at least a few of their fingers, whether upper or lower knuckle, and the person with hands entirely free of knots is rare indeed. This person is likely to be found in a convent or seminary if the fingertips are pointed.

Fingertips

The ability to recognize and identify various fingertip shapes is a tremendous asset to any palmist. Fingertips give a clue to the way the energy of each finger is being expressed. We know that each finger has certain characteristics, but the nature of *how* those traits are being put to use will be shown by the shape of the fingertips. The fingertips illustrate individual methodology. The fingers themselves show dexterity and patience. The fingertips show the style in which this dexterity and patience are expressed.

It is important to ascertain the current profession of the client to make sure you are not observing fingertips that are altered by any physical work the person is doing daily. For example, the fingertips of a man who pours cement may be radically altered by the work that he does. The lye in the cement compounds will often damage the fingertips as well as altering the shape and color of the fingernails. The fingertips of a musician may have callouses from holding down the strings of an instrument and so on. Therefore, it is important not to confuse fingertips that have been shaped by the person's profession with fingertips which have not been altered. If you see fingertips that are reddened by some form of work, do not embarrass the person by asking what kind of work would leave such an effect. A good palmist will never dwell on negative qualities found in anyone's hand.

If you find fleshy pads on the fingertips or callouses on the tips alone, the person is quite likely to be a musician. If there are only callouses on one hand it is a sure sign of a stringed instrument. If these callouses are accompanied by square tips, great emphasis is placed on rhythm and meter. A bass player would have such a development. Always inquire about the profession before beginning the palm reading.

Always correlate your fingertip findings with the Head Line of the person. The shape of the fingertips will give an added reference to the way the mind operates, and can serve as a back up reference for deductions about the Head Line. The fingertips themselves, however, should never be used as a singular reference for any conclusions. Information about the fingertips should be used in conjunction with other information, such as hand shapes and finger lengths. Remember, fingertips tell the style of execution, which is only a small clue when considering the person's behavior as a whole.

Conic Fingertips

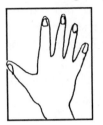

The conic fingertip is round in appearance and is the most common of all fingertip shapes. It is an especially prevalent shape for the fingertips of women. Conic tips illustrate the feminine qualities of whimsy and decoration. They also suggest that the person is impulsive, intuitive, quick-witted and devoted to beautiful, harmonious surroundings. The person will be impressionable, and life will be less a matter of work than a matter of enjoyment. Intuition is the greatest talent, and this person will not care to deal with figures or other practical matters. The greatest love is that which pleases the eye and the ear, and the world of reason and system will take much effort to acquire. To these fingertips, the regularity of the square-tipped person will be an annoying nuisance. The conic-tipped person will not care whether the things he or she buys are useful, so long as they are beautiful. These fingertips usually accompany fine skin, showing that refinement and taste are uppermost among their aspirations. Conic tips are often artistic, and indicate someone devoted to beautifying self and surroundings. This person is also idealistic, emotional and sympathetic.

Square Fingertips

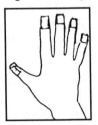

The square fingertip is less frequently found and is indicative of regularity, order, system, punctuality and precision. This person will rarely ever be haphazard, since disorder is positively abhorrent. He or she goes by the rules, follows instructions carefully, and is attentive to social custom. This type has difficulty understanding how people could operate otherwise, and this trait may be difficult to get along with. The individual is fussy and economical, and will buy products that are useful before buying something that is merely beautiful. Beauty is found in symmetry, and in things that are durable and lasting. The person with square fingertips makes a good scientist and mathematician, or might work at drafting, architecture, sculpting, and if medically oriented, plastic surgery. Remember, square fingertips show precision and a special affinity for working with plans and blueprints.

Square fingertips are often found on hands possessing knotty finger joints. This feature will give added patience and attention to detail, especially if the fingers are also long. In appearance, the square fingertip will usually be accompanied by cuticles that also appear square. The very tip of the finger itself will not be rounded as it is with the conic tip, but will be noticeably flat beneath the nail area. Always apply the Three Worlds of Palmistry to the fingers themselves, to see which area the square tip on this finger will operate — in the mental world, the material world or the physical world.

Spatulate Fingertips

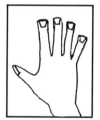

The spatulate fingertip is far less common than the conic or square fingertip, and is flared at one end, appearing noticeably wider or noticeably more narrow than the width of the first knuckle. These fingertips indicate active and original thinkers, who are prone to restlessness and over-enthusiasm. These people are constantly on the go, and very innovative in their way of thinking. Highly independent, they care little for the opinions of others and are not flustered by criticism. They are skillful and have a practical streak that will incline them to renovate and update old things, restoring them to their former use. Action, achievement, and originality are the three words which characterize these fingertips. These people have a fondness for animals, especially fast ones like racehorses and racing dogs. They will rarely shrink from a challenge, and love the excitement of gambling. Spatulate-tipped people will get things done in a unique way without wasting time.

Pointed Fingertips

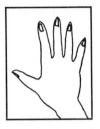

People with pointed fingertips are few and far between. Traditionally speaking, they are known as psychic types and are commonly found in the religious community. This type depends almost exclusively on intuition and first impressions. Theirs is a world of vibrations and inspirations. They are extremely idealistic and are inclined to be greatly influenced by dreams and omens. Highly sensitive and psychic indeed, people with pointed fingertips are not suited for the world of hard knocks and practicality. They are uncomfortable in the world of business, and seek to refine and beautify everything. If they cannot achieve this puritanical standard, they will withdraw completely into a world of fantasies. They are constantly on the alert for signs and omens, and seem high-strung and superstitious to all who know them. Their dreams are full of symbolism, and are often premonitions of things to come. These people are hypersensitive and horrified by crassness. If their surroundings are not harmonious, people with pointed fingertips will be nervous and irritable in the extreme. They are uncomfortable around loud, brash people and are apprehensive about challenges. They absorb information very quickly, but do not retain it for very long. They are quick-witted, but too timid to make much use of it. Be careful when speaking to pointed-tipped people as they are sensitive and superstitious and will hang on every word that you say.

Fingers which are all conic, pointed, square or spatulate are not often found on both hands. Most people have what is known as a mixed hand, a hand with more than one kind of fingertip shape. If one particular kind of fingertip predominates, be aware that the person is most likely to operate in the style indicated by those shapes. Always compare the tips of one hand to the fingertips of the other to see if the person is currently expressing him- or herself in the style indicative of that tip shape. (See Hand Comparison section for further information.) Remember also, that the middle finger—Saturn—is inclined to be somewhat square on most hands, and the pinky—Mercury—is inclined to be somewhat pointed on most hands as well. Therefore, these fingers must show extreme signs of squareness and pointedness respectively for those qualities to be considered.

──────────────── Fingertip Checklist ────────────────

□ Examine your own fingertips and note which kind of tip is found on each. List the tip shapes of the right hand and compare it to the tips of the left. Do the tips of the individual fingers enhance or hinder the other features found on that finger? How so?

□ Is the hand dominated by any one kind of fingertip? Which kind? Is this true for the left, right, or both hands?

□ Are the fingertips *all* the same variety? Which kind?

□ Apply the Three Worlds of Palmistry to the tip shapes of each finger. What does this tell you about the qualities of the individual fingers?

Fingertip Prints

The fingertips enhance our tactile sensitivity by forming a rough surface which aids the grip. They are also channels for the secretion of sweat. There are four basic patterns of skin development. These four basic patterns which the skin forms on the fingertips are shown in figure 3.

The Ulnar Loop is the most common formation found on the fingertip. It belongs to the conventional person, one who is not especially original in the way he or she thinks or operates. It does

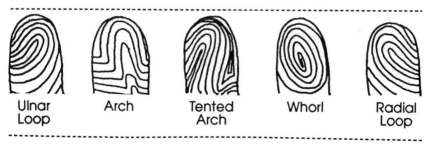

Ulnar Loop   Arch   Tented Arch   Whorl   Radial Loop

Figure 3. Basic fingertip patterns.

not have a specialized meaning as far as my research has concluded, however, according to Psychos, a noted palmistry writer, the presence of an ulnar loop on all the fingers can signify a person who is conservative, strong-willed, coolheaded in judgment, and possessing a tendency to be ruthless in business in the name of conventionality. The same would be true for radial loops on all fingers if you find them. See figure 3.

The Arch and Tented Arch (figure 3) are usually attributed to the more elemental type of personality, and indicate a crude, stubborn, defiant, insensitive person, who can be very hard-hearted. This person is rebellious, and unable to accept even the simplest social conventions. If this formation is found on only one finger, apply its characteristics to modify the qualities of the finger in question.

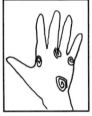

The whorl indicates an individualistic type who is very active and original in his or her thinking. The whorl will draw attention to the finger on which it is found and enhances the powers inherent in that finger. It also signifies a measure of artistic talent and restlessness, especially if it is seen on all the fingers. This person will have a great many ideas and a very active mind, but will often scatter efforts and spread himself or herself too thinly. This person is brilliant, but too easily distracted.

With whorls on the ring fingers—the Apollo fingers—of both hands the artistic abilities are highlighted. This person will desire to express and will do so with quick flashes of wit. With a whorl found on both pinkies—the Mercury fingers—the person is likely to be unconventional in matters of sex and money, and is clever, eager for action, and constantly tempted by dishonesty. Wherever the whorl is found, it activates the spot like a whirlwind. Whorls on *all* fingers show a very active and dynamic person, one who is original and unconventional in the extreme. This person is so restless that he or she must keep busy physically to keep from climbing the walls with nervous energy. A whorl found elsewhere in the hand has the same significance as whorls on the fingertips. It activates the spot where it is found with restlessness and originality. If a whorl is found between the fingers or dead center on a mount, it lends its immense creative energy to that area. A whorl is a blessing when found on the Mount of Saturn, beneath the middle finger, as it lightens the tendency for pessimism and gloom, and adds to the sense of humor.

The Thumb

The thumb is the most important of all the digits found on the hand. It is the pivot point for the activity of all the other fingers. It is the key to understanding the dexterity of the hand in question as all grasping is done with the thumb. To understand the thumb, a palmist applies a pressure test to assess its flexibility. This is done by pushing the thumb backward firmly and noting how far it will bend. Be sure to note the resistance, or lack of resistance, of the thumb while bending it.

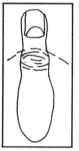

Traditional palmists use the thumb as a means of measuring tact and logic. The thumb will also gauge a person's willpower. It reveals determination and the capacity for leadership.

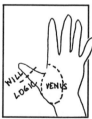

The palmist divides the thumb into three sections and examines each individually. The tip, or first phalange as it is called, represents the willpower and leadership ability. The second phalange (the area below the knuckle) shows tact, logic, and reasoning abilities. The third phalange of the thumb, also called the Mount of Venus, is located on the ball of the thumb in the lower third of the palm itself. This mount shows the need for romantic love, the depth of the person's sympathy, and the capacity for passion. The combination of all three of these areas reveals the sensual nature, and the logic, and willpower that governs it. The degree of flexibility of the thumb will show how readily these energies are expressed.

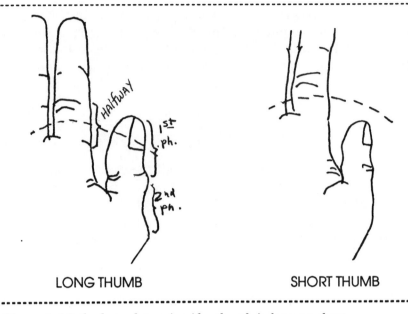

LONG THUMB   SHORT THUMB

Figure 4. Methods to determine if a thumb is long or short.

A good thumb is moderate in size, and well-proportioned to the rest of the fingers. A good thumb should be well-developed at the tip, with no flatness, paleness or excessive redness. It should be flexible, but not flabby or too easy to bend. The second phalange of a good thumb should be slightly waist-like, tapering inward like a woman's waist. Ideally, the good thumb should be somewhat low-set on the hand, and not held too tightly against the rest of the fingers. This would indicate a successful blend of will power and decision-making ability, with a measure of tact, stick-to-itiveness, logic and intelligence.

Note: Always use the thumb to back up other findings, i.e., check the Head Line when you are examining the intelligence of the person. This will show the powers of concentration, and the ability to remember and organize information. Then check the thumb for determination and logic before drawing any conclusions about intelligence.

A weak thumb is characterized by a thumb lacking proper muscle tone. It may appear flabby, puffy and pale. It may also bend too far backward with no spring to it, have a crooked appearance, lack a developed knuckle, or be noticeably mismatched with the other fingers. This kind of thumb shows a lack of willpower and one who is easily led. This person would rather have decisions made for him or her than make them. This thumb also shows a person who is easily discouraged. A lack of enthusiasm and poor staying power are additional traits which go with this kind of thumb. With a weak thumb, the person often has a weak Mount of Venus as well showing poor staying power in sexual matters. Poor muscle tone in the rest of the hand will indicate a flabby condition throughout the whole body, but these factors can be modified by other features.

To determine if the thumb is long or short in relation to the rest of the hand, have the person hold the thumb closely alongside the rest of the hand. If the thumb reaches beyond the halfway point of the third phalange of the index finger it is considered long. If it is shorter than this it is considered short (see fig. 4). Be sure to note whether the thumb is set high or low on the hand and apply its position to your assessment of the thumb's length.

Large thumbs show force of character, determination and will power. A short thumb shows a deficiency in these areas. A large thumb will add patience to short, critical nails and tone down a hot temper. The large thumb strengthens any weaknesses found in the nail characteristics, and will add strength and willpower to a poor Head Line. A large thumb adds persistence to knotty fingers and makes them more painstaking in their search for truth.

Large thumbs strengthen smooth fingers and temper their impulsiveness with reason and logic. The large thumb will give added determination to the square and spatulate tips, and render them more active and more practical. A large thumb tip decreases the impulsive qualities of the pointed and conic tips, and contributes logic and practicality to them as well. The conic and pointed fingertips are more likely to accomplish something tangible with a large thumb pushing them to greater exertion. The large thumb makes a person with short fingers quicker and more determined. A large thumb will incline a long-fingered person to carry out his or her ability for details with diligence and forethought. A large thumb shows a great reserve of energy and stamina. With it, you will find a love of history and one who seeks the useful and practical things. These people are not frivolous or flighty, they have a need to be authoritative, and will always show regard for the practical side of life. Small thumbs show a person who is guided by the heart and sentiments. It indicates a love of romance, and one who appreciates the beautiful, poetic, dreamy side of things. They have poor willpower, and succumb to temptation easily. Small thumbs show a lack of persistence and one who is inclined to take things for granted. This person is impulsive and must really make an effort to finish what he or she starts. Small, pointed thumbs show a dreamer who is adverse to effort of any kind, especially physical exertion. If the rest of the fingers are short, the accompaniment of a short thumb detracts from the energy. This person is less likely to complete things than someone with long thumbs, and is less likely to be thorough in executing plans. A small thumb with long fingers will not be much support for the love of detail that long fingers desire. Hands with smooth fingers and conic or pointed tips, when combined with small thumbs, show an artistic temperament, but without sufficient self-control to make practical use of it.

The supple and flexible thumb is distinguishable in that it bends back at the joints with spring and flexibility. It will also possess good pink color (or pink hue, if the person is not Caucasian) and good muscle tone. This thumb reveals someone who is enthusiastic, extravagant, versatile and at home anywhere. This person adapts easily to changing surroundings, and is sentimental, outgoing, generous, and sympathetic. This type is emotional in the sense that he or she is up one day and down the next. Success is achieved by brilliant dashes rather than by plodding and planning things slowly. This person is ambitious and aspires to surpass his or her own efforts as well as the efforts of peers. This thumb works best with square tips, a good Head Line and a good Mount of Saturn, to give more seriousness, and stronger powers of concentration. The conic, pointed, or spatulate tip will not be good with this kind of thumb, as it will contribute more impulsiveness to an already impulsive disposition. One should have sobering qualities (such as a strong Finger of Saturn) to make the best use of a supple and flexible thumb. If the thumb bends backward too far, the person is a pushover for one with a more forceful temperament. This person can't say *no*, and will be generous to a fault.

The stiff thumb will not bend backward at the joint when given the flexibility test. The hand itself is usually also rigid when pressed backward. This person is often pig-headed and uncompromising. He or she possesses a strong will and stubborn determination. A person with stiff thumbs is not likely to give or invite a confidence as there is an element of caution and reserve. He or she is practical, dogmatic, economical and, at times, stingy, weighing everything carefully, saving money and plodding along.

The stiff-thumbed person is appalled at waste of any kind, and is not inclined to be adaptable or change his or her mind once it is made up. Steady and serious, this type doesn't expect frivolity from life, and has a strong sense of justice and self-control. This person is not erratic and will stick to one task until it is finished; being very hard-nosed when crossed, this type usually does things by the book. The person with stiff thumbs is usually quiet, cautious, practical and reliable. If the stiff thumb has coarse skin, it will reduce the better qualities of the stiff thumb and render the person hard-hearted, stingy, and mean. Be sure to note the hand shape when analyzing a stiff thumb to see what other characteristics the person possesses before venturing an opinion. The stiff thumb is likely to argue with you, so be on your guard to comment only on areas which can be proven to the naked eye. The stiff thumb is always on the lookout for tangible evidence.

Always note the *color* of the thumb when considering how its shape will affect the temperament. (Remember when we speak of "color" it is usually referring to the cast or hue of the person's skin tone.) The white thumb describes a cold love nature and a lack of enthusiasm. The red thumb tells of ardor, and an excessive need to dominate others and be authoritative. Pink is the normal hue regardless of race, and shows good health, enhancing the qualities of any thumb. A yellow hue to the skin shows toxins in the blood, and will make the person touchy and easily upset.

The mounts should also be considered when examining the thumb. If a particular mount is emphasized elsewhere in the hand, a good or bad thumb will contribute to it in some way. The following is a brief list of effects caused by pronounced mounts combining with various thumb qualities:

□ The ambition, pride, and leadership of the Jupiterian would be brought to greater expression with the support of a good thumb. Ambition alone does not produce good results unless backed by a proper amount of reason and willpower. The Jupiterian qualities will be weakened by a small or pointed thumb.

□ The wisdom of the Saturnian will be employed to its fullest potential with a good thumb. The efforts of the Saturnian will become weak and vacillating with a weak thumb.

□ The brilliant Apollonian will be more-so with a good thumb. The person will be self-confident and good at business. With a small thumb comes the inclination for an artistic temperament, which may not find a creative outlet for its talents, due to lack of determination.

□ The shrewd and quick Mercury type with a large thumb will be sharp-witted and organized in business. This thumb will propel the person to excel in medicine or to become a high-powered salesperson. Much force will be lost if the thumb is weak though, especially if the hand is short-fingered. This will be a lazy type who uses cunning to cut corners and cheat rather than advancing through more conventional channels.

□ Mars will be even more determined with a good thumb. As an athlete, this type is unbeatable. Those ruled by Mars are aggressive. With a weak thumb, the Martian will have a chip on his or her shoulder and will be quarrelsome and lazy. This person will also be discouraged easily, and with coarse skin, will be a bully.

□ An emphasized Venus mount coupled with a large thumb will show a sensualist who is in constant pursuit of physical and sexual expression. This person is very dynamic and passionate when it comes to the love nature. With a small thumb, however, he or she will be too lazy to go after the sensuality necessary to be happy. This person is more inclined to fantasize sexual energy away. This type may be nonassertive and expect others to demonstrate love and affection without being willing to do the same in return. A good thumb makes the Venusian type more outgoing and more practical.

□ With a strongly developed Mount of Luna accompanied by a large, well-developed thumb, the person will have a great love of literature and a vivid imagination. The large thumb fosters this talent for self-expression and gives the drive to apply a wonderful imagination to the task of writing. This Lunar type will have a never-ending supply of poetic descriptions available, and a desire to interpret dreams through the use of literature. With a poor thumb and a strong Mount of Luna, the person has a strong imagination but is too lazy to apply it for practical use. This person is the dreamer who lacks the motivation to put dreams into action. This combination is sometimes found on the hands of the obese.

Thumb Tips

The following is a list of interpretations for thumb tips and other thumb characteristics. It is not necessary to read them all, but do feel free to keep them handy as reference material. It is difficult to fathom all the variations of thumbs unless you are actively engaged in the palmistry practice. It is then that you will see these thumbs close enough to distinguish one from the other, and the following list may be put to greater use. If the thumb tip is hard to classify, examine the cuticle shape for a clue. Press the thumb tip with your finger and note to what shape the fingertip returns after having been pressed.

Remember: The thumb tips are the most important tips of all the digits.

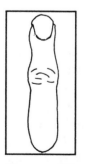

Conic tips found on the thumb will indicate that the person is impressionable. Although this fingertip does not add strength to the willpower it is not considered detrimental unless other factors found elsewhere in the hand agree. The conic qualities of impulse, idealism, and love of beauty will reduce the strength of the thumb's determination, regardless of its size. The conic tip suggests that the person can be easily led, and firm muscle tone or a measure of finger stiffness would be needed to offset this feature. The conic tip, when found on a very weak thumb, would indicate that the person is unstable and changeable. Always remember that the willpower of the person is modified and somewhat reduced if the conic tip is found on the thumb.

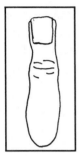

The square tip tells of practicality, common sense, and logic. If the thumb tip is excessively long and possesses a square tip, the person is likely to be obstinate. With a normal thumb length, the square tip enhances willpower and self-control. The person will be level-headed, pragmatic, organized, and factual.

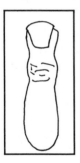

The spatulate tip, when found on the thumb, tells of independence and originality. The person is active and commanding. This kind of thumb tip will lend ingenuity to a long thumb. A spatulate thumb tip is a benefit to the weak thumb, but will contribute to the excesses of an overly strong thumb. On a bad hand, this tip can be a real menace, and will indicate an overly aggressive type who becomes dangerously brutal when provoked.

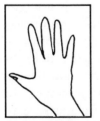

A thin, flat thumb tip shows a nervous and easily discouraged temperament. This thumb will usually be accompanied by many lines on the hand, a soft, flabby consistency, and fluted nails—all signs of nervous excess. This person will have problems implementing his or her wishes, and will have little tolerance for the differences found in others. This type is apt to have a short fuse, and if the thumb is also red, it will show someone who is argumentative.

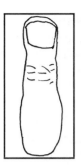

A broad thumb shows strong determination that is also supported by physical strength. This thumb is usually found on the hands of successful people and shows a firm and careful disposition. The liability of this thumb is that its owner can be a tyrant who is obstinate and even violent if the rest of the hand shows great stiffness or is overly red.

The elementary thumb is a shapeless non-symmetrical thumb which reveals a nature that is coarse and animalistic. Its owner is crass, tactless, and unconsciously rude. This can be a brutally willful person if other areas of the hand confirm. The elementary thumb is seldom found, but once seen, you are not likely to forget it. It is a shape-less thumb, lacking the distinction of a square fingertip, developed knuckle, or tapering lower half. The elementary thumb merely sticks out from the side of the hand as if it had no connection to the hand whatsoever.

There are two distinct ways in which the elementary thumb operates and this depends largely on the skin texture of the individual. With fine skin, the elementary thumb is likely to bend backward easily when pressed on. This will show a lack of will-power and self-discipline. It is also likely to have a short or otherwise deficient thumbnail, which would indicate impatience; with coarse skin, a short fuse, and readiness for violence. Because the thumb is such an important part of a person's anatomy, helping the hand to grasp and hold things, deficiencies found in the thumb should not be overlooked. The person with an elementary thumb and smooth, glossy skin will expect others to see his or her needs without making any effort to do anything for him- or herself. The thumb bending backward easily indicates a follower, not a leader. This person is likely to be a pushover for people who would like to make decisions for him or her and this person is particularly prone to being led into the realm of corruption and self-indulgence due to a lack of discipline. This person is inclined to find jobs where physical stamina is not required. He or she is blunt and obtuse when dealing verbally with the general public, and is far more comfortable with animals, where he or she can communicate without troubling to refine speech or mask true feelings.

If the skin is coarse with all nails short and the fingers stiff and thick in appearance, the elementary thumb will have more stubbornness, drive, and aggression. These hands are apt to be happiest doing physical labor. There is a temperamental streak that can easily turn to crime, using physical strength to satisfy an abundant appetite.

Second Phalange of the Thumb

Knots found on the thumb operate exactly as do knots found anywhere else on the hand. The thumb knot shows deliberation of thought. It adds strength to the Will Phalange (the tip) by reducing its impulsiveness and adding to its analytical qualities. Knots will also add strength to the conic or pointed thumb and increases the ability to reason and use logic. Knots reduce the laziness of a poor thumb tip, making the person more inclined to be thoughtful and considerate. However, if the second phalange of the thumb is thick and untapered, it will show a blunt and tactless disposition that is likely to jump to conclusions and look for arguments.

Remember, the second phalange is the indicator of the ability to perceive logic, exercise prudence, caution, and reasoning ability. It is important for the phalange to be in proportion to the rest of the hand. Note whether it is longer or shorter than the first phalange of the thumb. Normally, the second phalange should be slightly longer than the rest of the thumb, but it is also considered a good development when the first and second phalanges are of equal lengths. Remember that this phalange is the Director of the Will. With the second phalange in proper proportion to the rest of the thumb and the rest of the hand, the person will act from well-defined motives and will have a high level of competence. This type will be sure of opinions before stating them, and will apply willpower in a constructive fashion. A reasoning brain guiding a constructive will—a winning combination by *any* standard.

A long second phalange with a conic tip shows strength added to the reasoning ability. This will benefit the conic tip by making the person less impressionable.

The pointed thumb tip shows a lack of determination and one who tires easily. This person is extremely impulsive and has a difficult time sticking to a decision once it has been made. This impulsive quality can find a useful outlet in the practice of photography. A chameleon and a creator of whim and fancy, this thumb is suited for capturing a quick study. This person becomes bored easily and is constantly seeking change.

A thumb with a square tip and a long second phalange will add sound, practical judgment. A spatulate tip with a long second phalange will direct the original, innovative nature of the person into carefully planned channels. This combination adds forethought.

If the second phalange is shorter than the first, the individual will be inclined to act first and reason later. Willpower outweighs reasoning. This can be modified if the second phalange tapers gracefully adding tact to curb the will.

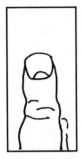

When the second phalange is short and thick, it shows a stubborn, headstrong person who acts without careful thought, and often makes mistakes due to impulsive decisions. This individual is not inclined to admit being wrong, and is unlikely to correct mistakes once they have been made. With the second phalange short and the thumb possessing a conic tip, the person is impressionable and lacks logic. This will detract from any of the thumb's better qualities. This person is easily swayed and prefers to have decisions made by someone else.

A short second phalange with a square-tipped thumb shows someone who attempts to show strength no matter what. The actor who believes "the show must go on" and the worker who goes to work when he or she is sick are likely to have this combination. With a spatulate thumb, the person will be fussy without producing any tangible results.

A flat and flabby second phalange is a nervous development. The person lacks sufficient strength to make logical ability operative. Greater physical strength is needed here. This development will weaken all other thumb qualities, and deplete the strength of the other fingertips.

With the second phalange coarse, heavy and thick, the person has only elementary reasoning. Low, common tastes will likely surface elsewhere in the hand and, will detract from the Will Phalange and the other fingertips.

With the second phalange slender, and the skin fine in texture, the person will possess refined logic and tact. This person thinks in a fine and delicate way, but loses no element of strength by this finesse. He or she reasons and plans tactfully and directs energy in refined directions. In a bad hand, this can render the person crafty and designing, but always clever.

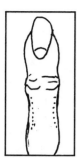 The second phalange, very narrow and waist-shaped in the middle, will show a tactful nature, with a wonderfully refined sense of logic and proportion. This person does things in an adroit and diplomatic way, has the ability to approach people in the correct manner, and will gain his or her ends by pleasant means.

———————————— Thumb Checklist ————————————

The following is a list of questions that will help you to examine your own thumbs:

□ What size is the thumb in relation to the rest of the hand?

□ What kind of flexibility does it have? If it is not flexible, would it be considered a stiff thumb?

□ What color is the thumb? Consider the color of all three phalanges. Do they differ?

□ Describe the Mount of Venus. Is it firm, flabby, pink, or pale in color?

□ What kind of a tip does the thumb have?

□ Are there any outstanding features on the thumb? What are they?

□ Is the thumb smooth or knotty at the joint? Describe the second phalange. Note the texture of the skin. Is the first or second phalange the longest? Is this true on both hands?

□ Compare the left thumb with the right. Are there any noticeable differences?

CHAPTER 3

The Mounts

The mounts are pads of flesh that sit at the base of each finger and protrude from the palm in various places. Their firmness indicates the condition of the muscles throughout the rest of the body, and their color tells us about the person's health and vitality. Traditionally, each mount is associated with a planet, and the attributes of that planet will have bearing on what each mount represents. An example of this is the planet Saturn. This planet symbolizes coldness and is one that moves very slowly. The Mount of Saturn is located under the middle finger, and both the mount itself and the finger attached to it are referred to as being both slow and cold in the way they affect other parts of the hand. More will be said about Saturn in subsequent chapters, but for now, just remember that a mount bearing the name of a planet will have that planet's attributes. It would be to the student's advantage to memorize the planetary features. See fig. 5 on p. 66 for a closer look at the mounts and the area of the hand they inhabit. Remember also that when you find a particular mount noticeably more developed than the others, the person will be the most influenced by the planet associated with that mount. If this mount is dominant in both hands, interests, work methods, and personal goals will be colored by the planetary features.

It is important to remember that the ball of the thumb (also known as the Mount of Venus) is usually the most developed

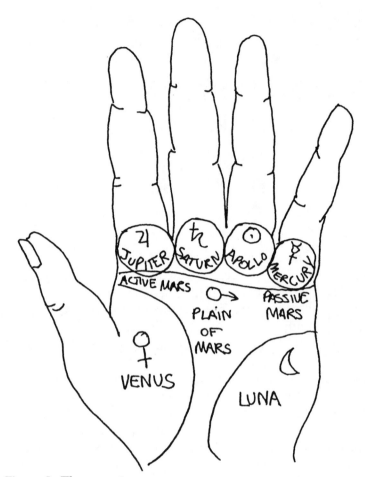

Figure 5. The mounts.

mount of everyone's hand. The thumb is the most active digit on the hand and its muscle development must be strong to support its activity. Therefore, it is advised not to be misled by the height of the Venus mount when comparing it with the height and development of other mounts.

When examining the hand for mount development, hold the person's hand perpendicular to your eye and bend it backward at the wrist. Look for the area of the hand that protrudes from the palm in the most noticeable fashion. When holding the hand at this angle it will be easy to spot the most prominent mount. The light will be hitting the hand in such a way that the high and low points of the hand will become quite obvious. Try this method with your own hand and record what you see. Read the height of these areas as if they were a topographical map, noting the locations of the highest and lowest areas.

When the hand is seen with mounts which are all equally developed, it shows a well-balanced character and healthy body. This is a broad-minded, even-tempered person who is usually amenable to reason. Not an extremist like someone with one mount overly developed, this person is well-rounded educationally and not likely to shrink from challenges no matter how tough they may seem. Cool-headed and fearless, this person will not be intimidated and is too practical to take foolish chances. This type greatly values health and will exercise discipline to keep in shape.

The Apex

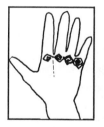

The apex is a curious marking found on each of the finger mounts. It is like a fingerprint for the mount itself, and its placement on the mount will give a valuable clue as to how the mount operates. In appearance, it will have the shape of a triangle made up of skin ridges. It should be directly beneath the middle of the finger to be properly located on the mount. If it is directly in the middle of the mount, it will show that the mount is operating to its optimum potential.

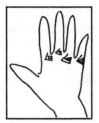

If it is placed to the left or the right of the mount, it will decrease the mount's potential and lend the energy of that mount to the mount toward which it leans. If the apex is located high on the hand — directly beneath the finger's connection to the palm itself — the more elevated qualities of the mount's character will be highlighted. If the apex is found low on the mount, the mount's qualities will be expressed in a more physical way.

When reading a mount, the vertical lines found there will enhance its qualities. Horizontal lines on a mount are usually detrimental. Lines crossing the mount horizontally prevent the energy from surfacing into the fingers. A grill — which is a combination of vertical and horizontal lines found on the mount — is considered a defect of the mount, and should be read as such, with the exception of a grill under the ring finger, which indicates a theatrical nature and a love of the spotlight.

Finger Influences on the Mounts

Accurately judging the degree of influence the fingers have upon the mounts is very important to the practice of palmistry. Although fingertips provide information about the mentality of a person, fingertips alone do not provide the complete picture. The clues which reveal the most are the character of the fingers and the development of the mounts which lie just beneath them.

When considering the character of a finger we are observing a number of things. We are looking first at the length and flexibility of the finger, then tip-shape and knots, and finally, its color and skin texture. In addition, we are also looking at the finger's erectness, and whether it is bent toward any other finger or if it is twisted on its axis. Then, look to the mount beneath the finger and examine its muscle tone, markings and apex. The character of the finger will enhance or hinder a good mount according to its nature. A good fingertip will not help if the finger is twisted or bent. A hand with well-shaped fingertips will have reduced strength if the fingers are pale and white, or if they are twisted on their axes.

These clues, used in conjunction with one another, serve as a check and balance system for proper assessment. Even if we are perplexed by the fingertip shapes, knots, or other features we can train our eye for the general character of the fingers and make accurate deductions. It takes a good memory to keep in mind all the tedious details that palmistry teaches, but we need not be discouraged as long as we can read the general character of the fingers. Consult this chapter often whenever examining a print of the hand. Try to commit these details to memory. Also, remember that any finger which is set low in the hand subtracts a portion of strength from the mount on which it is found.

 If one finger leans noticeably toward another finger, it gives a part of its strength to the other finger. If the finger is crooked, it adds shrewdness and a penchant for dishonesty to the mount on which it is found. To find out where this shrewdness is likely to surface, look to the finger phalanges, and measure the longest joint with your eye. Once again the Three Worlds of Palmistry will provide a clue.

If one finger is flexible while the others are not, apply the characteristics of flexibility to that finger only. For example: imagine examining a stiff hand with only the ring finger—the Apollo finger—appearing to have flexibility. We can safely deduce that even though this person will be stubborn and uncompromising on most issues, he or she will be remarkably flexible regarding matters of art, drama, and literature. These are traits from the realm of Apollo. The most flexible part of the hand will indicate the areas where the person will be the most flexible. The mount qualities will be enhanced by a flexible finger, and will operate more smoothly than will mounts accompanied by stiff fingers.

Look closely at the nails to see what health indications are given. If one nail looks brittle or otherwise defective, while the others appear healthy-looking, it will debilitate the operation of both that finger and its mount. Find the chapter concerning that particular mount and locate the paragraph that lists the illnesses connected with that mount. With only one nail defective, it is likely that the illness which caused the damage to the nail is the one associated with that particular mount on which the finger is located.

View the vertical lines found on a mount as channels through which the energy can escape. The effect of the mount is hindered by any horizontal lines that cross it.

Look at the nails when examining a mount. Both the nails and the mount should have a nice, healthy pink hue in both hands. If you find a healthy mount in the hand that represents the past, and an unhealthy one in the hand representing the present, draw your own conclusions accordingly. This will be useful when discussing what the past was like, and what the client has now become.

A health defect shown by the shape, texture or color of the nails on any finger brings out the health defects associated with its mount.

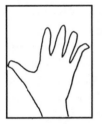

If all the fingers are short, and a single finger deficiency is found, remember the meaning of short fingers, and add the deficient characteristic of that finger to your assessment. Oftentimes, it is a trait of long or short fingers that acts as a precursor to the finger defect in the first place. For example, since the short-fingered person is hasty and has a short fuse, these traits will certainly contribute to the health of the person in terms of dietary habits and exercise patterns. This person will overexert in short spurts, overeat hastily, drink too much too quickly, and the nervous system and recuperative powers are affected accordingly.

Always keep the character of the fingers in mind when examining a hand for defects. The character will give you a clue as to where an illness originated. However, if the person does indeed have a short fuse, and you see that the thumb is also blunt or indicating a volatile nature, it may be best not to mention it at all. This person is likely to argue with you, denying the short fuse. Stick to the positive qualities and give an opinion regarding temperament only if the person asks you for it. This is especially important with spatulate tips. This person will be outgoing and demonstrative, and you do not need any demonstration of indignation! In the case of a short-fingered person, remember this type is inclined to act very quickly.

If the fingers are long, apply the slow, painstaking love of detail to the mount qualities found. If only one finger is long, apply these traits to the mount of the finger.

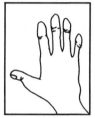

With only the first joints developed, remember the qualities of investigation, analysis, and patience that go with them and apply these attributes to the mounts themselves. This will add the strength of the top knot qualities to any mount that is well developed, and also strengthen deficiencies found in other mounts. These people will be well ordered in thinking habits, and organized as writers and researchers, but may not be as competent in sports or drama professions where spontaneity is required. Check the fingertips to see how the talents operate.

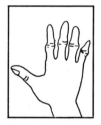

If the second knots (the lower knuckles) are very developed, you will know these people are systematic in business and orderly in the home. Add these qualities to the most developed mount and also to the fingertip attributes. If only one finger has this feature (developed lower knot) it will add strength to the mount beneath it. The same is true if both knots are found. Apply those knotty features to the mounts beneath the fingers on which they are found. These people will be slow and skeptical no matter what mount is most emphasized, and their manner of expression will always bear the stamp of the knotty-fingered style.

————————— Mounts Checklist —————————

Observe your own fingers and the mounts they are connected to.

□ What is the character of the fingers in general? Straight, bent, twisted?

□ Are the fingers knotty or smooth? Do one or two of the fingers have these features while the others do not?

□ Are the fingers long or short? Do one or more look this way apart from the others? Which ones?

□ Are there any fingers that have a coarse texture? Which ones?

□ Are there any fingers more erect than the others? Which ones? Is this so in both hands? What deductions can you make from this information?

□ What is the condition of the mounts? Is the muscle tone good or poor?

□ Are the mounts pink and healthy-looking, or are they flat and pale?

□ Where is the apex found on each mount? Are they well centered? If not, where do they lean? Are they high or low-set on any of the mounts? Which one?

CHAPTER 4

The Mount of Jupiter

 The Mount of Jupiter is located directly below the index finger and extends approximately to the area where the Life Line begins. A good Jupiter mount should have firm muscle tone and a centrally located apex. Markings which are considered beneficial to the mount would be a vertical line extending downward from the finger, a square, a trident, a triangle, a star, a ring which encircles the entire mount, or ascending branches from the Head, Heart, or Life Lines.

Unfavorable markings found on the Jupiter mount would be a grill, a dot, a deep Heart Line which divides the mount, an X, or any other lines that may cross the mount horizontally. If the mount is pale or discolored in any way, this will also detract from the mount's higher qualities. This will also be the case if the mount is flabby, flat, or indented in any way. The following is a list of Jupiterian qualities which should be memorized.

Jupiter represents: ambition, pride, loyalty, justice, religion, sociability, ability to lead others, expansion, dignity, protection and law and order. Jupiter was a god famed for his protection of children and small animals and is portrayed in mythology as authoritative and generous. He was an epicurean of great magnitude, and his rulership extends to the palate and the sensualism of eating. The negative side of Jupiter is ruthless, vainglorious, jealous, domineering and arrogant.

The Jupiterian Type

In the hand, the Jupiterian type is a leader. This is a very ambitious person whose commanding presence and love for high positions may lead him or her into politics. This type is also found in the military, as here again, the opportunity to hold a commanding position and to lead others is a powerful attraction. Religion is another strong attribute of the Jupiterian, so prominent clergymen and religious leaders often have this kind of hand. The Jupiterian love of nature may also foster an interest in climbing mountains or blazing trails in a pioneering spirit. The Jupiterian will always exert a sense of honor and love of challenge.

Jupiterian Appearance

In appearance, Jupiterians are of average height with a large frame and strong, firm muscles. As they age, they are inclined to become rather fleshy, but in their prime, Jupiterians are solid, strong, and well able to support their weight. They have a vigorous constitution. They also may have a lot of body hair; males have developed chests and are well-known for loud voices and lungpower. They are robust, attractive, and confident, and it is these attributes that enhance their ability to secure the devotion of the people they lead. They are self-sufficient types, who do not ask the advice of others. Jupiterians are aware of the ability they have to sway others, and this can sometimes lead to vanity and domination over others.

Jupiterians are warm-hearted people, and they are usually generous in a warm and charitable way. Always fair-minded, Jupiterians encourage honesty in business and relationships. They are gallant and attractive to the opposite sex. They can be extravagant, and positions of authority will attract them not just for money but also for authority. They have contempt for people who are petty and miserly.

Jupiterians prefer to have a refining, broadening, or uplifting influence on people they know. They are aristocratic, conservative, and fond of formality, pageantry and tradition. Jupiterians are easy to get along with and have a talent for making and keeping friends. They mature early and are inclined to marry someone of whom they can be proud.

Jupiterian Illnesses

The blustery, self-assertive, outgoing nature of Jupiterians predispose them to certain illnesses. They have great appetites with a preference for highly seasoned foods. They are fond of wine and tobacco, and a natural enthusiasm inclines them to overdo. Thus, later in life Jupiterians are prone to digestive problems. Gout, indigestion, and apoplexy are typical Jupiterian illnesses. Impure blood caused by rich foods and other toxins will take its toll on the lungs, which are frequently abused by the Jupiterian tendency to bellow and speak loudly. The liver is also overtaxed and the Health Line—running vertically under the pinky—should be examined with care when defects are found on the Mount of Jupiter.

Jupiterian Apex

If you suspect someone of having predominantly Jupiterian traits, examine the apex (the center of the skin ridges that converge beneath each finger) to see if this energy is emanating from dead center on the mount. If the apex is properly centered, the Jupiterian qualities will be evenly distributed. If the apex of the Jupiter mount leans toward the Mount of Saturn, the sobriety, slowness, and caution of the Saturn influence will restrain the typical Jupiterian ambition, and make the person less inclined to take risks. If the apex falls on the side of the hand nearest the thumb it is traditionally read as representing selfish aggression aimed at personal advancement, therefore this is a person who may step on others to get ahead. The effects of this marking can be modified by other factors in the hand, but the tendency will always be present. If the apex is connected to the Heart Line, the ambitions will be directed to love and security in the family. If the apex should touch the Head Line, ambition will more likely be directed along the lines of intellectual fulfillment.

Jupiterian Mount Color

If the Mount of Jupiter is very pale or white looking, the Jupiterian will be less magnetic, less attractive, and more inclined to be selfish. He or she will be without the Jupiterian charisma that people follow and applaud. The Jupiter mount should have a pink hue to bring out its optimum potential.

A red cast indicates excessive strength and ardor. It adds intensity to an already intense character, and increases the liability for health defects. This person is likely to have constant indigestion due to poor eating habits and a tendency to overindulge. In character, this person will be demanding, overbearing, at times tyrannical, and expects always to have things *his* or *her* way. To this person, "might makes right."

Yellow colored mounts are not often seen, but if yellow is found on the Mount of Jupiter it will indicate liver trouble.

A blue Mount of Jupiter will show a weak and congested heart.

The Jupiterian Finger

Observe the Finger of Jupiter carefully to discern which phalange is the most emphasized; once again, apply the Three Worlds of Palmistry as a gauge.

Jupiterian Finger Length

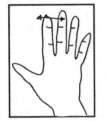

To measure the length of the Jupiter finger, note whether the index finger reaches to the middle of the first phalange of the neighboring Saturn finger. As long as the Jupiter finger is no longer than the middle of the first phalange of the Saturn finger, it indicates that the desire for power and leadership will not be excessive. If Jupiter is longer than the middle of the first phalange of Saturn, it shows that the desire for power and leadership will be very great indeed. If the Jupiter finger is longer than the Saturn finger it will show a tyrant who craves power and dominion beyond anything else.

If the Jupiter finger does not reach the first phalange of Saturn, it is considered very short and will deplete the higher

Jupiterian traits as well as the power of the Jupiter mount. This person will lack ambition, would rather follow than lead, and will also have a poor sense of self-esteem.

A crooked Finger of Jupiter adds shrewdness to the Jupiter qualities but is not necessarily a bad sign. This person will systematically plan all moves and will be cunning and calculating. He or she can be manipulative and will have a tendency to scheme, taking the covert route to personal goals.

The Jupiter Fingertip

If the fingertip of the Jupiter finger is conic, it will emphasize altruism and religiousness. This person will have great reverence for his or her faith and respect for the religions and beliefs of others.

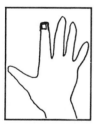

If the Jupiter fingertip is square, the person will use reason and common sense, and his or her ambitions are practical. Religious ideals will be plain and simple.

If the Jupiter fingertip is spatulate, this person is original and leans toward the agnostic. He or she will follow no particular creed or church and will have a domineering spirit that may be rather overbearing. The broader the first phalange, the more domineering the person will be, and the less religious.

Jupiter Finger Phalanges ———————————————

If the first phalange is long on the Jupiter finger, the person is ruled by the mental world and will be both intuitive and religious.

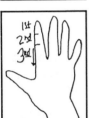

If the second phalange is longest, the person will be more attentive to the practical affairs of life. This person will be a money-maker and the Jupiter desire will be expended in the world of business and commerce.

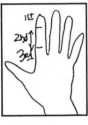

If the third phalange is the most emphasized in length, it will suggest that the lower nature of the Jupiterian will rule the ambitions. This is not a good sign, as it points to over-indulgence in flesh, food, and alcohol. The desire for rulership will have sordid motivations if the rest of the hand is a bad one. This person will not operate in a manner that is always refined. This development will coarsen the nature considerably.

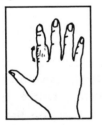

If the third phalange of Jupiter is long and thick, it is traditionally read as gluttony. If this is the most predominant phalange on the finger, these people will be ruled by the more common, sensual side, with ambition and desire for luxury utmost. They will overindulge in eating and drinking and bring on health problems peculiar to Jupiterians. People with this development will be more attracted to eating and self-indulgence than anything else. On a more positive note, this feature is often found on people whose palates are of great importance to their lifestyle—chefs, wine experts, and culinary artists.

 If the third phalange is long, but thin and waist-shaped, it indicates the opposite of the above. These people are more likely to achieve higher ideals without being distracted by indulgence of the senses. They are also not fond of cooking and eat sparingly.

Other Jupiterian Characteristics

Note the consistency of the hand to see if the physical energy will back the ambitions. A soft or flabby muscle tone to the hand, and especially to the mount, will cause the person to be more talk than action, and less likely to fulfill his or her ambitions.

Examine the skin to see if the Jupiterian qualities are refined or coarse. Note the flexibility of the hand to see whether a flexible mind is available to help carry the Jupiterian ambition forward. A hard, unyielding hand will show a stiff, uncompromising mind that will hamper the Jupiterian.

If the nail on the Jupiter Finger is very short, the desire to lead will be more intensified. The aggression natural to the Jupiterian would surface as excessive physical strength. This person will be short-tempered and criticize too much.

With light colored hair on the hand, the Jupiterian will be less ardent and less sensual, but very strong, determined and practical. Black hair on the back of the hand is more commonly found on the Jupiterian and indicates fire, vigor and enthusiasm. This person will have a large appetite and will be more prone to injuring his or her health through excesses.

Check to see what area is most pronounced using the Three Worlds of Palmistry. If the mental world is more pronounced, the ambitions will be for a literary career, or a career as an orator. If the middle of the hand is more pronounced, he or she will be a leader in business and in the affairs of the commercial world. If the lower zone is the most pronounced, an already sensuous person will become even more so. This person will indulge the appetite and tend to be obese. With refined skin, the person will be a connoisseur of wines, foods, and the opposite sex. Many fine chefs have this Jupiterian emphasis.

Knotty fingers will make the Jupiterian more analytical, more reasoning, and patient. This will help the Jupiterian plan his or her moves more effectively.

The best type of Jupiterian has a large, smooth Finger of Jupiter with a square or conic tip. The Jupiter finger should be straight and erect, and possess good flexibility and a broad, pink nail in order to function with optimum Jupiterian expression. The phalanges should be fairly equal, and the Jupiter mount below the finger, pink, and possessing good muscle tone. A good thumb would also contribute to the Jupiter finger by adding tact and logic to support ambitions. The rest of the hand should also have good muscle tone and well-cut lines without defects. With these features present, the best parts of the Jupiterian are likely to surface. He or she will be outgoing, well liked, healthy, conscientious and successful.

A Jupiterian with an otherwise bad hand would have some or all of the following features: a short Finger of Jupiter, coarse skin, a finger that is badly bent-looking or twisted. The mount will be pale and flabby. You will also see poor flexibility of the Jupiter finger and the rest of the hand.

With shallow lines and poor overall color, the health of the Jupiterian will be poor and the temperament will also be poor. Another feature which corrupts the nature of the Jupiterian will be overly long fingers, an overly red mount, short nails, and a bad thumb. With these features present, the Jupiterian love of command will degenerate into tyranny and sensualism, preying upon the weak, overpowering them with glee. This person can be overbearingly petty, or grossly extravagant for the sake of gratifying personal appetites. This person is selfish in the extreme, and will subject loved ones to terrible indignities. He or she will indulge the appetite for food, alcohol or the opposite sex.

─────────────── Mount of Jupiter Checklist ───────────────

Observe your own Finger and Mount of Jupiter and record your findings.

□ What kind of fingertip does the Jupiter finger have? What length of nail?

□ Are all the phalanges equal in length? If not, which one is longest/widest? Are there knots? On which joints? Is this true in both hands?

□ Is the finger flexible or stiff?

□ Is the skin refined, coarse, or medium in texture?

□ Is the Jupiter finger or mount the most prominent of any on the hand?

□ Are there any discolorations on the mount, finger or nail? What color? Where?

□ Describe the Mount of Jupiter. What color is it? What kind of texture does it have? What kind of muscle tone? Are there any detrimental markings on the mount? Which ones? Where?

□ How does the finger of one hand compare to that of the other?

□ How does the mount of one hand compare to that of the other?

The Mount of Saturn

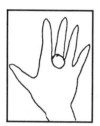

The Mount of Saturn is located just below the middle finger and should not be too excessive in its development. A good Mount of Saturn should have firm muscle tone and a centrally located apex. Good markings on the Mount of Saturn would be: a vertical line extending down from the finger, or a Fate Line that runs straight up the middle of the hand and reaches the mount with no unfavorable markings. A triangle, square, or ray-like extensions that reach downward onto the mount from the Finger of Saturn are also beneficial. Unfavorable markings would be: a grill, any kind of dot or dent in the Fate Line near the mount, a Heart Line that is broken just beneath the mount; an island, a ring that encircles the mount; an X, or lines which mar the mount horizontally. Other detrimental features would be a white or pale cast to the mount, a flabby mount, a yellow cast to the mount, a stiff Finger of Saturn, or a mount which is concave in appearance. A red or blue cast is rarely seen on the Mount of Saturn, but when found, is also considered detrimental and relates to illnesses of the Saturnian type.

The following is a list of Saturnian qualities which should be memorized: Saturn represents wisdom, sobriety, serious study, slowness, skepticism and frugality. Saturn is associated with the following occupations: research, the occult, mathematics, all forms of scientific pursuits where patience and detail is required, mining, geology, and one's sense of duty and responsibility.

Saturn rules the things which are buried or hidden deep within the earth. It is a cold, slow-moving planet, which was called by the ancient occultists a "malefic." Its effect is to retard, restrict, limit, bind, restrain, and investigate.

It may appear malefic, but everyone has Saturn influence to deal with. Without the influence of Saturn, there would be no discipline, and we would be swept away by frivolity, with no self-control. The Finger of Saturn is referred to by modern palmists as the "balance wheel" of character, and indicates the power to hold abundant enthusiasm in check.

The Saturnian Type

The Saturnian is sober, prudent, wise and serious. The Saturnian point of view is at times a gloomy one, and it causes the more spontaneous types to pause and think. Saturn is not at home in social surroundings, and is often referred to as a wet blanket. Saturn is cynical, irreverent, and a born doubter. Instead of seeking the company of others, this type avoids it, and has a strong tendency to withdraw from the social world altogether. The Saturnian prefers the country life to the city, and will choose to study agriculture, chemistry, or laboratory occupations where he or she can work alone in silence. The Saturnian doesn't mix well with others, and doesn't have much interest in attracting or keeping friends.

He or she does not succeed well in a business that depends on genial ways or attractive manners. This love of solitude is attractive for farm life, and the Saturnian is a natural horticulturist by virtue of a love for digging and exploring.

The Saturnian has a mystical streak. He or she is also very fond of occult studies, and is partial to mathematics, chemistry, medicine, and is usually successful in any of these professions. The Saturnian nature is deep, steady, and true. While others spend time on frivolity, he or she will be engrossed in deep thought and study. The Saturnian is conservative and does not do things hastily. Choices of business investments would be real estate, farms, and buildings. Things that endure the test of time is where you will find the investments of the Saturnian, and Saturn is called Father Time by the ancients.

The Saturnians are not known for affection, and often repel the opposite sex rather than attracting it. Warmth and passion are not strong points, Saturnians may not care to marry. Prudence gives a talent for saving money, but Saturnians can be very stingy and miserly about it. They are slow, patient, tireless workers, who will always do the job according to code. They love music, and can be fine composers. Musical tastes will be very serious and classical, with a tinge of melancholy. They prefer art that reflects an appreciation for natural scenery, such as landscapes and still-lifes; favorite literature might be traditional classics and history. Remember that Saturnians are very independent and dislike restraint.

In a bad hand, an emphasis on the Saturn mount will tell of a mean surly dishonest, villain. Always comb the hand for details which will counter this tendency. Saturn ruled people are often late bloomers in life. They have a great regard for education and are inclined to acquire many degrees, which they achieve with painstaking study that adds to the alienation they feel in the social world. People ruled by Saturn quite often have tremendous obstacles to overcome early in life, which also contribute to their shyness, studiousness, and disdain of social contact. But, not all Saturnian people are negative, cold, and morbid. Many have encountered hardships that have affected their personalities accordingly. Be patient when you find a true Saturnian, as these are rare and intelligent people, who are capable of love despite their prickly exterior.

The Saturnian Appearance

Saturnians are tall, gaunt, thin and pale, with thick dark hair and extreme features. The face is bony and narrow, with high, prominent cheekbones and deeply set eyes. The jaw is often quite square, and the eyebrows are thick and stiff, sometimes growing together over the nose. They have a deadpan expression, and an incisive wit that does not win many friends. They are inclined to be stoop-shouldered, and counter this posture by walking starkly erect, if possible. They appear gangly, with long arms and thin build. The walk does not show lightheartedness or enthusiasm, they do not portray exuberance, and often look undernourished. The blood circulation is not as vigorous as other types, and this detracts from their health and stamina. They do not have the warmth and magnetism of the healthy, vital Jupiterian, nor the quick brilliance of the Apollonian. They are slow, steady, and serious, content to remain that way without being compelled to improve the way they look. They are loners who prefer their own company to that of most anyone else.

Saturnian Illnesses

The gloomy, withdrawn nature of Saturnians predisposes them to certain illnesses. When observing the Mount of Saturn, remember the more developed the mount is, and the more square the finger-tip, the more pronounced the Saturnian features will be. A highly developed mount is a rarity, and in the majority of hands there is a concave appearance to this area rather than pronounced development. If the Finger of Saturn is very erect in the hand, or notice-ably longer than the other fingers, this will also indicate an emphasis on Saturnian qualities. Any Saturnian excess will make morbid, melancholy, gloomy people, who are both stingy and pessimistic. If the apex is well centered on the mount it brings out the more positive attributes of Saturn, such as durability, self-discipline, and good technical skills for research, invention, law, mathematics, and nutrition.

A Saturn mount with excessive grilling, a bad Heart Line crossing it, or with crooked, gnarled or inflexible fingers indicates that the more unfavorable attributes of Saturn are likely to surface. In matters of health, Saturnians are known for excessive bile. This gives a yellow tinge to the nails, palm, and mount. As bile in the blood creates intense nervousness, Saturnians are plagued by this as one of their many health problems. Colitis and ulcers are common among Saturnians, and at the very least, they will suffer from chronic indigestion. Note the Health Line and the nails to see how prevalent this nervous condition is. Rheumatism and stiff joints are also common Saturnian problems, along with varicose veins and knee problems. These are all due to the poor circulation and the constricting affect of Saturn. In old age the lower limbs are a great liability. The bones and teeth are also delicate. With dots or islands on the Head Line beneath the Saturn mount, people often have ear problems. Always remember that no one is ruled by one planet and that most of the time a combination of planetary factors will offset some of the problems indicated by Saturn.

Fine skin on the hand will modify the propensity for Saturnian illness, but crosslines and grills increase the liability for health problems. Flexible hands and elastic skin will also modify the severity of the Saturnian nature, but stiff hands will add to it. Stiffness will add to stinginess of the type, and will make Saturnians shun their fellow human beings with contempt and malice. If the hand is flabby, Saturnians will indulge all the morbid fantasies and will be too lazy to work. Soft hands will be a slight improvement and will elevate the ideals. As with all other planetary types, the flexible hand is the best, as it shows people who are more active and healthy.

Saturnian Apex

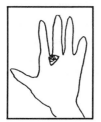 If the apex of the Saturn mount lies more toward the index finger, the wisdom and seriousness of Saturn will be added to the ambition of Jupiter. For Jupiter ruled people, this addition of Saturn qualities will render them wise and cautious, and will enhance leadership abilities. If the apex lies near the Apollo mount it will loan patience and seriousness to the pursuit of the arts and all other Apollonian qualities.

Saturnian Mount Color

A white or pale cast to the Mount of Saturn increases the coldness of the type, and this person's wit will be the bane of every party.

A yellow cast to the Mount of Saturn shows the presence of bile in the blood, a typical Saturnian health problem according to traditional interpretation. This condition is likely to sour the disposition and render the person quite irritable. It will also indicate poor digestion, and a likelihood for frequent gastric problems.

The red Mount of Saturn is rarely found, but my interpretation would be a flare-up of one of the Saturnian illnesses, or great stress caused by demands of rigorous study and research. Check all fingertips for a red pallor to verify the latter.

A blue Mount of Saturn is rare and would most likely be accompanied by blueness elsewhere in the hand, indicating very constricted circulation.

The Saturn Finger

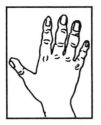

With knots on the finger joints, the Saturnian features are more pronounced, and there is added seriousness and patience. Knots will render the Saturnian a good judge, and will reduce whatever emotionalism and sentimentality he or she may have. Conic tips will lesson the seriousness of the knotty fingers, but the person will still be a hard-core realist. Smooth fingers will bring out the musical side of the Saturnian, and he or she will be less despondent and decidedly more happy.

Saturnian Finger Length

Short fingers will make Saturnian types faster, and easier to approach socially. Long fingers will make them more tidy, but also indicate they will be fussy, suspicious, and criticizing. Look to the thumb to see what kind of willpower and logical ability these people have, as well as the kind of love they are capable of (the ball of the thumb or Mount of Venus). A short thumb makes Saturnians indecisive. A large thumb will add to the determination the type already possesses. Square thumbs will also add determination as well as practicality, and pointed thumbs will detract from the strength possessed by the Saturn mount.

The Saturn Fingertip

The fingertip of Saturn will be important in showing how the mind will operate. If the fingertip is very square looking, the person will be serious and scientific. The conic fingertip will lighten Saturnian tendencies considerably, and make the individual more amusing and open-minded. If the fingertip is long, it will emphasize the mental world, and an inclination for scholarly pursuits. With a pointed Saturn fingertip, the person will be extremely superstitious, and likely to be ruled by dreams, signs, and omens.

Saturn Finger Phalanges

With the second phalange longest, agriculture, chemistry, physics, and all forms of scientific investigations will be most favored.

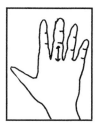

If the third phalange is longest, the more base side of Saturn will be uppermost. This would surface as a form of money worship. In a hand which is otherwise good, with no detrimental markings on the mount, we can use this long third phalange to indicate a penchant for economy.

Other Saturnian Characteristics

A concave Mount of Saturn shows an absence of Saturnian elements. This person will have poor self-control and a lack of discipline.

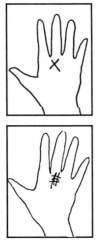

An X on the Saturn mount shows a despotic temperament and a proclivity for all Saturnian illnesses.

A grill on the Saturn mount would be similar to a ring in its effect, but this person would be irritable and disagreeable. The grill would heighten nervous tendencies and increase the chances for digestive and circulatory problems. Traditionally this grill is read as an indication of a worrier who worries himself or herself into ill health. It can also indicate a tendency for gout or rheumatism, if it is prevalent in other family members. Be sure to ask the person if this is true.

Dots on the Saturn mount would increase the proclivity for gout and rheumatism, as well as herald a liability for gastric trouble and infections.

A ring encircling the Saturn mount shows an emphasis of the more negative Saturnian features. This person will be melancholy and withdrawn, gloomy and skeptical, and needs a great deal of solitude. He or she will challenge anyone who threatens his or her independence. This type is inclined toward scientific research and mathematics, and will work long hours without wishing to be disturbed.

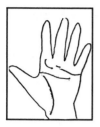

A Heart Line that is broken beneath the Mount of Saturn shows a disappointment from which the person never fully recovered. During this time the emotions were channeled into the gloomy style of Saturn.

──────────── Mount of Saturn Checklist ────────────

Look at your own Finger and Mount of Saturn and write down your observations.

□ What kind of fingertip does it have? Is this on both hands?

□ Are all the phalanges equal in length? If not which one is longest or widest?

□ Are there knots? On which joints? Is this true in both hands?

□ Is the finger stiff or flexible? Is this true in both hands?

□ Is the skin fine, medium, or coarse in texture?

□ Is the Saturn finger the most prominent of any on the hand? Which hand?

□ Is the Saturn mount the most prominent of any on the hand? Which hand?

□ Are there any discolorations on the mount, finger, or nail of the Saturn finger?

□ Describe the Mount of Saturn in each hand. What color, texture, and what kind of muscle tone does the mount have?

□ How does the Mount of Saturn in one hand compare to that of the other?

□ Are there any detrimental markings on the mount? Which ones? Where are they located?

□ Are there any favorable markings on the mount? Which ones? Where are they located?

□ How does the Finger of Saturn in one hand compare to that of the other?

□ Is one finger longer, wider, smoother or more erect than the other? Which one?

CHAPTER 6

The Mount of Apollo

The Mount of Apollo is located directly below the Apollo finger—the ring finger—and is ruled by the Sun. To bring out its best, the mount should be well-toned and pink with a Finger of Apollo that is equal in length to the Jupiter—index—finger. The finger itself should be straight and erect, not bent laterally toward any other fingers, or twisted on its axis. The Mount of Apollo describes artistic talent and creative self-expression. If the Apollo mount is even slightly pronounced in the hand, it will indicate a measure of talent. The way this talent will manifest will be indicated by the next greatest mount in the hand. Perhaps Mercury will add verbal skills to an already bright-minded Apollonian, or Jupiter will add ambition and a sense of command. The palmist is looking for the planet which contributes a backup form of energy and contributes itself to the Apollo influence.

Strengthening signs found on the Apollo mount are stars, triangles, squares, circles, a trident, a ring which encircles the whole mount, and a single vertical line. Defects on the mount are shown by crossbars, grills, a single cross, an island, a dot, a Heart Line which breaks beneath the Apollo mount, or any line which dents or mars the mount.

Apollo represents the artistic ability of the person—luck, potential for fame, and wealth—in relation to emotional self-expression. Traditionally, this mount was linked with the heart.

Any defects here are read as relating to the circulatory system, the lungs and the eyes.

The Apollonian Type

Typical Apollonians are healthy, vigorous people who are genial, happy and attractive. They are spontaneous and versatile, and often quite brilliant. They love the beautiful, and do everything with flair and artistry. They are partial to beautiful clothes, beautiful surroundings at home and in business; they love art. However, unless they have a finely developed mount with a centrally located apex, do not assume they are always the creator of it. They certainly look the part of the artist whether actively artistic or not, and it is easy to be misled by their appearance, as they take great care to dress well and travel in the "right" circles. Apollonians are usually successful in business, and their convivial nature draws people, rendering them very well received socially. They are flexible by nature, and easily adapt to the demands of the public. They are tasteful, and apply this taste to business pursuits, which in turn makes money.

Apollonians are sought out by all classes of people; they are the life of the party, the hero of the athletic field, players with brains and style who risk it all for a win. They are full of brilliance and versatility, and anything that lacks beauty is repulsive to them. Apollonians are not afraid to openly speak their minds. The Apollonians' intuitive faculties aid them in understanding occult matters, at which they can become quite proficient. They are usually cheerful and happy but can be subject to quick bursts of temper which disappear as quickly as they arrived. They are not likely to evoke any long-term hostility or harbor a grudge. Apollonians are not inclined to make lasting friends, but will temporarily attract and captivate everyone with quick wit and versatile self-expression. They also have the uncanny ability to win over enemies.

The Apollonian Appearance

Apollonians are handsome, muscular and athletic. The men are light and supple with graceful curves, well-proportioned features, and good, clear skin. The eyes have an honest expression, and twinkle with a love of pranks and mischief. Other facial features are well-proportioned. They convey a healthful and intelligent countenance and whether healthy or not, they will be the picture of the "good life" in both looks and dress.

Apollonian men are highly intuitive and likely to apply keen perceptions to the field of art and literature. They do not labor painstakingly like Saturnians, as this mind grasps things quickly. They are more apt to take a tidbit of information and exploit every angle. They often get credit for knowing a great deal more than they really do, but Apollonians are great actors and never let on. They are often the center of attention in a group.

Female Apollonians are brilliant and have a glow that can only be described as electric. They are quick-witted, intelligent, tall, and possess comely, symmetrical features. They love excitement and are often found in show business or in demanding professional positions. Apollonian women hold their own among ambitious male counterparts in the business world. Their beauty, stature, and good taste are also valuable assets.

On the negative side, Apollonian women can rely too heavily on their looks to get them what they want. They can be seen as vain, overly ambitious, ruthless and demanding. Homelife and children are not their primary interest; they are always on the go and plan family activities with the same sharp scheduling they would apply to a business meeting. Their pursuit of the glamorous fast-life would incline them to spend a great deal of money on their appearance and in acquiring an impressive home or car. They are convenience-oriented, and when a relationship becomes less than convenient, they will end it and remain aloof, knowing full well that another relationship is just around the corner. They spend so much time in the world of the persona and on the go from place to place, that they may end up shallow and superficial with estranged families who hardly know them.

Apollonian Illnesses

Apollonians are usually very healthy, but the temperament may predispose them to certain illnesses. These illnesses are sudden high fevers, weak eyes and other eye problems, infections, and heart disease (if the hand shows this tendency elsewhere), bronchitis, and all illnesses which are common to those with delicate lungs and respiratory systems.

Apollonian Apex

To identify people with strong Apollonian traits, check the size of the mount's development in both hands. Examine the mount for the location of the apex. If it is well centered with no detrimental markings, and a long shaped finger with fine skin or with a deep, long Apollo line present, then strong Apollonian tendencies are likely. The ring finger should be erect and flexible, and quite possibly longer than the index finger. It should not be bent, twisted, or discolored in any way for the true Apollonian features to surface.

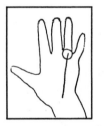

If there is a single vertical line on the Apollo mounts, this will be a very good sign indeed. Its presence indicates an open channel for the wit, charm and talent of the Apollonian qualities. Traditionally, this line is read as the hallmark of a fortunate career, with wealth, fame and recognition as typical by-products. It indicates a sense of style, and if it is well marked, with ascending lines, triangles or stars, it shows eloquence and the ability to achieve deep personal desires. It also signifies a good constitution, and aids the Heart Line and the recuperative powers.

Apollonian Mount Color

A red Mount of Apollo will show quick temper, one who plunges into things and takes risks. This person will have a liability for heart problems if the Heart Line is also defective in the area of Apollo.

A white or pale hue to the Mount of Apollo will detract from its spontaneity and sparkle.

A yellow Mount of Apollo will tell of infection to the eyes or lungs.

Mount of Apollo Markings

A ring that encircles the Mount of Apollo is another good sign. It shows a zest for living and highlights the brilliance and self-expression of Apollo. It also shows loyalty in marriage.

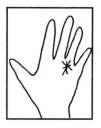

The star on Apollo is traditionally read as fame. At the very least, it signals recognition and applause, and is considered one of the most fortunate markings a hand can possess.

The trident is another of the more magnificent markings, and indicates tremendous achievement, and great success due to personal efforts. It indicates lofty achievement, rather than achievement for the sake of money or prestige. This person will do something that will benefit all human beings, and will be required to put forth a tremendous effort to complete the project.

Squares show a talent for architecture and a keen eye for line and form. This person will have a brilliant skill for organizing, and a fine administrative ability. If the person is an artist, he or she will be a brilliant sculptor, architect or conceptual artist. This will be especially so if the fingertips are very square looking.

Circles found on the Mount of Apollo are rare, and there is not much written by traditional palmists to explain their true meaning. However, in the course of my own studies, I have come upon circles on the Apollo mount several times. They are always found in the hands of brilliant and talented people, who had achieved fame as a result of a pursuit of excellence. I interpret the circle on the Apollo Mount as a halo. It is a marking that shows someone who strives for self-mastery and is not afraid to try and try again. Dauntless, is a good word to describe the character who wears the halo, and this person will want to take all his or her friends along on the road to success. The only liability with this marking is that the people I have encountered have eye problems. Defective markings on the Apollo mount, especially an island on the Heart Line beneath the mount, can also indicate eye problems. I will not make any permanent conclusions about this marking until I gather more data. For now, I will refer to it as a halo. I invite anyone who wishes to contribute to my study of this marking to write to me care of the publisher.

Defects on Apollo hamper self-expression and delay success. A grill on the Mount of Apollo can be a debilitating defect. It is traditionally read as vanity and arrogance, a love of show and a love of applause. The updated version of this marking indicates one who craves the spotlight and who will go to great lengths to attain it. This denotes someone inclined to worry about achieving fame and will not be content until he or she gets to the top of his or her chosen profession. The grill may also indicate a delay in the person's success. In a hand with poor health indications, it confirms a nervous temperament and indicates disorders common to high-strung types. Such disorders, if confirmed by other indications in the hand, would be bronchitis, asthma, and allergies.

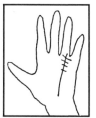

Crossbars which deeply cut the Mount of Apollo hamper the higher qualities of the mount, and are likely to accompany the above-mentioned illnesses. The crossbar is more detrimental than a grill as it interrupts the vertical line which may be running upward on the mount by cutting across it. The grill merely blends in with them. Cross lines would suggest that there were specific obstacles to the success of the chosen profession. They should be read as hidden obstacles that arose unexpectedly when the person was very close to reaching a goal. Each cross line is a setback, but check the Fate Line to confirm this factor before commenting. If the Fate Line does not confirm this assessment, assume the cross line indicates health setbacks.

A cross on the mount at the end of the Apollo Line is traditionally read as a blemish on the career—a final block of energy when the person was very close to success. However, I have seen too few of these crosses to verify this interpretation. Crosses found elsewhere in the hand are usually read as detrimental markings, and signify death of a loved one, disappointments, or health problems, such as accidents.

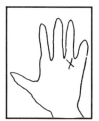

A cross which looks like an X is read as some form of damage to the eyes, or an accident that caused a shock that affected the eyes. If the X is very red, it indicates recent eye surgery.

A dot warns of eye infections and someone susceptible to high fevers. Traditionally, a dot is read as a career ending in disgrace, but I have not verified this traditional interpretation to my satisfaction, as I have encountered so few of them.

The Apollo Finger

Examine the Finger of Apollo to see how the Apollo energy is sent out.

Apollo Finger Phalanges

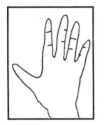

Is the first phalange, the fingertip, longer than the rest of the joints? If so, this person will have excellent taste. He or she will have fine clothes, a love of jewelry and luxurious surroundings and will be fond of plays and short stories where wit and humor are abundant. This person will strive for a good education, and the Apollo features will surface in an intellectual fashion.

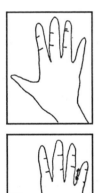

With the second phalange longest, the person will display brilliance in the business world, and will be the dashing entrepreneur or the successful stockbroker, providing the finger and mount are also good.

If the third phalange is longest, it can detract from the better qualities of Apollo. An emphasis here would tell of a show-off who is always trying to impress people. Taste will be flashy and gauche, and though this person may very well be successful, he or she will inspire envy and avarice in others in response to garish behavior. A thick third phalange will show someone who is vain, boastful of accomplishments, self-indulgent, and in love with money. He or she is likely to be a schemer who craves notoriety for shady techniques.

Apollonian Fingernails

The fingernail on Apollo should be pink, and any discoloration found there or on the mount will deplete the energy of Apollo considerably.

A square nail is wonderful on the Finger of Apollo. It enhances the sense of economy and the practical side of the person. It will show someone who is attentive to artistic details, such as drafting and sculpting. As an artist, this person will be meticulous and concise. It also shows an ability for organization and administration.

The Apollo Fingertip

The conic tip on the Apollo finger is the most common fingertip found. It shows heightened idealism and artistic sensibility.

The pointed fingertip on the Finger of Apollo will show a very quick wit, and an inclination to pursue the world of comedy. The person will not have the discipline to put this wit to use unless a prominent thumb, good flexibility, and sturdy muscle tone are also found.

The spatulate fingertip on the Finger of Apollo would be an asset and would indicate a very innovative artist. Spatulate tips are often found on the hands of athletes and artisans, both of whom are energetic and restless at times of inactivity. The person with this fingertip needs constant action to express this creative energy.

Apollonian Deformities

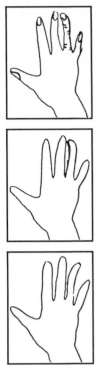

If the finger is crooked or bent, it is a bad indication and will affect the Apollo mount negatively. It will show common tastes. The person will be crafty and shrewd, and is not above doing something dishonest to find success, especially if the skin is coarse.

If Apollo leans toward Saturn it will give some of its warmth and gaiety to that mount and lighten Saturn's seriousness. It will also add an element of intuition to the Saturnian efforts at research and study.

With Apollo leaning toward Mercury, it will contribute brightness to the Mercurial sense, and a love of medicine. This will certainly be an asset when found on the hand of a doctor, as it will loan Apollo's quick wit to the shrewd verbal skills of Mercury. This person will be devastatingly funny, and will be very well-received socially.

Other Apollonian Characteristics

Coarse skin on the Apollo finger or mount will coarsen the tastes and make the person a faddist. This person will prefer loud colors, and will love to be seen and complimented.

Flabby skin found on the Apollo finger or mount will signify a great love of luxury, but one who is too lazy to achieve those things personally. These are people who marry for money. They have fastidious taste, and are full of beautiful visions while being very impractical.

With a glossy, refined texture to the skin, the tastes will also be refined and the mental world is emphasized. This person will favor the world of beauty and art, and may be found in the world of fashion or hairdressing.

Flexible hand consistency will enhance any development of the Apollo finger or mount. This person will market creativity and use charm to enhance business dealings. The commercial world will receive this person well, and he or she is likely to be successful. This person will work by fits and starts and create in direct response to sudden inspiration. Improvisation will come easily to this flexible mind.

The hard hand, when found with a strong Apollonian influence, will coarsen the higher qualities, and the individual may be uncompromising and even conceited.

——————————— Mount of Apollo Checklist ———————————

Test your own Finger of Apollo and its mount and write down your findings.

□ What kind of fingertip does the Apollo finger have?

□ Are all the phalanges equal in length? If not, which one is the longest? Widest?

□ How does the Apollo finger compare in length to Jupiter, the index finger? Is the Apollo finger longer or shorter than the index finger?

□ Are there any knots? On which joints? Is this so in both hands?

□ Is the finger flexible or stiff?

□ Is the skin refined, coarse, or medium in texture?

□ Is the Apollo finger or mount the most prominent of any on the hand?

□ Are there any discolorations on the mount, finger, or nail? What color? Where?

□ Describe the mount. What color? What texture? What kind of muscle tone?

□ Are there any detrimental markings on the mount? Which ones? Where?

□ How does the finger of one hand compare to that of the other?

□ How does the mount of one hand compare to that of the other?

C H A P T E R 7

The Mount of Mercury

The Mount of Mercury is located directly below the pinky and extends downward as far as the Heart Line. The outside of the hand just above the Heart Line is also considered the domain of Mercury. A good Mercury mount should have firm muscle tone and a centrally located apex. Favorable markings on the Mercury mount would be a square, a triangle, a star, a good line of Mercury that is deep and well cut, or a ring that encircles the whole mount. The mount itself should be firm and pink, with no X's, cross lines, grills, dots, or other unfavorable markings. Lines which rise up to the Mount of Mercury from the Heart Line or Head Line are considered favorable. Any paleness or discoloration of the mount will detract from the mount's more favorable qualities, as will any flatness or flabbiness.

The Mercurian Type

The planetary attributes of Mercury are: the power of speech, swiftness — both physically and in thought — dexterity, commerce, medicine, shrewdness, deals and schemes, the mentality, and the written word.

Mercury is associated with quick wit and fast talking. His talent for languages makes him an excellent translator, and powerful orator. The Mercurian has a natural affinity with the sciences, especially medicine. The Mercurian can be very tactful and has a great deal of business sense. Commerce is his forté and he has a very practical approach to life. He is usually successful in business where there is a challenging opportunity to barter and dicker for the best price. He is often found in the import-export business, but is equally at home in a court of law, or any profession where shrewdness and understanding of human nature can be of use. He is active and tireless, and skilled in all games where dexterity is required. He is keen and versatile, and has a good mind for facts and figures. He is highly intuitive, and shows a nervous and some-what hyperactive attitude. His knowledge of people and a cunning wit provide a constant temptation to dishonesty, and there are no better liars, cheats, frauds and swindlers than the bad Mercurial type. The versatility of the Mercurian creates great actors, mimes, and mimics. He likes children and is inclined to marry early. He is also fond of home life and is skilled with the hands. The Mercurian has a restlessness and an inclination for traveling. He is also fond of nature.

The Mercurian Appearance

Mercurians are rather small in stature, compactly built, trim and tidy looking. They are often found with curly hair, a high fore-head and very animated facial expressions. The eyes are dark, expressive and restless. They have good voices which carry well, and lean limbs enabling swift movement. Mercurians have stamina and are well-known for endurance and agility.

Being the quickest and most active of all the planetary types, Mercurians are fast learners and enjoy whatever will test the quickness of their mental skills. This includes a love of study, scientific investigation, and mathematics. Keen powers of speech will give them many opportunities to advance in business. Tact and quick wit will win many friends. Constant schemers, Mercurians will use the powers of shrewdness, intuition, and speech to get through the world.

Mercurian Illnesses

Mercurian temperament is predisposed to thyroid disorders, problems with the reproductive organs, digestive disorders due to nervousness, bladder and kidney weaknesses, and hypertension. Mercurians are also adversely affected by pollution in the air.

Mercurian Apex

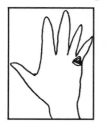

When the apex of the Mercury mount is centrally located, the best Mercurial qualities are highlighted. These people will be fast and humorous speakers with a fluency in at least one, if not several, foreign languages. The languages of computer sciences and chemistry are also favored, including slang and colloquial figures of speech. If the apex is on the outside of the hand, they will employ aptitude to their advantage and will be rather selfishly inclined. If the apex should lean toward the Mount of Apollo, these Mercurians will be devoted patrons of the arts, and the business is likely to be art- or music-oriented.

Mercurian Mount Color

When the Mount of Mercury is pink in color, it adds warmth and vigor to the personality. It heightens the keenness and the sense of humor, and also the agility.

Red color will make an individual a strong worker and a strong force in the community. This person will be pushy and aggressive, and up to date in the world of technology.

A yellow color on the Mount of Mercury often signals poor health. This Mercurian will have very delicate digestion and may suffer greatly from processed foods or various kinds of pollution. He or she is likely to be irritable and nervous in temperament. Apply these color factors to the nails as well.

The Mercury Finger

Smooth fingers will add impulse and intuition to an already quick person who has an ability to read human nature, and who is extra keen and intuitive to begin with. This person loves beauty and is fond of the arts.

Knotty fingers will add their power of reason and analysis and thus, the Mercurial person will be systematic and neat. He or she will use deductive reasoning rather than intuition and apply careful thought to any project.

Mercurian Finger Length

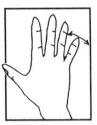

If the Finger of Mercury extends to the first joint of Apollo it is considered average in length. If it extends beyond the first joint of Apollo it is considered long.

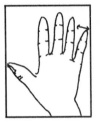

The long Finger of Mercury will show a strong Mercurial influence and will emphasize meticulousness and love of detail. This person will prepare thoroughly, and apply professional expertise with the utmost care. These people make good lawyers, radio announcers and translators as their ability with language is greatly heightened.

If the Finger of Mercury is shorter than the first phalange of Apollo, it is considered short. The person will be impulsive, intuitive, too spontaneous, and volatile. Any aberrations in a short Finger of Mercury will indicate some form of speech impediment, stage-fright or fear of talking in front of a crowd.

Mercury Finger Phalanges

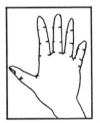

Next examine the finger joints and apply the Three Worlds of Palmistry to the most emphasized section. If the first phalange is longest, the mental world will be the most active, and with the already mental Mercurians, this would be one quick mind, but one easily driven to boredom. The emphasis would be on languages and all facets of speech and communication. This person will be an excellent orator or writer, will have the gift of eloquence, and has a quick wit. The Mercurial intuition will bring the talent to read non-verbal clues, and this person will be a sharp judge of human nature. This person will have great respect for knowledge and is likely to seek out a good education. The communications field (translators, computer technicians, linguists, salesmen, writers, and critics) would be the most likely profession for one with a long fingertip on the Finger of Mercury.

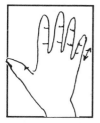

If the second phalange of the Mercury finger is the longest, it will enhance shrewdness, and contribute business acumen to all commercial pursuits. It will also intensify practicality and common sense. This person will be very innovative and may not do things according to the existing rules. This energy can also enhance an aptitude for scientific studies, such as medicine—perhaps even exploring new cures.

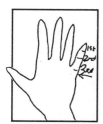

If the third phalange is longest on the Mercury finger, the shrewdness will be intensified and the person will be a wheeler-dealer type with a great appreciation for those who cheat the "system." He or she will use cunning in unconventional ways and may dabble in dishonest practices. He or she will usually have a commercial occupation and will most likely be a salesperson of some kind.

Mercurian Deformities

If the Finger of Mercury is long and crooked, bent or twisted, be on guard for a potential criminal. Examine the hand closely for grills on the mount, and check the Heart Line to see if affection will compensate for the heartlessness this formation implies. These people cannot resist the opportunity to take advantage of others. They are intensely superstitious. They are also likely to gamble frequently and even cheat when they can.

Traditional palmists have viewed the Finger of Mercury as a window into people's ability to make and keep partnerships. It also represents the ability to maintain intimate relationships with others. Sexuality can be a force that creates harmony. If these people don't adjust well to the sexual role in life, it can cause tremendous disharmony. Traditionally, the Finger of Mercury was said to reflect the relationship with the parent of the opposite sex.

 If the finger is bent or twisted, it indicates disharmony in the sexual life due to a general dishonesty in relationships or an intolerance of the opposite sex. Often these people come from homes where the parents did not agree, or where one parent was absent, or completely dominated the rest of the family. This bent or twisted finger will indicate people who are poorly adjusted to the opposite sex, because of difficulties with the parents, or a parental fixation.

On a woman's hand, if the twisted finger is very pronounced and long, it could indicate frigidity. It is certainly a noteworthy factor to be considered by the palmist on whatever kind of hand it is found. The twisted Mercury finger should be regarded with suspicion, as many problems of sexual adjustment are lurking below the surface, as well as a proclivity for dishonesty.

Mercurian Fingertips

Observe the fingertips to see what influence they exert upon the Finger of Mercury. Broad nails will show a strong constitution, narrow nails will show a delicate constitution.

The pointed fingertip will add its power of idealism and imagination to the Mercury finger. These people will indulge in flights of fancy and charm the world with a quick use of language. They tend to spend lots of time on the phone and may even be in a profession where phone work is their mainstay. They will be inclined to gossip and are talented with foreign languages. The conic tip will make them more artistic. If the tip is square, they will use the talking ability for practical subjects. Facts and figures, common sense and reason will be the forté. If the Fingertip of Mercury is spatulate, then they will be magnetic speakers who can charm masses of people.

Mount of Mercury Markings

Observe the Mount of Mercury for any special marking which may be found. A flat mount will show laziness and a lack of diligence.

A square on the Mercury mount shows practicality and strict attention to procedure. These are the technicians who approach things in a scientific and organized manner. They will be very concise when they talk, and thus, will have teaching ability in scientific areas.

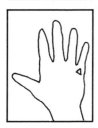

A triangle would enhance the Mercurian's love of art and indicate people who are good draftsmen or cartoonists. The quick wit of Mercury would be enhanced by a love of art and skill in executing it.

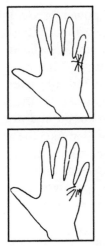

A star would show a brilliant scientific discovery, or a person known as a brilliant orator.

Little ray-like extensions from the finger onto the Mount of Mercury are traditionally called the "Medical Stigmata." They show an affinity with the healing arts, and one whose profession involves the study and practice of medicine. Energy, studiousness and scientific aptitude, combined with keenness in judging human nature, makes the Mercurian an excellent diagnostician and medical practitioner.

Grills on the Mercury mount are indications of very poor health. If they are found in an otherwise bad hand, they indicate criminality. The liver will be the target of poor health, and at the very least, the digestion will suffer as well.

Crossbars will also show obstacles to the health which affect the digestion and sour the disposition.

Other Mercurian Characteristics

Note the consistency of the hand to see if it is stiff, flexible or flabby. With a stiff hand, a person with a prominent Mercury mount or finger will be hardheaded and pragmatic. This is someone who will drive a hard bargain, and won't give an inch when holding out for a price. He or she will be old-fashioned and stingy, and will apply this shrewdness to every occasion whether it is called for or not.

Flabby hands are highly unlikely to be found on the Mercurian as laziness is not a typical characteristic. This feature will always inhibit chances for success and slow down a naturally quick wit and gift for gab.

The flexibility of the hand will add to the agility and cleverness of the Mercurian, and will always increase vitality and endurance. Flexibility heightens enthusiasm and sociability no matter what type of hand it is found in.

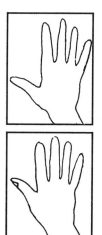

Always look closely at the thumb when you find a Mercurial personality. If it is low-set on the hand, it will tell of advanced mentality (or the inclination to use reason rather than intuition to make judgments), and if high-set, this decreases. Its shape and skin texture will tell if coarseness or refinement are present. The thumb of a Mercurian has a tendency to be stiff, as they love money and may have difficulty sharing it. They are generous with close family relatives, but will not be lavish or extravagant by nature.

The length of the first phalange of the thumb will tell of a person with willpower, and this will indicate whether the Mercurian will carry out his or her schemes or let them fall by the wayside. The thumbtip characteristics have strong influence upon the Mercurian and will help to verify any signs of brilliance or criminality.

———————— Mount of Mercury Checklist ————————

Test your own Finger and Mount of Mercury.

□ What kind of fingertip does the Mercury finger have?

□ Are all the phalanges equal in length? If not, which one is longest?

□ Is the finger long, short, or average in length?

□ Are there any knots? On which joints?

□ Is the finger flexible or stiff?

□ Is the skin refined, coarse, or medium in texture?

□ Is the Mercury finger or mount the most pronounced in the hand?

□ Are there any discolorations on the mount, finger or nail? What color? Where?

□ Describe the mount. What color, what texture, what kind of muscle tone?

□ Are there any unfavorable markings on the mount? Where? Which ones?

□ Are there any favorable markings on the mount? Where? Which ones?

□ How does the Finger of Mercury on one hand compare to the finger of the other? How does the Mount of Mercury on one hand compare to that of the other?

CHAPTER 8

The Mount of Venus

The Mount of Venus represents the love nature, passion, the emotions. The Venus mount is located on the ball of the thumb, and it is read according to its firmness, its color, and its height in the hand. Crosslines, grills, stars, dots, and discolorations are all considered detrimental to the Mount of Venus, and will inhibit its optimum expression. With a prominent Mount of Venus, the person is likely to be warm, sentimental, compassionate, and emotional. With a poorly developed Mount of Venus these qualities will be lacking.

The Mount of Venus rises into the palm and is larger and more prominent in height than any other mount. The Venusian qualities are love, sympathy, tenderness, beauty, melody in music, gaiety, joy, health, and passion. All of these attributes render the Venusian very attractive and liable to many temptations. If the mount is prominent, red in color and deeply grilled, it is considered an excessive development, and the Venusian features will be the most dominant in the personality. This mount should be in proportion to the rest of the hand to have an evenly distributed measure of Venusian qualities. If there is an absence of development, and the Mount of Venus appears flat, pale, or flabby, it is considered a deficient mount and the Venusian qualities will be in short supply. Between these two extremes, there are many degrees of development of the Mount of Venus.

The Venusian Type

Venusians have a plentiful supply of good, healthy blood and a strong heart to pump it. Consequently, the Venusian type is a healthy one, and good health begets good looks. There is no hint of gloom, or coldness in their nature. They are warm, attractive people with strong, physical passions. Venusians must have a strong Head Line (self-control and good judgment) and a good thumb (determination) to keep from succumbing to the many passionate temptations which beset them. Venusians are feminine, be they man or women, and they possess qualities that refine and elevate human nature.

In a man's hand, a strong Venus mount can operate in two ways. He may appear somewhat effeminate looking, very sensitive and emotional, compassionate and prone to tears. This will be especially so if smooth fingers, conic tips, and soft consistency are in evidence. The other way a pronounced Venus can operate in a man's hand is to emphasize his fiery, more passionate side, making him very sensuous and physical. He will not be effeminate at all, but will be very macho and protective. If the hand is also hard in its consistency, this person will indulge his desires without restraint.

Venusian women are hard to describe because all women have a measure of Venusian characteristics. Venusians love to cook and are often found in the food and beverage business — as successful caterers or confectioners. They have warm, generous natures and this can cause them to give away their profits, adopt too many pets, or inadvertently encourage too many houseguests. They are very fond of children and will most likely have them early in life and indulge them heartily. Marriage is important as they need tenderness and a mate to care for. They are very attractive to the opposite sex, as they are feminine, soft, vulnerable, silly, warm and inviting, and have strong sexual appetites. Because of this appealing, friendly nature, they are comforting to the opposite sex, and are at times pursued and tempted, regardless of marital status. Venusian women are likely to be very close to the family throughout life, and will have many close relationships with other women. They are inclined to beautiful surroundings, as they have artistic natures that seek harmony and comfort. Therefore, it is not unlikely to find them in the world of glamor — hairdressers, makeup artists, fashion designers, wardrobe mistresses, and interior decorators.

Grills will excite the Venusian passions to an increased degree. Traditionally grills on the Mount of Venus are read as worry and grief caused by a sexual partner. Palmists of yore read this marking as a person marred by venereal disease. A person with a smooth Mount of Venus will still be attracted to all things Venusian, but will be more refined and less prone to excesses. This kind of Venus mount will indicate a love of flowers, music, color, painting and beautiful scenery, but not necessarily a strong sexual passion.

Glossy smooth skin on the mount with grills creates a heightened sexuality, but the person will be very high strung, and there will be a proneness to frustration and exhaustion. If the mount is developed and grilled in a woman's hand, she will be highly sexed, and may be inclined to promiscuity if other signs agree. In a man's hand, it means that he is more likely to indulge his sexual passions without the social restraints that women have been obliged to exercise. If the Mount of Venus appears puffy and deflated looking, it tells of people who have freely indulged their passions until their passion became diminished and the person was forced to cease sexual activities due to exhaustion and self-abuse. This person will have a resigned attitude about sex and will tire easily.

The Venusian Appearance

Venusians are graceful, shapely, and well balanced, with an easy manner. Their beauty is feminine in quality. The skin is white, fine-textured, soft and supple. The face is round or oval in shape, finely proportioned, and often with dimples. The forehead is high and gracefully rounded in front. The hair is abundant, silky and fine in texture. The eyes are round or almond-shaped and have a sympathetic expression. The hands of Venusians have a pink cast, are soft and fine in texture, with conic tips, and large, smooth Venus mounts. The fingers are usually quite short, which emphasizes impulsiveness.

Venusians possess a love for humanity and are usually steadfast to one true love. To them, living is a joy and they are always cheerful and outgoing. They have no rancor in attitude and no malice toward anyone. Good health encourages a good disposition, and the world looks bright through Venusian eyes. They are popular and loved for their spontaneity and enthusiasm. Venusians are fond of amusement, dancing, gallantry, and all forms of entertainment. A lack of seriousness often inclines them to pursue pleasure to the exclusion of business.

Venusians value riches for the comfort and luxury they can buy, but are careless and irresponsible about handling of money. Venusians are warm, vivacious and genial, but are neither profoundly studious nor particularly ambitious. Beautiful clothing, home decor, flowers, and art in every form attract these people. Venusians find it more important that a thing be beautiful and enjoyable than useful or durable.

Harmless and passionate, love to Venusians is an inherent part of their very existence. Venusians are honest and truthful, not schemers for money or high position. They make good friends, and readily forgive an injury. They are inclined to see things from the other person's point of view, often to their own disadvantage. They hate quarrels and strife and would rather suffer an injustice than engage in combat—verbal or otherwise. Venusians love to give pleasure to others and will put forth all their power to amuse as long as the audience is entertained and appreciative. Music appeals very strongly to them and a well-developed Mount of Luna will bring additional musical taste. They often write well and although they appear warm and cheerful, their writing is often tinged with melodrama. In whatever way Venusians expend their talents, we find that they touch the heart, be it through music, writing, acting or art.

The Venusian is inclined to marry early, and being robust and healthy, grows to physical maturity sooner than peers. Venusians are attracted to strong, decisive people and to those in good physical health. People ruled by Mars are strongly attracted to the Venusian type and vice versa. Physically active and highly sexed, the Venusian is very likely to bear children, and is often found with a large family. There are no chronic ailments peculiar to the Venusian, as good health and strong vitality are their most prominent attributes.

With low-octave Venusians whose good qualities are overshadowed by self-indulgence and promiscuity, we find venereal disease prevalent, which will be shown by black dots or brown patches appearing on the mount. Excessive grilling on the mount may indicate venereal disease. This person may be apprehensive about sex. Other markings in the hand mentioned elsewhere will also confirm this.

On the Bad Side

In the lower type of Venusian, the baser desires will rule. In appearance they will be short in stature, and stout, with prominent abdomens. The grace and beauty of the other type of Venusian is not here. Excess is evident everywhere, and self-indulgence is the most important objective. The lips are thick, red and sensual, the face has coarse skin and the Mount of Venus is very hard, prominent, red, or dead white. The fingers are short and smooth, with the first phalanges deficient and the lower phalanges excessive. This person is likely to have crass taste, excessive appetites, warped ideas and will pander to the gratification of his or her animal desires.

Between the lower octave Venusian and the one mentioned previously there are innumerable grades of Venusian development. An overly red mount, excessive grilling, a very hard mount with stiff and short fingers are signs to watch for when observing this type.

Venusian Mount Color

The overall color of the hand is very important. White color reduces the Venusian warmth and attraction. This person will be less sympathetic and less ardent. The passion for beauty and art will be decreased. He or she will be less attractive to the opposite sex, and more liable to the follies of the typical Venusian, even if the Venus mount is strong. A pink cast will show good health and vivaciousness and will heighten the Venusian's better qualities.

Red color in the hand shows excess. With a Venusian, red will add fuel to an already flammable personality. This person is easily excited and greatly attracted to the opposite sex. He is so ardent and passionate that when aroused, all thoughts of consequence are lost. If the mount is full and deeply grilled, with the color very red, be on guard for excesses in all the Venusian traits. If the fingers are thick in the third phalanges, and the palm developed at the base, their excess will be quite extreme. This person will stop at nothing to accomplish his desires.

Yellow color is not common for a Venusian. The Venusian is usually healthy, so when yellow is found, it is quite abnormal. This person is likely to be cross and fretful. Nervous tension destroys the sympathy and attractiveness, replacing the warmer qualities with temperamentalism.

Blue is not terribly uncommon with Venusians as their overly emotional nature inclines them to heart trouble. However, this is not very often found as most Venusians are abundantly healthy. If blue is found, check the nails for verification of the condition. If a blue vein appears to jut out on the Mount of Venus, a pinched nerve in the spine (usually the lower spine) is likely to be the problem. This will inhibit digestion and cause people to tire easily. A trip to the chiropractor may help alleviate this problem.

The Thumb

Knotty fingers will greatly reduce the impulsiveness of the Venusian. If a Venusian is found with knots on all the first phalange joints, it will show an intelligent, systematic person. The second knot (the knuckles) will make a person tidy, unusually careful in appearance, and orderly in everyday life. Both knots will make the Venusian analytical and fussy about clothes, decor, and appearances.

Smooth fingers are the most likely fingers to accompany the Venusian. The artistic, impulsive, spontaneous ways of the Venusian are doubly emphasized by smooth fingers.

Long fingers are unusual, as the Venusian does not love detail and is not necessarily known for patience. This person prefers to have someone else see to the planning and systematizing of things. The Venusian is more hypersensitive and suspicious with long fingers, and this is not a natural feature of this type.

The thumb will be a very important factor in judging the Venusian. If it is small or pointed, the person is likely to be indecisive and weak. The desire will rule and the person is likely to be easily led by others. The natural laziness of the Venusian will be increased, and determination may be seriously lacking.

If the thumb tip is strongest (the Will phalange), the person will have determination but not necessarily good judgment. If the Will phalange (thumb tip) is pointed, the impressionability is increased, and the willpower weakened. If the thumb tip is square, there is more common sense, practicality and stronger willpower. If the thumb has a spatulate tip the willpower is very strong, however, if it is unsupported by a good Head Line and second phalange, this willpower will not be brought into operation. The second phalange of the thumb must be long and well-proportioned to give the best results to the Venusian. Reason and good judgment are needed to keep the Venusian level-headed.

On a Venusian, a large thumb gives good judgment and the determination to hold in check any amount of strong desires. The Head Line must be clear, well-colored and unbroken to give the best results, as the Venusian needs self-control and clear judgment to steer clear from emotional pitfalls.

Venusian Fingernails

Broad nails, pink in color and fine in texture will show good general health, and a frank, honest disposition. Narrower nails will show a less rugged constitution. If the nails are very thin and narrow-looking, it shows a very delicate constitution, and the good health of the Venusian will be affected accordingly. Short nails are not very prevalent on the Venusian but when found, the more critical, pugnacious side of the Venusian is apparent. Fluted nails will show nervousness. If this feature is prevalent on the Venusian hand, the person will be excitable and flighty, especially if the hand is flexible, with long, smooth fingers and pointed fingertips. Bulbous nails, in whatever degree, will warn that bronchial trouble is present.

Venusian Fingertips

With pointed fingertips, idealism and a dreamy quality will render these Venusians impractical but loveable and fascinating. Conic fingertips are the most common tips for the Venusian to have, and show artistic taste and sensitivity. Square fingertips make the Venusian more practical, more regular in habit, tidy in dress, and methodical. Spatulate tips add energy, fire, and originality. This person is rarely caught off guard, and is quick and clever in ideas and speech. The spatulate fingertip is a good feature for the Venusian as it indicates a humane and sympathetic individual. This person is intensely fond of pets and children. He or she is constant in affections, original in ideas, active in games, skillful, graceful, charming, and has a gentle, tender side to the personality.

Other Venusian Characteristics

With finely textured skin, the Venusian is refined in love matters. With a coarse texture, the love nature is more aggressive and animalistic. The Venusian with coarse skin is more inclined to be selfish, and will indulge personal pleasures without regard to others, especially if the thumb is stiff as well.

The mount's consistency will show the energy level. If the Venus Mount is flabby, the person will be a pleasure hunter, and no thought of usefulness or ambition will activate him. Soft hands will show more energy than the flabby hand, and will be more practical, though lazy.

Flexible skin texture is a fine attribute, showing the more refined Venusian qualities directed by intelligent energy. It renders the person less sensual, more practical and more realistic. This consistency inclines the person to action, thus the lower side is less likely to develop. To test skin-flexibility, squeeze the flesh on the back of the hand and pull slightly.

Hard hands show a pig-headedness directing Venusian energy. The person will be less refined and more argumentative. This Venusian will have strong desires and is likely to gratify himself or herself in unintelligent ways. With this person, love, sympathy and generosity are secondary to desire.

Flexible hands show open-mindedness. Flexibility coupled with a strong Venus mount makes an intelligent, gifted (though high strung) person who is versatile but extreme. This Venusian will be too fond of admiration and pleasure for his or her own good, and will need the balance of a strong Head Line and a large thumb to keep these traits in line. With these assets, he or she would be less inclined to indulge in the pursuit of pleasure and more inclined to be self-controlled.

The stiff hand shows a stiff, uncompromising mind. Coupled with a prominent Venus, this person is more apt to be sensual, self-indulgent, coarse, unprogressive, bordering on the selfish and full of what we call lower desires.

———————————— Mount of Venus Checklist ————————————

Test your own Mount of Venus.

□ Is the Mount of Venus prominent in either hand? Which one? In what fashion? (Note color, height, markings, texture, hardness.) What does this tell you?

□ Is the Venus mount lacking in either hand? In what fashion? Which hand?

□ Are there any detrimental features which would hinder the mount's operation? Which ones? (Grills, cross lines, paleness, blueness, etc.)

□ With an emphasized Venus mount, are there any other features which will modify the Venusian excesses? What are they? (Strong Head Line, knots on the fingers, strong thumb, etc.)

CHAPTER 9

The Mounts of Mars

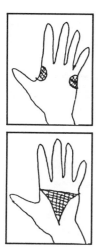

The next type of personality we will discuss is ruled by the planet Mars and is called Martian. The portions of the hand that identify the Martian type are the two Mounts of Mars. The upper Mount of Mars is located on the Percussion, the outer edge of the hand where the Mount of Mercury borders the Heart Line. The lower Mount of Mars is located just under the beginning of the Life Line, and just above the Mount of Venus. There is also a triangular shaped area which occupies the middle portion of the hand called the "Plain of Mars."

All crosslines, stars, crosses, or grills in the Plain of Mars increase the inflammability and temperamental nature of the person. Markings on the lower Mars area are read as chance lines, directly connected to the Life Line, which indicate early influences in life that shaped aggressions and confidence of the individual.

The Martian Type

The Martian type embodies the element of aggression and resistance, consequently this is a great fighter and notorious warrior. Martian types are often found fighting their way against adverse elements and circumstances in the physical world. People with a strong influence from Mars will always be vigorous and pushy with whatever interests them, and will very stoutly resist the efforts of any person who seeks to force his or her way upon them.

In almost all hands we find some Martian development, as life demands that we learn to find courage and aggression whether we want to or not. If Mars is noticeably underdeveloped in muscle tone, pale in color, or noticeably deficient in other ways, the person is easily discouraged, and likely to be overwhelmed easily in his or her struggle for existence. The Martian qualities of aggression and resistance are necessary elements that build character and individuality. Without them, this person — no matter how brilliant — will be trampled underfoot, and his or her brilliance will never be brought before the eyes of the world.

There are two kinds of fighters: those who are the aggressors, forcing their way in the world, and those who act in self-defense, or resist the pressure brought upon them. This separation of Martian qualities is distinguished by the divisions of upper and lower Mars. The upper Mars mount shows resistance, and the lower mount shows aggression. When both mounts are strongly developed, the person has both aggression *and* resistance. He or she will push forward with great persistence, and will resist vigorously any attempt to be imposed upon. The person with both mounts developed simply shoves away obstacles, and is usually endowed with the physical strength necessary to do so. This person does not accept that he or she is beaten, and permits no one to think that his or her defeat is a possibility. Athletes who compete will have very pronounced Mars development in the hands.

If the Plain of Mars is largely developed, or if crossed by fine red lines, this will show a person capable of sudden temper. This development, if combined with large development of the other two mounts, will make a dangerous combination, as it will add inflammability to an already strong aggression and resistance instinct.

The absence of the lower Mount of Mars is likely to result in poor self-confidence and lack of stamina, as the person will allow others to push past him or her by the sheer force of their own aggression. A good thumb will help offset this characteristic.

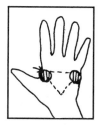

The three sub-divisions of the Martian are resistance—upper Mars, aggression—lower Mars, and temper—the Plain of Mars. The Martian, according to this development, becomes a three-sided person, and you will have no trouble in estimating this type properly if you carefully note which development is most prominent. Muscular hands, short, stout fingers, and a red cast to the skin are usually the most obvious clues to a Martian personality. Red hair on the head and backs of the hands is another indication. When the upper Mount of Mars is developed so far as to curve outwardly at the Percussion of the hand, it is considered a strong mount. When, in addition, it is so strong, that it forms a perceptible pad on the inside of the palm, it is considered overly developed.

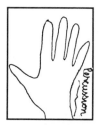

When the Percussion, or outer edge of the hand, is straight, or has a depression that gives the area a hollow, concave look, the qualities of the Mount of Mars are definitely absent. This would incline the person to give up easily when hardpressed, taking a passive approach and becoming easily discouraged. In moments of danger, he loses his head; when he falls down, he does not get up.

Thus you can see what a wonderful power the upper Mount of Mars gives us through this faculty of resistance, and what a loss the lack of it can mean.

A deficient Mount of Mars is likely to be found on the hand of the suicide victim. A person with only the upper Mount of Mars developed will not force a fight, but will be content to resist opposition, and to overcome it when it appears.

The lower Mount of Mars, when strongly developed, will show a person who pushes his or her plans to their fullest extent, does not stop to consider the feelings of others, and who forces his or her way in most matters. This person seeks out strife, loves it, and is always the aggressor who is full of drive. If you find a hand with the lower mount strongly developed, and the upper mount lacking, the person will be a great bluffer, but, not having resistance, will back down easily if pressed. So, when judging the Martian, consider whether he or she is the aggressor, the resistor, temperamental—or all three—according to which respective mounts are developed.

The Martian Appearance

Martians are of medium height, very strongly built and muscular looking. They carry themselves erect, and always look like they are able to defend themselves. The head is small, bullet shaped, and the back of the neck is broad and red looking. The face is usually round. The skin is thick, with a strong red cast often presenting a mottled appearance. The hair is short and stiff, and of an auburn or red color. The eyes are large and bold-looking. The eyes have a bright expression and sometimes appear rather bloodshot, due to an abundance of circulation.

Mounts of Mars Checklist

Examine your own Mounts of Mars.

□ Which one is the most prominent? Upper, Lower or the Plain of Mars?

□ Is this true for both hands? If not, how does the development of one hand differ from that of the other? Which area of Mars is reddest? Palest? Is this true in both hands?

□ Are there any special markings found on any of the three Mars Mounts? Which ones? Where? Is this so in both hands?

CHAPTER 10

The Mount of Luna

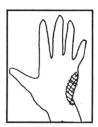

The Mount of Luna is located on the side of the hand beneath the little finger. It begins below the Mount of Mercury and extends downward as far as the wrist. Luna represents the Moon, the tides, the imagination, the power of divination, and the faculty of intuition. The realm of the Lunarian is the world of imagination, and the power of the imagination is what makes these people original. The lack of it shows an inability to express themselves and this type will have difficulty rising above the earthbound characteristics of human nature.

In the hands of great fiction writers, composers and linguists, we find the Mount of Luna most strongly developed. Although too much imagination can be a menace, the lack of it can render their outlook very hopeless. Hope is one of the higher qualities of human imagination. Devoid of this feature, the Lunarian will be certain that life is a vain struggle, an illusion, and that tangible happiness is only a shadow.

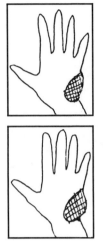

When we find people with a well developed Mount of Luna, they express themselves well, and deeply enjoy the pleasures of fantasy and imagination.

When we find this mount deficient or badly marked, we see people who can picture very little to themselves. If the mount is excessive, we see people who easily become flighty and imaginative to a dangerous degree. People with excessively developed mounts are capable of losing control of their mind entirely. Therefore, it is important that we find no excess nor deficiency with this mount.

A good, well-proportioned development is best, showing the presence of a healthy imagination without excess. The Mount of the Moon must be judged by the strength of its curve outward onto the Percussion, and by the size of the pad it forms on the inside of the palm. If it is seen to form a decided bulge outwardly, it is called a well-developed mount. If, in addition, the Mount of Luna is exceedingly thick, forming a large pad on the inside of the hand, it should be regarded as a *very* strong mount. If the outward curve and the inside pad of this mount are both unusually large, there is excessive development. In this type of mount, vertical lines strengthen it, and cross lines deplete its energy. One single vertical line extending lengthwise along the Mount of Luna will indicate added strength. If the mount is very well developed, and this vertical line is very deep, it will add to the excessiveness of the mount's qualities.

The Lunarian Type

Lunarians are controlled by imagination, consequently, they are dreamy, fanciful and idealistic. They build air castles and plan great enterprises. These enterprises rarely materialize because they have little or no practical value. Lunarians are lazy in the extreme, preferring to live in cloud-land rather than toil upon the earth. They are constantly prey to their imaginations and often imagine themselves ill. They are fickle, restless and changeable. They find it hard to settle down to a humdrum life, as they are always yearning for things beyond reach. Therefore, they are rarely satisfied to remain long in one place, but desire a continuing change of location and scenery. This restless disposition inclines them to spend their last dollar on traveling. The more lines there are on the Mount of Luna, the more restless Lunarians become, and the greater their desire to drift from place to place. They are very superstitious, believing in signs and omens, and have wonderful visions which can border on hallucinations if the mounts (in both hands) are excessively developed. Also check the Head Line and the thumb to see if this characteristic is mitigated. Lunarians are extremely sensitive, imagine slights where none were intended, and shy away from company. They do not love nor seek the approval of society, and are likely to retire to the woods or other secluded places where they can enjoy themselves alone. They love nature, the sea, birds, flowers, and all things that elevate the senses and excite the imagination. They are fond of poetry, and deep classical music, are also very fond of the water. If able, Lunarians will live near or on the water and are likely to be good sailors and naturalists.

Lunarians lack self-confidence, and prefer to remain aloof from the active pursuits of everyday life. Their energy and perseverance fluctuates with the Moon and consequently they feel inappropriately placed in the business world. They are not known for generosity, and a reclusive selfishness can sometimes be seen as part of the character.

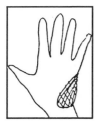

They will be greatly assisted if they have a long Finger of Mercury, especially if the first phalange is long. This combination, with the addition of conic fingertips, will add to the imagination and enhance their writing ability. Imaginative pursuits will become more practical if the tips are square, and the imagination will be more original if the fingertips are spatulate. Thus we see Lunarians as peculiar people in whom the imagination and fancy are always the dominating motives.

On the Bad Side

Badly aspected Lunarians are talkative, apt to be untruthful, often allowing the imagination to run rampant, and thus, deceiving others as well as themselves. They can be mean, selfish and cowardly. They lack physical passion, but seek amorous pleasure nonetheless, in order to gratify their world of flagrant fantasy. Nymphomaniacs are not uncommon among Lunarians. They can be hypocritical, and are likely to slander anyone who incurs their displeasure. They can be insolent and disagreeable, and rightly earned the ancient title of Lunatic. Always check the Head Line to see if it is straight, deep, and possessing no unfavorable markings. When the Mount of Luna is excessively developed, this will offset the less desirable features of the Lunarian and give them intelligent direction for their abundant imagination. Also check the thumb for good power of self-control.

There is an important matter to consider in connection with a Mount of Luna that is excessively developed. An excessive Mount of Luna was called the hallmark of the insane by ancient palmists, and this is not so far-fetched if we consider the effects the Mount of Luna represents. With an excessively developed mount, there may be mild spells of hallucinations if the skin is refined. With coarse skin, there can be a dangerous mania. Excesses of this mount will give way to excesses of the imagination.

The Lunarian Appearance

Remember, most people are ruled by a combination of planetary influences rather than by one planet alone. People who are purely ruled by Luna are not commonly found. Usually another planet will be more prominent and the Moon's influence will add inspiration to the other planet's qualities. Lunarians are often looked upon as dreamers, and are regarded by conventional society as impractical, unrealistic misfits. Lunarians are tall, fleshy, with thick lower limbs. They are often quite stout, the flesh is not firm, and the muscles are not strong but are soft and flabby. Rather than muscular vitality, this flesh has a spongy feeling. The complexion is dead white in caucasians, and pasty-looking in other races, which marks them as victims of very poor circulation, making them likely candidates for anemia, kidney trouble and diabetes. The head is round and thick through the temples, with a low forehead bulging over the eyes.

The eyes of the Lunarian are round and staring, often bulging and frequently watery. The eyelids are thick and flabby, giving them a swollen look. The voice is thin and high-pitched. The hand is puffy looking, flabby in consistency and pale in color. The fingers are short, smooth, and the first phalanges are often pointed or deficient in length.

Lunarian Illnesses

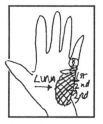

To assess the Mount of Luna properly, we divide it into three sections. The upper, the middle, and the lower, corresponding to the Three Worlds of Palmistry. Each section enables us to locate the health difficulties of the type. These health liabilities are to the throat—the upper third, the kidneys—the middle third, the bladder and female organs—the lower third. Grills, crosses, badly formed stars, islands, dots, chains, or wavy, illformed lines will help locate the health defects, and the degree of their seriousness. It is important to consult the Life Line and the color of the nails for confirmation of the health defects.

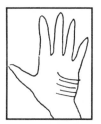

The liability of intestinal disorder is shown on the upper third of the Mount of Luna by lines running horizontally, grills, badly formed stars, and dots which mar its surface. A paunchy abdomen shows that the same flabby condition is present in the intestines and in the muscles. This condition makes them prone to many illnesses. Lunarians often suffer from appendicitis, bowel trouble, peritonitis, and all other inflammations that are related to the intestinal tract. Always examine the Life and Health Line for confirmation of any serious illness. Also check the nails. Lunarians are also predisposed to gout, rheumatism, and diabetes. These will be indicated by defective markings in the middle third of the mount.

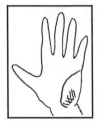 Defective markings in the lower third of the Mount of Luna will indicate kidney or bladder trouble in men. On a woman's hand, weak kidneys and bladder problems detrimental to the female organs are also indicated. Kidney problems are most often shown by spindly horizontal lines which cross the mount. When female organ problems are present, there is often a star on the Health Line in the area where the Health Line crosses the Head Line. Look to this spot if the client inquires about reproductive problems.

Lunarian Mount Color

Pale and pasty is the typical pallor of the Lunarian. If it is very pronounced, the aloofness of the type will be strongly marked, and health defects should be carefully studied. If the hand has a more pink pallor, it will show the coldness of the Lunarian lessened. The heart will be stronger and the blood richer, reaching the skin in good supply. With this pinkness, there will be less selfishness, and a warmer, more practical nature. Red pallor on the hand will greatly influence the more positive aspects of the Lunarian, indicating he or she is warm and ardent. The person will be easily excited by suggestions that appeal to the imagination. Yellow pallor will show a disagreeable sort who is cross, selfish and cold, and who views life with a sour approach. With yellow color, gout, rheumatism, and instability are strong liabilities. Blue tone to the skin is a typical result of poor circulation. When this blueness is found, it is not unusual for it to be accompanied by diseases of the bladder and sexual organs. Check the lower third of the Mount of Luna and the Health Line for further clarification.

The Lunar Finger

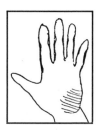

Knotty fingers reduce the Lunarian's fanciful nature to a marked degree. The combination of reason and imagination produces a practical writer, teacher and deep thinker. This person is not tied down by materialistic motivations and has better reasoning ability than other Lunarians.

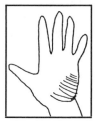

Smooth fingers with their impulse and intuition, their artistic sense and their distaste for analysis, exacerbate Lunarian qualities. The imagination is heightened, usefulness becomes subservient to beauty, and the result is a highly unrealistic nature, full of poetic ideals. These people love romance and fiction. They are likely to be continuously changing their ideas and occupations, and usually avoid applying their brilliance to its best advantage.

Long fingers and their element of slowness added to the already slow Lunarian, impart an element of suspicion. These people are likely to be careful in the way they dress and in the design of their surroundings. They are fanciful in conversation, but long-winded, and they are inclined to take offense where none is intended. They make good writers, as they are attentive to detail and have limitless imagination.

With excessively long fingers, the mental world will dominate the Lunarian, and the highly charged imagination will be devoted to language. This person may become a linguist, or will devote time to literary studies. If the middle zone of the hand is well-developed, the Lunarian will have good business sense, a characteristic that is not typical for the Lunarian ordinarily.

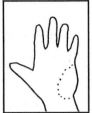

Short fingers make Lunarians quick, impulsive and likely to fly off the handle. They also incline Lunarians to be careless in appearance. They are apt to rely entirely on inspiration, planning schemes which are impractical, and not likely to be brought to completion.

A large thumb will show strong willpower and reason, adding strength to the whimsy of the Lunarian. A short thumb reduces both willpower and reason, and makes a visionary who is indecisive and weak. This is especially true with a pointed thumb, however, this combination does make an excellent photographer.

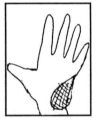

Check to see if a thick, coarse thumb will be affecting the Lunarian's power of imagination, or if a delicate, refined thumb is present to elevate the ideals of this type.

Note the Head Line. If it goes straight across the hand, the ideas are more practical. If it drops to the Mount of Luna, it adds melancholy and moodiness to a personality that is already inclined to this kind of behavior. If the Head Line is clear, well-marked, and of good color, it indicates a strong mind, self-control, and a healthy imagination. With a poorly marked Head Line, or weak, frayed-looking one, combined with a well-developed Luna, there will be poor concentration, a lack of firmness in decision-making, and a vivid imagination that does not work to the person's advantage. Such a person is likely to be continually changing his or her mind, being restless, indecisive and never satisfied. This person will be on the verge of imbalance most of the time.

Thus, the Lunarian ranges from a highly gifted person, to an out and out Lunatic, all indicated by the size, character, and markings on the mount, as well as the numerous variables that accompany the mount's development.

Lunarian Fingernails

The nails must also be considered. When broad nails are found, it indicates strong general health, and will make the person less liable to the health defects of the type. If the nails are narrow, it will show a delicate constitution, and the mount should be carefully examined for health defects. A badly crossed mount with fluted or brittle nails shows a highly sensitive, irritable, discontented person. Short nails will make the Lunarian pugnacious, cranky and critical.

Lunarian Fingertips

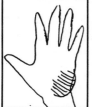

Pointed tips make the person prey to great idealism, religious excesses, and impracticality. Superstition and a tendency to mentally drift will make this person unsynchronized with the work-a-day world and indicate an eccentric or odd individual.

Conic tips are normal to Lunarians and their intuitive qualities tinge these people with romance and fancy.

Square tips will make Lunarians more practical, and common sense oriented, rather than idealistic. They will be more predictable and self-controlled than other Lunarians, and more inclined to follow the rules. Here we find a healthy imagination, which, when coupled with practical ideas and common sense, produces successful people.

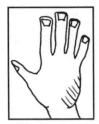
Spatulate fingertips add activity to an already restless nature, especially if the mount is grilled or riddled by crosslines. These people have original ideas, and are entirely unconventional. They are inclined to become rovers in search of a place where they can exercise their wild ideas.

Other Lunarian Characteristics

Texture of the skin will bring out the refined or coarse influences when a well-developed Mount of Luna is found. If the texture is soft and fine, it will undoubtedly be found with flabby consistency. Although these people may be refined and imaginative, they will also be lazy, and less likely to accomplish a great deal. They may not have the drive necessary to finish what they start. Their ideas will be high and their tastes refined. Coarseness will indicate the reverse—much drive accompanied by coarse tastes.

The medium skin texture is best when finding a well-developed Mount of Luna, as it will indicate more energy and more practicality. Flexible skin and good muscle tone is good to find in conjunction with a well-developed Luna. It will tell of a healthy imagination, with ingenious, original ideas, and people who are clever, versatile, good talkers, and who are not bound by rules and formalities. These people will not sit idly and make nothing of their ideas, like so many others with a strong Mount of Luna. Instead, they will energetically work to see them through.

Flexible muscle-tone and flexible fingers will add to the Lunarian imagination and will reduce the danger of extremes. The mind will not become prey to the imagination as easily, but will be directed into more practical channels. The stiff hand will indicate the lower qualities of the Lunarian. This type is likely to be miserly, lacking in sympathy, and the imagination will satisfy itself by hunting the mysterious and the superstitious.

 If the lower third of the hand is the most developed, the imagination would lean toward base topics, and the appetites would be vulgar. This person will imagine suggestive things where none were intended. If the upper part of the mount is the most developed, the imagination will be of a higher order. Students should be aware that modern palmists have given this lower area of the hand a new name in the 20th century. It is called by some the Mount of Pluto and represents the ability to regenerate oneself and to transform others. I have not found this interpretation to be accurate and prefer to apply the traditional Lunarian attributes, as they have proved quite accurate in the course of my observations.

——————————— Mount of Luna Checklist ———————————

Test your own Mount of Luna:

☐ What features does Luna contain in your hand? Describe them.

☐ Is the mount properly proportioned to the rest of the hand?

☐ Is it bulging noticeably in any one area? Apply the Three Worlds of Palmistry. Is this true for one or both hands?

☐ What color is the Mount of Luna?

☐ Are there any areas which appear discolored? Where? On which hand?

☐ Are there any unfavorable markings? Where? On one or both hands?

C H A P T E R 11

The Lines of the Hand

The lines in the hand are a map of a person's temperament and natural energy. When mental or physical changes are great enough to alter someone's habitual behavior, the lines in the hand are likely to change as well. The palmist, therefore, believes that the lines in the hands are a direct reflection of mental and physical habits, and that the mind can control and alter them. From a more technical point of view, a noted English palmist, Beryl Hutchinson mentions the following hypothesis from Professor Wood Jones in his *Principals of Anatomy as Seen in the Hand* (London, 1946):

> We know that the hand is covered with thousands of fine nerves which find their cortical termination in the nerve cells in the central sulcus or Fissure of Rolando, which divides the brain like a walnut. Latest discoveries suggest that all messages to the intelligence arrive via the spinal column. These messages, which require our knowledge, memory, acceptance and consideration of action go forward to the front part of the brain, thus crossing the area of the terminals of nerves to the hand. All such messages are basically electrical impulses. The hypothesis therefore, is that as we think in our brain, thoughts pass across nerve endings of the hand which are located in the same vicinity of the brain. The nerves must be excited frequently or dramatically to show and retain the habitual path of thought on the palm.

Only matters that are hereditary, or are natural tendencies within the individual, or those things that have created a profound impression on the mind will be shown in the hand. For example, early conditioning from the father and mother, shortages of food, living in a war zone, will all leave tremendous impressions on the mind, the physiology, and consequently on the hands.

No two hands are alike, not even the two hands of the same person. However, the more alike two people are, the more alike are the lines and shapes of their hands. Thus, we often find similarity in the hands of children and parents, but there is always a difference in some particular. This is because parents pass on their thinking habits to their children via conditioning.

My own definition of the lines is that they are a network of nerve endings, and anything that leaves a profound impression on the nervous system will reflect that impression on the lines of the hand.

Strange as it seems, lines often change in color, length, depth, or even direction as people alter their health habits. Abrupt changes in health will be most evident on the Life, Heart, Head and Health Lines, but no statistical research has been done to verify whether the lines are consistently lengthened or shortened by any one health condition. It is important not to use one single line to assess a person's health or character without correlating its evidence with information found on other lines. Always cross-reference a line with the others before concluding anything.

I have been told by medical doctors that the lines fade and nearly vanish altogether when people are in a coma. I have yet to verify this with my own eyes, but I suspect it is quite true, as no thoughts, movement, or habitual messages are being transmitted.

Examine the hand yourself and consider for a moment where the energy that is so abundant in the hand comes from — and where does it go? Does this energy come pouring out of the five fingers or does it circulate like electricity consolidating its power? Does energy enter the body from outside sources as well as from internal sources? These are questions whose answers are better left to the scientist, however, I do believe from my own personal experiences that energy does indeed travel *into* as well as *out of* our two hands. A good example of this would be the feelings of energy we pick up in our hands after giving a massage.

Character of the Lines

Knowing the character of the lines is a wonderful way to assess vitality and enthusiasm at a glance. Generally speaking, when all the lines are deep and there is an absence of crosslines, people are healthy, with good strong constitutions and cheerful, enthusiastic dispositions. These people like to work, and usually work very hard at what they do. They are quite outgoing and when ill, their recovery powers are strong.

If the lines are shallow, the opposite of the above is true. With shallow lines, people are apt to be delicate, hypersensitive, unenthusiastic, and liable to catch cold easily. These people do not have much stamina. They are shy, reserved and can also be quite superficial. Socially, they are likely to be shrinking violets. They are not the kind of people who employ their brawn at work. They are easily hurt in the realm of the emotions—high strung and protective when it comes to matters of the heart.

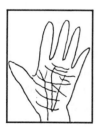

If the hand looks like a tangle of lines, with the major lines shallow, and a variety of shallow lines criss-crossing them, the people are likely to be confused about life and where they fit in. Thinking is muddled, and the ability to make decisions is impaired. Health is likely to have many ups and downs, and the outlook on life is highly inconsistent. These people lack determination and are inclined to worry about every trifle.

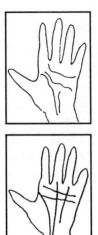

When all their lines appear wavy, people are inconsistent and get confused easily. With wavy lines, health problems will be more likely than with lines which are only tangled.

When all the lines appear straight, people are straight and uncompromising in attitude. They want everything their own way and do things by the book. They are staunch and stodgy, and argue with anything that deviates from their conventional approach.

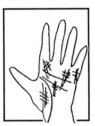

An abundance of grills in the hand shows a constant worrier, whose health is depleted by endless stress. These people suffer from inferiority complexes and never seem to get enough rest. They are easily defeated and pessimistic. Worry takes the place of more constructive thought, and they are hard-pressed to complete what they start. These people are preoccupied with their problems to the exclusion of more positive channels for their energy.

Depth, Clarity and Course of Line

It is important to observe the depth of a line to assess the vitality of the area in question. A deep line would show a strong channel for the energy particular to that line (see fig. 6). A deep line stresses the importance of that line. If the Life Line was the most deeply cut line in the hand, it would indicate a strong vitality and a need to express this energy in a physical way. It indicates a healthy constitution. A deep Heart Line would indicate a strong emotional nature and a need to express it adamantly through the personality. The clearer the line, and the less hindered by unfavorable markings, *i.e.*, shallowness, or a line that wavers, the more wholesome and unhindered will be the expression of that line.

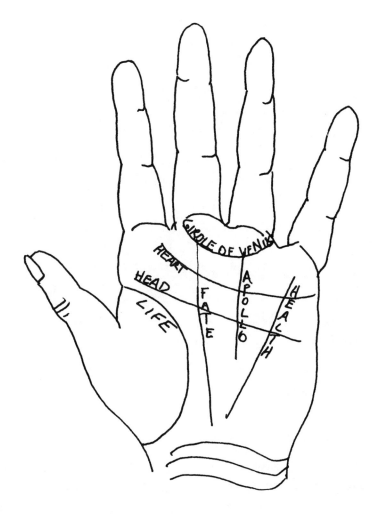

Figure 6. A palm showing deep, clear lines.

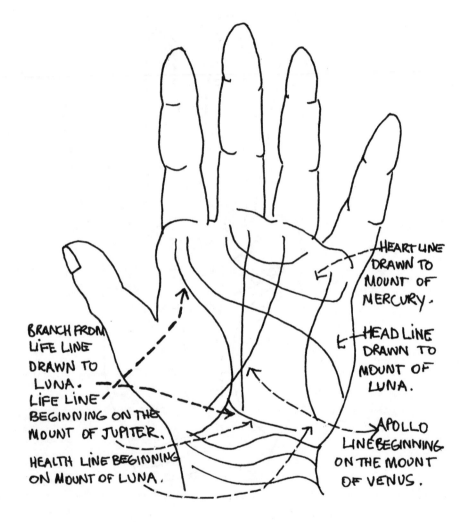

Figure 7. Lines drawn toward other mounts that are not their usual destination. The mount will influence the expression of that particular line.

If the line is drawn toward a mount which is not its usual location, the energies of the line will be expressed through the qualities of that mount (see fig. 7). The mount qualities will also lend themselves to the expression of that particular line. If the mount is not appropriate for the expression of that line, there will be problems. For example, if the Heart Line were to end at the Mount of Saturn (not its usual place) the love nature and the emotions — represented by the Heart Line — would be hampered by the restraining influence of Saturn. In such a case, it is important to check the hand for other factors that may mitigate this effect. See the chapter on the Heart Line for more information on this marking.

The beginning and the ending of the lines are important. The beginning of a line shows the origin of that line's energy. For example, with a Life Line beginning under the index finger, also called the Mount of Jupiter, the vitality, represented by the Life Line, will use Jupiter's ambition and self-assertion as one of its sources of original energy. The Jupiterian qualities will greatly influence how the person manifests vitality. See fig. 8 on page 148 for examples of the various ways lines may begin and end.

The same is true for other lines that do not begin in the normal starting position. Special attention should be given to the place the line begins. The palmist can then interpret the line in conjunction with the properties of that mount.

The color of each line also provides a clue as to which line is most emphasized. In addition to this, it shows the vitality of the line in question. A good example would be a red Heart Line. This tells us that the heart organ is very active, perhaps overly so, and that the emotions are affected by heightened circulation. This is a person who is apt to become emotionally charged without much provocation. Red lines are a sign of abundant energy. Pale or blue lines show just the opposite. Blue is especially significant because it shows a constriction in the circulatory system. Yellow lines have been read traditionally as indicating too much bile in the system, but they can also show an excess of nicotine and other toxins.

Always note which line is deepest and clearest to ascertain the line that is the most influential to the person's character. If one line is noticeably more red than the others, special attention should be given to that line. Color is the equivalent of very pronounced or deeply-cut lines.

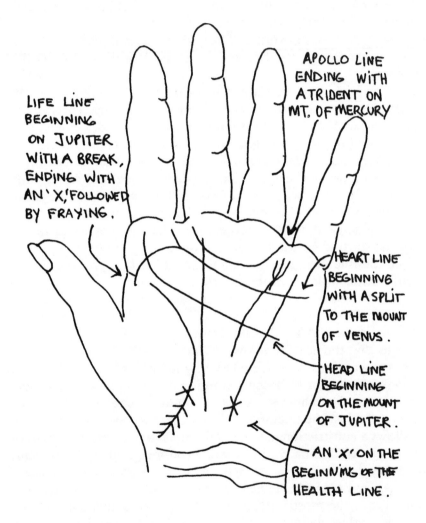

LIFE LINE
BEGINNING
ON JUPITER
WITH A BREAK,
ENDING WITH
AN 'X,' FOLLOWED
BY FRAYING.

APOLLO LINE
ENDING WITH
A TRIDENT ON
MT. OF MERCURY

HEART LINE
BEGINNING
WITH A SPLIT
TO THE MOUNT
OF VENUS.

HEAD LINE
BEGINNING
ON THE MOUNT
OF JUPITER.

AN 'X' ON THE
BEGINNING OF THE
HEALTH LINE.

Figure 8. Various examples of the beginning and endings of the major lines.

Line Markings

Markings found on the lines are highly significant. We know the lines are channels for various kinds of energy, so when a line is altered by some form of marking, the energy represented by that line is also likely to be altered (see fig. 9 on page 150). If the line is broken or damaged-looking, the energy represented by that line will also be disrupted. If a sister line or some other favorable marking accompanies that line, the energy that the line represents is enhanced. The following discussion explains the more traditional markings and how to read them when they are found on a major line. This will help the palmist determine whether the line's energy is being put to its optimum use or not. The most important line markings are islands, dots, squares, triangles, X's, breaks, sister lines, fraying and splits. Occasionally a line may contain two or more markings as seen in fig. 10 on page 151.

Islands

Islands indicate a division of energy found in that line. An island hampers the continuity of the line and dilutes the line's intensity for the duration of time indicated by the island's size. Measure the island's size using figure 11 on p. 152 to gauge how long its affects will last. An island is usually created by a health trauma, and the way the health has been affected will be determined by the line on which it is found. If an island, which disrupts a line, also falls on a particular mount, it will detract from the higher qualities of the mount. When assessing the character and vitality of the person, an island is not to be overlooked. Check the hand for any repair signs which will compensate for the island's influence. For special information pertaining to islands found on particular lines, check the subsequent chapters referring to individual lines.

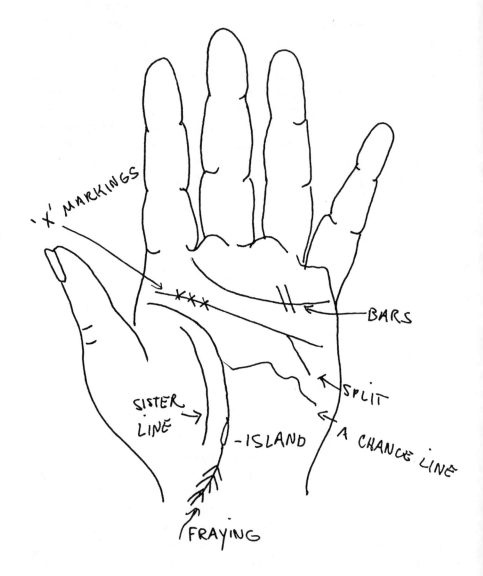

Figure 9. Markings on the lines of the palms. Each marking—islands, dots, squares, triangles, X's, sister lines, fraying and splitting—has an effect upon the line's energy.

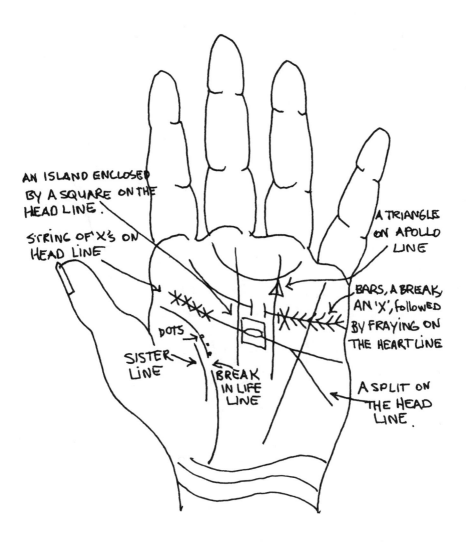

AN ISLAND ENCLOSED BY A SQUARE ON THE HEAD LINE.

STRING OF 'X's ON HEAD LINE

A TRIANGLE ON APOLLO LINE

BARS, A BREAK, AN 'X', followed BY FRAYING ON THE HEART LINE

DOTS

SISTER LINE

BREAK IN LIFE LINE

A SPLIT ON THE HEAD LINE.

Figure 10. Extensive markings on the hand lines.

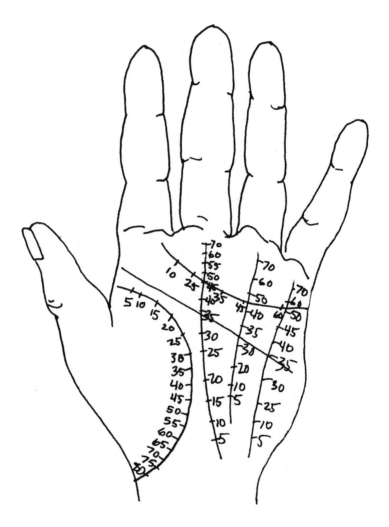

Figure 11. Age as seen on the lines. Use this figure to measure the size of any markings on the lines in order to get an idea of how long an interruption will last.

Dots

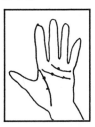

Dots show a shock to the nervous system. They indicate a high fever if they are found on the Heart Line, or an infection if found on the Life Line. If the dot is found on the Heart Line beneath the ring finger, Apollo, it indicates an eye infection. The dot refers to a physical event which left a gravely memorable impression on the nervous system. A dot accompanied by an X is almost a sure sign of an accident which had drastic and shocking affects upon the entire body of the person. A broken bone with a subsequent fever or infection is a typical occurrence which would leave such a mark. When a dot is found on the Health Line it will also indicate an infection, but in this case, to the stomach or kidneys. Be sure to ascertain the nature of the illness for future reference. Not every marking found in the hand has been adequately documented, and every bit of information can be put to use if proper methods of questioning are employed.

Squares

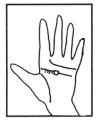

Squares are a repair sign and show restoration to damaged lines. Traditionally, they are called preservation marks and indicate repairs made to a disrupted Health Line. When a square is found on the Life Line, it is traditionally read as a period of confinement in an institution—usually a hospital, but in a bad hand, it could also indicate prison. Activity is restricted during this time period, and the person is likely to have been (or at least felt) very isolated from the rest of the world. If an X precedes such a marking, an accident is likely to have been the cause. In a case such as this, the person's recovery time is commensurable to the size of the square.

Triangles

Triangles are a sign of creativity. They proclaim talent in whatever area they are found, and show an ability to incorporate mental skill with physical dexterity. When found directly on a line they activate the line's higher qualities, and highlight the talent and creativity of that line's potential.

X's

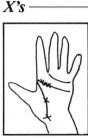

X's are important markings not to be overlooked wherever they are found. Their significance varies according to their depth, clarity, and location; but generally speaking, they indicate a shock to both the nervous system and the skeleton as well. Do not confuse chance lines which crisscross haphazardly over the hand with an X. A proper X is deeply marked and stands apart from other lines and markings in the hand. Broken bones are always a shock to the nervous system and are the most common causes of X's on the Life Line. If an X is found on the Head Line, the shock was confined to the head and neck area. I have personally seen this marking many times on the Head Lines of those who have suffered a fractured skull, a concussion, or broken neck.

An X on the Life Line that appears to cut the line, impeding its continuity, will tell of an accident which greatly jeopardized the life of the person. Another form of shock to the body which is reflected by an X is surgery. This is likely if the X is very red in appearance. Be sure to ask if the person had any recent surgery when inquiring about an X found in the hand. It is important to look for repair signs when an X is discovered. A square would show that the scattering of the life-current was contained. Sister lines show that although the energy of the line was drastically disrupted, this energy was re-routed and loaned a measure of support from other areas of vitality within that person. A sister line acts as secondary support system to that line which it accompanies. The size of the X will show how long the affects of the shock have lasted.

 Often a string of X's are seen on the beginning of the Life Line. These are signs of childhood shocks and illnesses that were certainly disruptive to the health, but were too numerous to define. Illnesses such as measles, mumps, strep throat, and chicken pox all cause tremendous shock to a child's immune system when they are encountered. Although they leave a permanent impression on the nerves, the child recovers, grows up, and thinks nothing of it. The person, at that time, was too young to recall what caused these X's to appear, so it is best to overlook them unless there is one specific X that stands apart from the others. If a string of X's appear in a row on the Head Line, it is a sure sign of recurrent headaches such as migraines. The intensity of these headaches is commensurable to the depth and size of the X's themselves.

Hand Line Checklist

When assessing the lines there are several things to be considered. The following is a checklist of factors which help the palmist to draw conclusions:

□ Note the depth and clarity of the line.

□ Note the course of the line, whether it wavers or is drawn to any particular mount, or whether it runs in a straight line fashion.

□ Note the beginning and ending of the line and what mounts they are found on.

□ Note the color of the line, or any discoloration found thereon.

□ Note any markings found on the line.

□ Note if there are any sister lines, splits, or chance lines connected to it. Use this checklist to analyze your own lines. Compare the findings of the lines seen on the right with those on the left. How do they differ?

The Life Line

The Life Line is of tremendous importance when trying to ascertain the physical vitality and disposition of the individual. Markings found on the Life Line are not to be overlooked. The current of life energy which this line represents should not be broken, split, or impeded in any way. Other lines which cut the Life Line, dangle from it, dent it, or alter its natural direction are to be carefully noted and compared to the Life Line in the other hand of that person. The Life Line is metaphorically equivalent to the human spine. In prenatal infants, the Life Line has been photographed as early as the first sixteen weeks. After personally viewing more than 20,000 hands, I have never seen a hand without a Life Line. It is interesting to note however, that the Life Line fades dramatically in the hands of people who are in a prolonged coma. Its depth and direction may be altered many times throughout the life, but when the Life Line is seen as broken, blocked, cut, wavering drastically, or ending with an abrupt or unusual marking — such as a star or a cross-line — that blocks its flow toward the wrist, the good palmist will interpret it carefully!

The Life Line begins just below the index finger and sweeps downward alongside the ball of the thumb toward the wrist. The area nearest the index finger represents the earliest part of the life, while the other end of the Life Line represents the latter part of the life. Therefore, when reading this line always begin by reading it from the top down.

The Life Line is considered the most important line on the hand. It reveals basic vitality and the measure of enthusiasm that accompanies the person's present health circumstances. It also indicates what kind of stamina the person has, and whether he or she is socially outgoing or withdrawn. In addition to this, the Life Line provides us with a chronological record of the person's illnesses, traumas, and changes of residence. The Life Line provides the following information about an individual:

1) The Life Line shows the approximate timing of illnesses and traumas;

2) It shows the past health habits of the person, and future health potential;

3) It shows the nature of the present disposition, such as enthusiasm, physical activity, lethargy or ambition;

4) It shows the person's stamina and recovery power;

5) It shows changes of residence, and how these changes affected the person.

To read the Life Line, a palmist should observe the line with several things in mind. First, the depth and clarity of the line should be considered. The depth of the line is the point of reference for stamina and enthusiasm. A very shallow Life Line would indicate that these qualities are lacking. A Life Line that is inordinately deeper than the rest of the lines on the hand may be a mixed blessing. It indicates an abundance of physical strength and enthusiasm that is not backed up by an equal measure of concentration as disclosed by the Head Line. The Head Line should be equal in depth to the Life Line.

If this deep Life Line is accompanied by a shallow Heart Line, a lack of self-control is indicated, despite the fact that the person's vitality — as seen from the deep Life Line — will compensate for poor circulation implied by the shallow Heart Line. Remember that an overly deep Life Line shows a persistence bordering on pig-headedness. A simple test of finger flexibility would verify this finding. If the fingers are very stiff, stubbornness is assured.

The clarity of the Life Line is also very important, as it reveals whether the vitality has been impeded, at what age, and by

what event. Lines which muddle the Life Line, cross it — or interfere with its course in any way — inhibit the vitality and impede the
expression of the person's enthusiasm. A good, clear Life Line
that is deep and uninterrupted by crosslines is the surest sign of
excellent health.

The direction that the Life Line travels is also
significant. If the Life Line swings way out into
the center of the palm, it shows a warm, outgoing
nature, and optimism.

If it hugs the ball of the thumb, it shows introversion, reticence and stinginess.

The next thing to look for when judging the Life
Line is to discover where exactly it begins. Normally, the Life Line begins on the side of the hand
near the thumb.

If the line begins directly beneath the index finger, it is considered a sign of ambition and determination. If the Life Line begins on the ball of
the thumb — the Mount of Venus — it is traditionally read as timidity and sentimentality. This person will seek to insulate his or her life with a kind
of motherly protection. If other factors bear it
out, this marking is likely to indicate an inferiority complex.
Remember, however, that in the case of complexes, phobias, and
other mental problems, no one factor is conclusive without proper
confirmation in other areas of the hand.

In this discussion of the important characteristics shown in the Life Line, it would be advantageous to commit this section to memory. The beginning of the Life Line is considered the well-spring of people's vitality. The ending of the line hints how this vitality will expend itself.

A short Life Line does not necessarily indicate a short life. It does tell us, however, that longevity was not a feature inherited from both parents. If the Life Line is short in both hands the person is likely to run on nervous energy after the age indicated by the end of the line. The exact age of this transition from vital energy to nervous energy can be determined by using the age guide to the lines featured in figure 11 on page 152.

A long Life Line does not guarantee a long life, but it does show an inherited trait of longevity passed on through the blood-lines of the parents. This inherited tendency can be changed, however, by poor living habits, careless behavior or accidents.

A branch extending from the Life Line to another area in the hand will provide a clue to where the vitality is being channeled.

The normal place for the Life Line to begin is the Active Mount of Mars. The Line beginning here indicates a healthy constitution with good staying-power and self-control. It shows people who are endowed with enthusiasm, and who are not afraid of hard physical work. These people are tenacious and strong-willed, and have a sturdy constitution to fight off illness.

When the Life Line begins on Jupiter, beneath the index finger, it shows people who are ambitious and who will show undying stamina in satisfying their goals. If the line rises from the top of the Jupiter mount near the finger, the ambitions will be quite lofty. Special care should be taken to see where, exactly, on the mount the line begins. If it is the bottom of the Jupiter mount, the lower qualities of the

Jupiterian will be emphasized. Indulgence of the physical appetites would be likely and there will be a great appreciation for rich, highly seasoned foods. (For more information on the Mount of Jupiter see the chapter about Jupiter on page 73ff.)

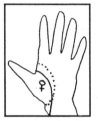

If the Life Line begins on the Mount of Venus, it describes people who are "clinging vines." They are likely to be timid and conservative, are not overly enthusiastic, and will often go through life feeling inferior about issues of personal potential. These people are more likely to limit vitality to issues that are emotionally safe. When the Life Line begins here, it indicates an introverted temperament and people who restrict energy in the name of caution and security.

The ending of the Life Line is also an important area to consider. The normal ending for the Life Line is at the base of the Mount of Venus. The nearer the wrist, the better, as this implies longevity.

If the Life Line should extend across the other side of the palm and end on the Mount of Luna, it is traditionally read as a life that ends in a far distant place from where it began. This ending also suggests that the person will have traveled widely during the course of life. I have no way of verifying this assessment, but I feel it is important to include all the traditional interpretations because recorded information on this subject is so difficult to come by.

The Life Line ending on the Fate Line is difficult to interpret, although it is quite often found. Since the Fate Line is read from the bottom up, and the Life Line is read for the top down, there is some confusion about the time periods that each of these lines refer to. In my opinion, these two lines merging would indicate a time period during the latter part of life when the career—Fate Line—becomes as important as life itself. At this time, people are likely to concentrate all their vitality to satisfying career goals.

I will advise the palmist to make as few comments as possible regarding the ending of a person's life. Some clients will press you for a comment about this area, but a good palmist will know how to decline a comment without being rude.

Life Line Markings

The Life Line is usually the deepest line on the hand, and it is very significant when there are favorable markings which enhance its character. The Life Line speaks to us about our vitality, and the general course of our life, its assets, its interruptions, and any physical affliction we may encounter along the way. Unfavorable markings to the Life Line can indicate major health traumas, as they impede the vitality which the line represents. The Life Line also helps us to corroborate the timing of significant events and illnesses that may be in evidence elsewhere in the hand. Read further to find the meanings of some of the more commonly seen markings that positively or negatively influence the Life Line.

Islands

Islands on the Life Line are considered a serious health debility. They show a time in life when energy was divided and vitality low. During this period, it is likely that these people experienced a period of seclusion or they were discouraged because of their physical condition. The island suggests nervous strain and exhaustion at the age indicated by the island's location. If the island is found in the hand of a woman at age 45–50, it is likely that menopause is the cause of the distress. An island on the Life Line is traditionally read as a serious and prolonged illness with a protracted recovery period which depleted the vitality. The length of the illness is commensurate with the length of the island itself. Check the hand carefully to identify what the cause of the illness might be. Consult figure 11 on page 152 to ascertain the age of the person at the time where the island is located.

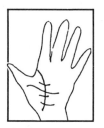

Little lines that cross the Life Line and appear to cut it indicate annoying illnesses caused by nervous tension. These may take the form of allergies, skin eruptions, asthma, or any other health debility aggravated by nervous tension that occurs with regularity. Traditionally, crosslines on the Life Line indicate family worries that deplete the health because they create constant stress.

Dots

Little dots on the Life Line tell of high fever. Infections are often accompanied by a dot. These dots can also indicate a puncture wound such as a gunshot, but a trauma like this would also be accompanied by a star or very distinctive fraying around the dot. These dots appear to indent the skin and are not to be confused with red or other colored spots that merely rest upon the skin's surface.

Tassels

Tassels on the line represent a dissipation of energy. This applies wherever the tassel is found, whether it is on the lines or on the mounts. On the Life Line, tassels suggest depleted vitality at the time indicated. (See figure 11 on p. 152 on how to tell time by the lines.) Fraying of any kind found on the Life Line is a sign of dissipation.

Breaks

The importance of breaks in the Life Line cannot be stressed enough as they show a drastic disruption to the vital current of energy found in that line. Breaks are usually caused by a very serious illness that endangers the person's life. A break in the Life Line is the most significant of all breaks. It shows that the vital current of energy was prevented and re-routed. Examine the break carefully to see if the line resumes, and in what fashion. If the Life Line resumes in a wavering fashion after a break, it shows poor recovery from the event which caused the break. This will also be the case if the line is shallow or badly marked after it resumes. Fraying of the line after a break shows that the health was greatly depleted by the health trauma that caused the break. The condition still depletes the person who has not yet fully recovered. If the line continues deeply and evenly after the break, it shows that the person has made a splendid recovery, and that the problem which has caused the break has been overcome. Be sure to look for repair signs such as squares or sister lines to assess the person's recovery. Never hesitate to ask what the nature of the illness was if it is not apparent.

Breaks usually occur after a brush with death when the person's life fell into serious jeopardy. Any drastic interruptions of the Life Line are traditionally read as having threatened life. The way the Life Line resumes after a break is a valuable clue to how well the person recovered. If the line becomes fainter after the break, the person never really fully recovered health after this danger period. If the line resumes deeply and becomes pink in color after a break in the Life Line, the person has recovered splendidly with renewed determination.

This marking also indicates that the person took an active part in correcting health habits after the break occurred. Consult the Health Line, and any defects found in other areas on the hand to discern what the nature of the illness was. Whenever the Life Line looks altered, it is correct to assume that the health and the lifestyle were both altered. Breaks in the Life Line are considered one of the most serious markings and indicate a very traumatic time during which the life and health were radically threatened.

There is one special case where a break may appear in the Life Line without a health defect having caused it. This is when the person has a drastic change of residence. Once again, the continuity of the lifestyle was interrupted by a move to a different climate or culture. This kind of break will usually resume as strongly as the rest of the Life Line without any other indications to confirm it as a health defect. It may simply represent a big adjustment in habits. This would be corroborated by a break or an abrupt change in the Fate Line as well. Use the age guide (see fig. 11 on p. 152) to assess the age of the person at the time in question, then check the age period on the Head and Fate Lines. Splits in a line show that the vitality of that line has been diverted. The energy has been channeled in two directions, and the energy of the line has been depleted as a result. The divorce of parents may cause such a marking — representing a division within the personality — as the two parents attempt to go their separate ways.

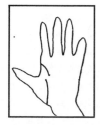

If the Life Line hugs the ball of the thumb after a break it indicates that the life resumed in a more conservative way after the age at which the break occurred. This marking indicates a change in attitude which restricts the person's enthusiasm and spontaneity. It is considered by palmists as a turn for the worst regarding the person's attitude.

If the Life Line swings wide — out into the middle of the palm — after the break it is considered a turn for the better. This person became more outgoing, amiable and open after the break.

Fraying

Fraying shows stress which defeats the vitality of whatever line it is found on. The person's nerves are weakened by this condition and enthusiasm wanes quickly. This marking is similar to that of the tassel.

Sister Lines

Sister Lines are a repair sign wherever found. They add strength to any depleted line and compensate for lost energy. They indicate that a correction has been made. If a Sister Line is found accompanying an undamaged line it doubly emphasizes the vitality of that line. The line which the Sister Line supports will be the most emphasized line on the hand. If a Sister Line runs parallel to the Fate Line, it indicates two careers.

Wavering Life Line

A Life Line that wavers or is inconsistent in its depth shows a highly changeable person whose health is also inconsistent. These people have poor concentration and have a hard time making up their minds or sticking to one thing. These people also tire easily, lack individuality, and are very prone to psychosomatic illnesses.

Life Line Checklist

Test your Life Line with this simple checklist of line characteristics. Be sure to compare traits found in the left hand with those found in the right.

□ Where does the line begin?

□ Where does it end?

❑ Is the line deep or lightly traced in the hand?

❑ Does it have forks or branches? Where? Where do these branches end?

❑ Does it have any breaks? Where?

❑ Does it waver or is it inconsistent in depth?

❑ What are its various markings?

The Heart Line

The Heart Line is located in the upper third of the palm and is the closest major line to the mounts of the fingers. Palmists differ on whether the Heart Line is read from the outer edge of the hand inward, or vice versa. I have always read the Heart Line as if its beginning were located under the index finger and its end located under the little finger. Bear this in mind when considering the line's beginning and ending. This is the traditional way the Heart Line has been read even though modern palmists seem to prefer turning things around. See figure 12.

When reading the Heart Line keep in mind the following points that are illustrated by it.

1) The physical action of the heart itself.

2) The excitability of the emotions.

3) The quality of the blood and circulation.

4) The degree of sympathy and compassion the person possesses.

 The Heart Line reflects the condition of the heart organ itself. Because the heart organ controls the bloodstream, we look to the Heart Line to give us clues about the emotional temperament of the individual. Palmists believe that the emotions are a direct reflection of the circulation. If the circulation is impeded, so, too, is emotional expression. If the blood is contaminated by pollutants, it will be

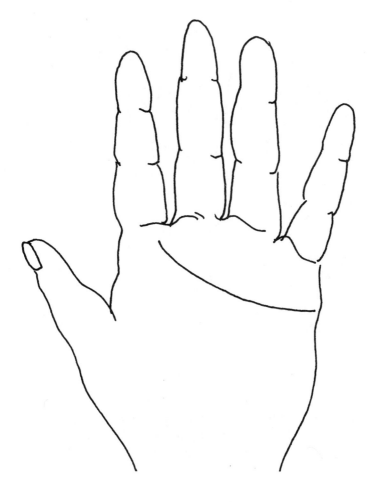

Figure 12. A normal, healthy Heart Line.

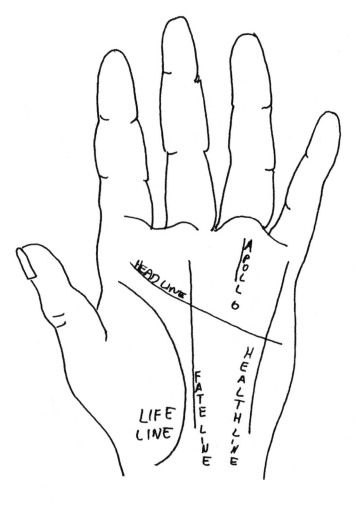

Figure 13. A hand with no Heart Line.

reflected by irritability in the emotional disposition. If the blood supply is too limited, as in the case of low blood pressure, the emotions will be far less receptive to enthusiasm and the person will be less inclined to be passionate, demonstrative and active. Rather than mistaking the Heart Line for a key to passions, the palmist should consider the Heart Line an index of emotions and circulation.

Traditional palmists agree that if the Heart Line is faint or shallow it describes a weak heart organ and poor circulation. The faint or shallow looking Heart Line will also suggest a lack of enthusiasm and a proclivity for blood and heart-related illnesses. This kind of Heart Line is usually accompanied by a shallow Life Line and the person is not known for generosity or hospitality.

It is very rare to find a hand without a Heart Line altogether (see fig. 13) but if this should be the case, the traditional interpretation would be a severe lack of affection and sympathy. This person is probably selfish, cold-blooded, and inclined to acquire success at the expense of others. The absence of a Heart Line, is not to be confused with a Heart Line that merges with the Head Line. Known as the "Simian Line" by medical doctors, this merging line indicates a person who has difficulty separating the emotional world from the mental world. With an absence of a Heart Line, the person would be ruled by the mind rather than by the cooperative blending of heart and mind. With the mental world predominating over the emotional, thoughts rule over sentiment. This also indicates a heart that may be weak in its physical nature, and special attention should be given to the care of the heart throughout the life.

Aggression, or the lack of it, depends greatly on the blood supply, its impediments, and the quality of the blood itself. Poor circulation and toxins in the blood are two of the worst assailants of good health. One of the most common affects of poor circulation is a hampering of the digestive system. Colitis and hemorrhoids are two typical problems resulting from poor circulation and emotional stress. These are minor compared to paralysis, varicose veins, spasms and migraines which are also results of impaired circulation. The sentiments suffer considerably when drastic ailments such as these occur in the body with regularity. Abrupt mood swings will affect enthusiasm and the sex drive. Poor circulation indicates someone prone to inconsistent behavior from day to day.

With overly active circulation, there are other liabilities which upset health and temperament. High blood pressure is one of the most common precursors to heart attack and many other heart conditions. The way this affects the temperament is manifold. The person will have a short fuse and will fly off the handle at the slightest provocation. This person is pushy, and the most likely to commit a crime of passion. A very deep Heart Line coupled with an excessively red pallor to the palm would be indicative of such a condition.

A palmist must be careful when dealing with one of these hot-headed types, as he or she loves to argue and has the physical strength to back it up. Remember that this person is emotional, temperamental, jealous, and competitive. In a thick hand with short fingers, an overly deep, red Heart Line will increase the potential for violence. This person needs to be constantly busy to be happy, and will suffer terribly in a job where the robust physicality is not utilized. This person is also a passionate lover and is ardent and enthusiastic in sports.

Basically, the Heart Line represents the origin of our primary emotional impulses. There are several common starting points for the Heart Line and each gives a clue to the emotional nature. The first starting point we will discuss begins under the index finger. Because the index finger is the finger of self-assertion, the Heart Line beginning here will signify ambition. The person will seek status, prestige, and authority in love relationships. The finances of the marriage partner would be important as this person seeks comforts that only money can buy. This starting point indicates an outgoing love nature and this person can be very aggressive when going after a mate. This origin for the Heart Line indicates a feisty kind of dedication and an inclination to be staunchly loyal.

If the Heart Line is straight across the hand instead of gently curving, this person can be the jealous type in love matters, and a very demanding one, as well. The index finger rules the religious nature, so, with the Heart Line beginning here, the person is inclined to be very much affected by religious convictions. If the Heart Line begins high on the Mount of Jupiter, directly under the finger, the more lofty qualities of Jupiter will be favored. This is a common marking for preachers and community leaders, where devotion and reform is important. If the Heart Line starts lower on the Mount of Jupiter, it will indicate a dauntless, though idealistic approach to love. The influence of Jupiter will enhance the circulation considerably.

If the Heart Line should begin under the middle finger, the Finger of Saturn, the characteristics of Saturn will greatly influence the line, both in terms of sentiment and in terms of health. Saturn is the planet of duty and responsibility. Its cold and restraining nature affects the Heart Line in this fashion. The Saturnian attributes restrict the warmth and sentimental qualities of the affections. This marking indicates a person who is reticent and undemonstrative in love, and someone to whom the practical world comes before the affections. This individual may also choose an orthodox religion or guru who seeks to structure and discipline the spontaneous compulsion of the basic love nature. The person is likely to be easily discouraged and will assume the worst first in affairs of the heart. This individual may be a late bloomer in the world of love, and is likely to postpone marriage and emotional commitments until later in life.

The circulation will be hampered with this marking and the passions will be restrained. Slow and cautious, this person will be more inclined to sensualism and emotional detachment than the simple caring and sharing of a less constricted emotional nature. There is a proclivity for gout and knee problems when Saturn afflicts the Heart Line, as Saturn rules the knees and would exert a strong influence upon the circulation there.

The Saturn connection to the Heart Line indicates someone serious and dutiful in love matters, but who demands punctuality and realism from a mate. Not frivolous or light-hearted by nature, this person can be a wet blanket when it comes to loving. Check the Heart Line in the other hand to see if these effects are mitigated by a Heart Line with a different emphasis.

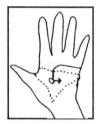

If the Heart Line begins on the Mount of Mars, the attributes of Mars will expend themselves via the Heart Line. The emotions of this person will be highly charged and aggressive. The person will be demonstrative, domineering, passionate, argumentative, and will fight to defend the honor of a loved one. Mars is the warrior spirit, and this quality will permeate the emotional behavior. Constantly seeking challenges, there will be a passion for fighting and all forms of aggressive behavior; the Mars influence will not take no for an answer. A strong Mars influence on a criminal hand reveals a bully who is likely to force his or her way wherever possible. Traditionally, this beginning for the Heart Line is read as the sign of an inferiority complex and a jealous love nature, but in my opinion it merely shows one who is touchy about affection and who will take offense quickly if affection is not returned. Demanding and dominant, a person with a Mars emphasis on the Heart Line will rely on aggression to express the need for love, rather than being able to love calmly and kindly.

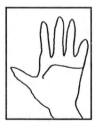

If the Heart Line begins on the Mount of Venus, it shows people who are greatly influenced by sentiment. These people could be described as hypersensitive, and life is ruled by emotions and love. Insecure and easily hurt, these people can be very possessive. They are prone to love at first sight, and emotions take precedence in decision-making. They are likely to have specific ideas of what they want from a relationship, and will take it to heart if a lover falls short of these expectations. The Venus influence will grant a pleasing appearance, and the disposition will be warm and loving. Romance is an irresistible attraction to these people; the drama of being swept off their feet is a constant temptation. In an otherwise bad hand, this feature would indicate a willful demanding sort easily enraged by the opposite sex.

If the Heart Line begins between the index finger and the middle finger it is a good sign. It indicates a good balance between the practical and the idealistic. These people will not be swept off their feet by a pretty face or by the romance of the moment. They are steadied by the Saturn influence of the middle finger, without being overwhelmed by its more negative factors. This marking shows people who are patient and thoughtful in love matters. It increases the loyalty and enhances the sense of responsibility.

Traditionally speaking, a single, clear, uninterrupted Heart Line makes the affections more self-contained. If the Heart Line is deeper and clearer at its starting point than where it ends, it is more likely that the affections will be possessive. The Heart Line is better when it begins with a fork or other ray-like extension. The more the Heart Line branches out at its beginning, the more the affections go out to others.

A double Heart Line shows a dualistic nature in love and a proclivity for having more than one relationship at a time. This extra line is read as a Sister Line to the Heart Line, especially if it runs the whole length of the Heart Line. The additional line strengthens the heart against any defects which may be evident, and adds vigor and resilience to the constitution. A certain fickleness will attend the romantic nature, but the person will be lively and animated.

A Heart Line located high up in the hand, near the fingers, is a sign of unquestioning loyalty. This person is likely to run his or her life around the lover's demands and there may be a lack of perspective.

If the Heart Line is joined to the Head Line at its beginning, the traditional interpretation for the marking is that the mind is more dominant than the heart. Practicality comes first. Reason and fact rule the emotions. This is a good marking for business, but not so good for the artist who must rely primarily on emotions. The same is true for a Heart Line that droops or extends toward the Head Line, however, but its influence is not as pronounced as when the lines are joined. This is also true if the Head Line is deeper and clearer than the Heart Line.

If there is only a Heart Line and no Head Line, the person is dominated by the emotions and very unlikely to be practical. These people are driven by sentimentality and passion, and the worlds of reason and logic are alien to them.

If the Heart Line is joined to the Life Line, this would indicate an early tragedy which deeply touched this person's emotions. This marking is not commonly found, and is usually seen as a line that descends downward from the Heart Line and touches the Life Line. If the lines are actually joined as in the illustration, this person is emotional, sentimental, sensitive, and very touchy about his or her feelings. Often emotions will get the better of him or her and he or she is apt to make decisions according to feelings rather than intellect. This person will be very attached to home and family, and any losses among loved ones may affect him or her so deeply that health may suffer. Remember that any lines drooping down from the Heart Line show disappointments to the heart in terms of affection. This is particularly so if the Heart Line—or a line extending from it—actually touches the Life Line.

The following is a list of interpretations for the ending point of the Heart Line. As you learn to observe the many varieties of Heart Line endings, you will see that the ones mentioned here are the most often seen. There are numerous endings for the Heart Line which have not been mentioned, but should be noted in your own references for future study. Remember that the ending of the Heart Line gives a clue to emotional makeup, and the way people respond to emotional challenges of all kinds.

With the Heart Line ending under the Finger of Saturn there is a coldness and a reticence toward love and sentimentality. Suspicious and overly serious, these people often choose not to marry. They are socially withdrawn, and their enthusiasm would more likely be devoted to mental pursuits than to emotional ones. There is a tendency toward rheumatism, gout, bone and tooth problems, as well as poor circulation and sluggish digestion. Another form of expression for this kind of Heart Line is in the form of complete religious or spiritual devotion, where emotional desires are given over to the world of sacrifice. For example, a nun or a monk may be involved in reclusive religious or spiritual service.

A Heart Line ending under Apollo, the ring finger, can show a liability for heart disease if the Heart Line is weak-looking or poorly marked. Eye problems are also likely and this person will be highly prone to infections. Asthma, allergies and other forms of breathing disorders are not uncommon with this marking. With a Heart Line ending under the ring finger, the person is very dedicated to the

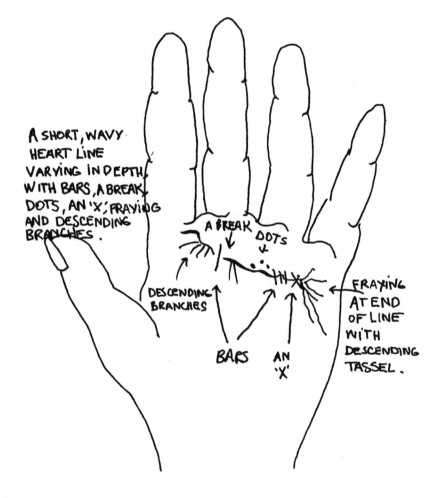

Figure 14. A poor Heart Line with examples of how markings disrupt the flow of energy.

arts and will expend the greater portion of his or her passion in pursuit of artistic expression. If this person works in the arts he or she will have a great deal of enthusiasm and stamina, but placed behind a desk or in another type of job, the individual will feel like a caged eagle.

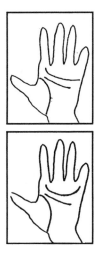

The Heart Line ends normally at the Mount of Mercury. If the Heart Line should curve upward, ending on or directly below the Finger of Mercury, the pinky, it implies cunning and shrewdness in love matters. This person is constantly tempted with dishonesty and will manipulate the opposite sex with shrewd use of language. He or she will have a passion for business but is not above cheating customers!

Heart Line Markings

Markings on the Heart Line are important clues to the personality and health. Be sure to corroborate any findings on the Heart Line with information found elsewhere in the hand. See fig. 14 for an example of a poor Heart Line with numerous markings. The Heart Line indicates the condition of the heart organ itself, as well as the quality of affection and sympathy exhibited by the person. The nails will provide additional information regarding the purity of the blood and the circulation, therefore, heart-related health problems should always be cross-referenced with them. So when a questionable marking is found on the Heart Line, look first at the nails to see if the marking is indicative of a blood related problem. If the nails look healthy, the problem will more likely be emotional in nature.

Islands

Islands found on the Heart Line are important markings that should not be overlooked. Islands show a division of a line's vitality. When found on the Heart Line, we can surmise that the circulation has been impaired during the time span represented by the location of the island. Note the location of the island in reference to the finger under which it is found. The planetary rulers associated with each finger will give a clue to what the nature of the illness may be. For example, an island under the middle finger (the Finger of Saturn) will suggest a Saturnian type illness that is blood and heart related. Rheumatism, a classical Saturnian problem affecting the circulation, will be a typical ailment associated with this marking. Always refer to the pages related to illness of the mount-type if there is a question.

An island found on the Heart Line under the Finger of Apollo, the ring finger, tells of eye problems. This is especially likely if there is also fraying of the line in the area. An island on the Heart Line under the Mercury finger, the pinky, tells of digestive problems.

I have found no written information on what an island on the Heart Line found under the index finger might mean, and I have not seen this marking often enough to verify what it might indicate.

Dots

If we find a dot on the Heart Line, it indicates a permanent impression on the nerves via the heart or circulatory system. A dot usually indicates an infection. When found on the Heart Line, it would be very important to corroborate its meaning with the Life Line and Health Line. Also the finger under which it is located will give a clue as to where the infection was found in the body. Remember, a good palmist should never be afraid to ask the client about the nature of an illness if he or she is stumped, since this will always be helpful in future readings. A dot accompanied by an X would indicate the medical condition known as shock.

Squares

Squares are repair signs, and when found on the Heart Line they indicate an illness which has been overcome. Since squares may also refer to institutions which may have confined the individual, it is also likely that the square was a result of hospitalization, which repaired the heart or circulatory system.

If the person is highly emotional, with very red palms, but with no sign of any serious illness, read the square on the Heart Line as a "feeling of emotional isolation." The square usually represents a period of confinement and recovery. This person is likely to have been withdrawn and secluded during the time period indicated by the square. This type will have nursed their emotional wounds very privately.

Triangles

Triangles are not often found on the Heart Line, but since they are indicative of creative talent, we can assume that the talent they represent is of an emotional nature. Acting would be a likely outlet for this kind of talent, but there are many other forms of creative self-expression that a triangle might represent. It is helpful to ask the profession in order to interpret the triangle's affects according to that person's work. Remember, as a palmist, you are not required to know all. If the person's profession is not apparent, you need not apologize for being unable to discern it. Sometimes a person is talented at one thing, and is in a profession which has nothing to do with that talent.

Xs

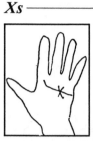

An X on the Heart Line is a very serious marking. It shows a drastic interruption of the circulatory functions. Since an X is indicative of shock when it is found on the Heart Line, we can deduce that the heart has been the recipient of the shock. This marking is often seen in the hands of people who have had heart attacks or those who have suffered a tremendous upheaval in the circulatory system. When the X is very faint toward the end of the Heart Line, it shows a proclivity for this kind of problem and should be guarded against very closely. With an X at the beginning of the Heart Line, ask the person about surgery to the heart or other illnesses to major arteries which may have occurred during childhood. Faint X's on the beginning of the Heart Line are traumas whose importance has faded over the years. Always cross-reference any X's found on the Heart Line with the Life Line for verification of their importance. A very red X on a Heart Line which is also deep, will very likely represent open-heart surgery. X's often appear on the Heart and Life Lines after surgery. The more red looking the X, the more recent the surgery. A string of X's which run faintly along the Heart Line indicate persistent allergies. When found under the ring finger these X's mean asthma, or if blue in color, bronchitis. This is especially likely when accompanied by small dots on the Heart Line.

Breaks

Breaks on the Heart Line are considered serious markings. They show an interruption of the circulation which could be close to fatal. The Heart Line must continue strongly after the break for the person to be out of danger. A break could indicate a severely restricted artery, but this condition will also be accompanied by a line that crosses the Heart Line deeply, appearing to cut the line, or look like an X. The break in the Heart Line represents a time when the heart ceased to beat, either due to an emotional upheaval, or to an impediment that endangered the person. If there is a Sister Line accompanying the break, it shows the circulation was indeed interrupted, but that it has been successfully re-routed. A blood clot or heart murmur would typify this type of heart irregularity.

Alterations in the emotional life of the individual are likely to follow suit. When the Heart Line resumes strongly after a break and the line appears to have strengthened or changed its course, the person's attitude will also have changed greatly. If a Heart Line that looks weak breaks, and then becomes deeper and clearer after the break, it shows a devoted effort to improve the health of the heart and circulatory system through exercise and diet.

Bars

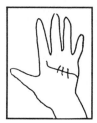

Bars on the Heart Line that appear to have cut it represent serious impediments to the heart action and the circulation. This person is likely to have had some form of heart disease.

Fraying

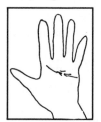

Any fraying found on the Heart Line tells of poor health habits that impede the strength and regularity of the heart's action. This fraying also suggests that the blood is likely to be polluted with toxins. This marking is often seen in the hands of heavy smokers. People with frayed Heart Lines are also prone to allergies and skin eruptions, and their stamina is likely to be of short duration.

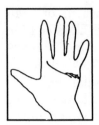

Fraying at the end of the Heart Line is traditionally read as affections that pour out to others,
and is read as generosity and warmth.

Splits

Splits in the Heart Line would indicate a diver-
sion of the circulation but without significant
damage to the heart, unless the line is completely
broken. Note where the splits extend for a clue to
the part of the body which was affected by this
misplaced heart energy.

Color

The color of the Heart Line is very important, whether accompanied by any of these markings or not. If the line is pink, it shows a
good supply of blood and a healthy circulation. If the Heart Line
is red it shows too vigorous a circulation, and heart action that is
overactive. These people are likely to hemorrhage profusely, and
are also liable to high blood pressure. They will also be temperamental and argumentative and have more energy than they know
what to do with. When the Heart Line is pale it shows the opposite, and indicates poor nutrition, poor circulation and someone
who fatigues very quickly.

Depth

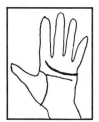

When the Heart Line is deep, it shows strong heart action, and a demonstrative love nature. These people, however, can be a little too ardent in expressing their affections, and are likely to appear domineering and aggressive.

A shallow Heart Line should be closely watched, as it indicates a delicate heart action, and the emotions will be that way as well. This person will be susceptible to infections and other blood problems, and is likely to be lacking in enthusiasm and physical stamina.

Other Heart Line Characteristics

If the Heart Line is set very low in the hand, it is traditionally read as if the Head Line were pulling the Heart Line toward it. The heart action and emotions will be greatly influenced by the individual's mind. In this case, the mind rules over the heart, and the circulatory system may be affected by stress and other events which tax the mind. These people tend to be afflicted by psychosomatic illnesses.

If the Heart Line should begin with a fork that extends to both the Saturn and Jupiter fingers, it shows a balanced approach to love matters. These people have both the idealism of Jupiter and the discipline of Saturn, which keeps them from being carried away by emotions. They know the meaning of give and take, and are fair in matters of the heart. Domestic harmony is important, and they will make compromises to achieve it. This influence of Saturn impels them to search very deeply for a meaningful form of love.

A triple-pronged fork indicates a dynamic emotional nature. A sense of drama accompanies the affections. The deepest of these three prongs will show the avenue of expression most favored by the person. Note the mount under which the deepest prong of the fork is found.

The curving Heart Line shows a need to act out and express what is felt. This person will be demonstrative and enthusiastic by nature.

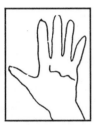

If the Heart Line is wavy, it shows one who is inconsistent in love matters and one who is also subject to irregular circulation. This person is likely to be unsatisfied with routine, somewhat unpredictable, and fickle.

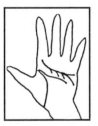

Descending branches from the Heart Line show disappointments to the affections, and how far they fall from the line will tell how far the spirits fell at the time. Rising lines show an uplifting of the spirits in relation to the emotions.

Chaining on the Heart Line is also a serious marking. Physically speaking, it shows a very inconsistent heart action, and susceptibility to heart and circulatory problems of all descriptions. But beyond this, a chained Heart Line shows a person whose very heart is subject to physical disturbances whenever the emotional life is put under stress. These people are emotional in the extreme, easily excited and easily swayed.

Comparing the Heart Line in Both Hands

If I were to see a healthy Heart Line in the hand which represents the past, and one with a break which represents the present, my counseling would be as follows: "Your heart, Sir, was very strong and healthy as a youth, but neglect and poor health habits have weakened its good health as of now. This condition has created a liability for heart ailments. Typical ailments for this kind of marking may surface in the form of poor circulation, or you may be prone to infection, colitis or hemorrhoids. If this neglect of your heart continues, you may overtax it enough to run the risk of an actual heart condition, or even a heart attack much later on. Do not assume that I am suggesting this terrible thing will befall you, but remember that your heart is your friend, and you should pay more attention to keeping it healthy. Ten minutes of aerobic exercise each day will strengthen your heart and circulation. Try eating less red meat and foods which are high in cholesterol. Quit smoking and increase your intake of green vegetables. Try to be more conscientious about your heart, sir. It is the only heart you have, and it has always been good to you. Also, remember that your heart is what you love with, and if you damage your heart, you will inadvertently damage your ability to love and receive love as well."

Always try to make your advice as inviting and as agreeable as possible. Never condescend. Remember, you are not a doctor. As a palmist, you are an observer, and your love of good health and good health habits is what motivates you. If the person feels he or she is under attack from your advice, or by your tone of voice, he or she will run to the nearest cigarette, and despise your advice with every breath. Remember that your client is listening attentively, and wants to hear the positive things most. The client doesn't want to be scolded or reprimanded, and doesn't want to be treated impersonally either. If you want your advice to be well received, you must be willing to send it out with a little sugar-coating from time to time.

When a defect is discovered on a line in one hand, and the marking is repeated in the other hand, the health danger is more certain. In this case, the palmist's advice should be more direct and must now counsel the person as to the gravity of the health problem. Explain that you are going to be frank. Your counsel, in this instance, must be firm if you are to protect your client from any imminent health dangers. Observe fig. 10 on p. 151. In situations like this, it is your duty to be very serious and specific.

A large red X found on the heart line in both hands radically disrupts a Heart Line and is a serious marking. It is quite likely that the client has already experienced some kind of heart ailment in the past, and with the marking resurfacing in the hand which represents the present and future trends, it is likely that this problem will continue. Ask the client about the heart history to verify your assessment. Tactfully explain that you are using the classical methods of palmistry when explaining these markings. Inform the person that it is time to take action against this problem in a decisive way. In this case, the chances of a recurring heart condition are rather high. Suggest that a complete change of diet and a carefully planned exercise plan prescribed by a doctor should be followed to the letter. Explain to this person that the heart organ is in a delicate state. He or she will verify the condition, as markings such as these are not likely to be found unless the person has had a brush with death as a result of a heart malfunction. Take the time to explain that each of us is the captain of our own ship, and that safe, careful sailing is the captain's business. One of the greatest gifts we palmists have is our ability to use metaphors and allegories to deliver our messages gently.

The client will then be anxious to know what the solution is, and glad to discover that there are things which can be done. Advise the person that good health habits take time to cultivate but pay off in the long run. Have good medical and alternative health sources for your client. Emphasis should be placed on finding the way back to good health before the heart condition weakens any further. Palmists must be conscientious about the way they deliver their information. If the doctor has been unsuccessful in steering the client toward the road to better health, suggest the client change doctors. A person with severe markings such as these must be told that the condition is a serious one.

The study of palmistry is the study of humans, and one must be dedicated to these humans if one is to seriously pursue the subject of palmistry at all. If your client has a stiff or a hard hand, he or she is not going to receive this information too readily. Therefore a palmist must use strategy before giving advice. One approach would be to tell the person, "Yes, I have the solution to your problem, but you are not going to want it." Curiosity will render the person anxious to receive this information, but you must wait to be asked for it. "Try me," the person says. At this point, the palmist can let go of the advice, and be assured that the person is listening closely to whatever is suggested. This is where the artistry of the palmist comes into play. And this is where the palmist has an advantage over a doctor. To the client, you represent an informed, non-condescending approach to better health. You are an alternative to the American Medical Association's bureaucratic point of view, and your observations are often more detailed and personalized. You are also less expensive than a doctor, and the client will be glad to have made your acquaintance. If necessary, recommend that the client go to a doctor when you note areas of the palm that are considered serious indicators of illness.

─────────── Heart Line Checklist ───────────

It would be helpful to memorize the following points and apply them one step at a time to any Heart Line you may be reading.

□ Note the depth and clarity of the Heart Line. A good Heart Line should be as deep as the Life Line with no breaks or impediments. It should not droop or have any portion of it drooping. It should make a graceful curving motion, beginning on or near the index finger and ending on the far end of the hand beneath the little finger.

□ Under which finger does the Heart Line begin?

□ Note the character of the Heart Line. Is it wavy in its course, does it have a variance of depth, is it too shallow or too straight?

□ Does the Heart Line have any forks or branches? Where are they found?

□ Does the Heart Line have any special markings? Which ones, where?

□ How does the Heart Line of one hand compare with that of the other?

The Head Line

Many things are revealed as we read the Head Line. Its depth and direction are important features, particularly when compared from one hand to another. When we look to the markings in the Head Line, much detail is provided regarding the condition of the skull, itself, and any injury or operation it may have sustained. In addition, markings to the Head Line can indicate periods in the person's life when concentration was improved or impeded.

We will now discuss common markings which may be seen on the Head Line. At times, other markings may be found which are not listed here, and you need to make deductions based on the condition of the line in the area *after* the marking to see if the Head Line re-emerges deep and straight, faint and wavy, or in some other fashion. Always look to the other hand and compare the two before venturing an opinion. If necessary, don't hesitate to ask the person what the difficulty may have been during a certain age (see figure 11 on page 152), and try to remember this uncommon marking for readings that you do for other people.

The Head Line is the third most important line in the hand. It is located just below the Heart Line, and runs horizontally across the upper third of the palm. The Head Line is an important feature for assessing character as it reveals the capacity to remember and concentrate. It also shows the manner in which the person thinks. Using the Head Line, we can assess the ability to study and retain information, and the ability to organize information and apply it logically. In addition to this, the Head Line reveals the condition of the skeletal head, and any injuries which may have befallen it. Markings found on the Head Line are read the same way as one would read any other line in the hand. The only difference is that these markings apply to the thinking faculties and the head area.

The Head Line is the "window of the mind." It indicates the nature of the mental talents and tells which qualities of the mind will operate in the person most strongly. The character of the line will disclose the strengths or weaknesses of the mind as well as its capacity for concentration. The deeper and clearer the Head Line is, the stronger are the powers of the mind. A strong Head Line would grant clarity of thought, concentration power, and a good memory. The length of the line shows the capacity for memory and logic. The depth of the Head Line shows the concentration ability. The straighter the line, the more fixed are the ideas, and the more unswerving are the convictions. The straightness of the line also shows the degree of practicality and common sense.

Be sure to note the Three Worlds of Palmistry when considering the Head Line, as well as the thumb and the fingertips. These will help correlate any findings which may be questionable on the Head Line. The thumb will tell of willpower, and willpower is an essential ingredient for success, regardless of how brilliant the person may be. If someone does not have sufficient willpower to bring ideas to fruition, a good Head Line will be of little use. The Head Line reveals:

Concentration ability;
Memory;
Logic faculties;
Mental vigor;
Independence or lack of it;
Attitude.

To judge the Head Line accurately note its beginning and ending, depth and clarity, markings (favorable or unfavorable), character, and compare the lines on both hands.

A good Head Line will be well-cut; as deeply marked as the rest of the major lines. It will be unwavering in depth or direction and will have no descending branches or other unfavorable markings. It is not a bad sign for the Head Line to slope gently toward the lower part of the hand, as long as it is not a drastic slope which plunges downward abruptly. The deeper the Head Line, the more the person is inclined to intellectual pursuits. Try to assess if the Head Line is deeper than the Heart Line. This will reveal whether the emotions, shown by the Heart Line, or the intellect, shown by the Head Line, are foremost in influencing behavior. These two lines should be equal in depth to have good balance between emotions and the mind.

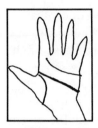

A Head Line which is deeper than the Heart Line shows that the mental world rules over the emotional. This individual is cool-headed in love matters and, if other areas of the hand agree, calculating. Logic will always rule over romance. A Head Line which is deep and well-cut and accompanied by a good thumb shows a person who is cool-headed and firm.

Depth variance of the line shows superficiality and a reduced ability to concentrate. Note the mount on which the depth becomes the most shallow and apply the defects of that mount to the general features of the Head Line.

A thin, narrow Head Line shows a clever mind but a lack of enthusiasm and staying power. The person is easily distracted and concentration is poor.

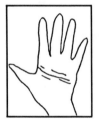

A broad and shallow Head Line shows one who is not firm, courageous or resolute. He will have a poor memory, a short attention span and poor concentration. It also indicates undisciplined thinking habits, a lack of determination, self-control and self-reliance. This person will be easily distracted and easily discouraged. A gently curving Head Line shows a flexible mind and a love of literature.

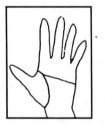

If the Head Line cuts a course straight across the hand, it indicates a person who has an imperturbable power of concentration and a good memory. This person will be good with facts and figures, and he will be very thorough in doing research. If the Head Line is too straight—stretching straight across the hand—it shows one who is rigid and dogmatic in thinking habits and one who is set in his or her ways. The person with this straight Head Line is very exacting, overly intellectual, and not apt to change.

A straight Head Line shows one whose ideas are fixed and unswerving. This is intensified by stiff fingers. In a bad hand, this marking shows an abundance of concentration power, which unfortunately is applied in a cold way. If it extends straight across the hand, the person is always calculating, rarely relaxes, and is inclined to exhibit a flagrant disregard for others.

The person with a straight Head Line will always do things "by the book," and is inclined to follow orders and procedures with the utmost attention.

If the Head Line wavers, it tells of inconsistency in the mental world. This is the opposite of the features mentioned above. This person has a hard time making decisions, and thinking habits are undisciplined, vacillating from one interest to another. The powers of concentration are easily distracted. A wavy Head Line shows someone whose moods are constantly changing. This person will have poor concentration and a wavering attention span. He or she is sensitive, indecisive, and unable to stick to a decision once it is made.

A Head Line that starts low in the hand shows a lack of self-confidence and self-reliance. This person depends heavily on others.

A deep dip in the Head Line shows periods of depression that last for the time indicated by the line's irregularity. If the Head Line dips at the end, it shows a moody, sensitive person who becomes gloomy and remote quite frequently. This marking indicates despondency, discouragement and a lack of self-confidence.

A chained Head Line shows a weakened mind with poor judgment and memory. These people should avoid emotional and academic pressure as their minds are easily taxed. They are scatterbrained, inconsistent, with a short attention span. They are easily deceived and misled. They are also fickle and flirtatious. They need a structured environment to sustain mental discipline.

The length of the Head Line is used by palmists as a gauge for assessing the ability to memorize things. It shows also the mental staying power.

A long Head Line would extend all the way across the hand and end under the Finger of Mercury. This suggests many interests, good aptitude for facts and figures and an excellent memory.

If the Head Line droops drastically or turns downward toward the wrist, it indicates someone whose imagination takes precedence over logical faculties. The unconscious world and the imagination will be favored—sometimes to the exclusion of the world of facts. Signs, symbols and fictional literature will be a powerful attraction.

When the Head Line droops very drastically to the lower part of the hand known as the Mount of Luna, it shows a person who can be completely carried away by the imagination, who is moody and easily depressed. This kind of depression is so all-engulfing and so deluding that traditional palmists call it the "mark of the suicidal." It also shows that the person is easily discouraged and inclined to be withdrawn and reclusive. These people are often preoccupied with the unseen world of their dreams, imagination, and spirituality, and they find the practical world of logical thought intolerable.

A Head Line ending on the Mount of Luna shows a fertile imagination and a talent for poetry. These people tend to be somewhat introverted and often lock themselves away from the harsher aspects of life through the world of their fantasies.

If the Head Line begins on the Plain of Mars (in the middle of the hand), it signifies a quarrelsome rebel. This person will start things with great enthusiasm and gradually lose interest. He or she is aggressive and frequently in trouble.

With the Head Line beginning on Jupiter, under the index finger, the person will be very ambitious, confident, self-reliant, and have a good capacity for leadership. With a strong clear Head Line, the person is diplomatic, magnetic, has good powers of concentration, is successful and would make an excellent politician.

If the Head Line ends under the Finger of Saturn, it is considered a short line. This person will have a one-track mind and will tend toward some form of specialized knowledge. The influence of Saturn, the planet of serious study, inclines to a study of deep or historical subjects without the distraction of more diversified interests.

A Head Line ending with an upturned hook under Mercury, the little finger, is traditionally read as a penny-pincher.

Depth variance on the Head Line indicates a reduced ability to concentrate. Note the mount on which the depth becomes the most shallow and apply the defects of that mount to the qualities of the Head Line in general.

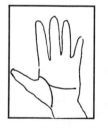

If the Head Line is connected to the Life Line at its beginning, it shows that the thoughts were not independent from the family's influence until the age indicated by the separation of those lines. This person's thoughts and thinking habits were overwhelmed by the prevailing attitudes of the family.

A Head Line joined to the Life Line and continuing in a connected fashion shows someone who is timid and conventional. Caution staggers the impulses. The person had a hard time separating from the home and mother. The home life is so absorbing that it is difficult to act independently in the outside world.

 A Head Line widely separating from the Life Line at its beginning indicates very independent, headstrong individuals. They act on their own initiative and have their own ideas. Self-reliant and sometimes pushy, they need long fingers to curb impulsiveness. They are so self-confident that it borders on conceit.

 If there is a wide separation between the Head and Life Lines, it shows a very independent thinker. This person was unique and different from his or her family from a very early age. This is the sign of the innovative thinker, one who is not inclined to be swayed by what others think.

A Head Line that separates widely from the Life Line, but is short and weak-looking, traditionally reads as jealousy and carelessness.

 A Head Line that appears in a hand with no Heart Line shows a person overwhelmed by the mind. The mental world rules without the benefit of the emotions to balance things out. This indicates a person who is very mental and who has a hard time opening up emotionally.

 If the Head Line and Heart Line are joined as one line, this is known traditionally as the "Simian Line," a medically recognized marking commonly found in the hands of mongoloids. It is not that rare a marking and does not always indicate an impaired mentality as severe as mongolism. It does indicate, however, that the person has difficulty separating the mental world from emotional impulses. Concentration powers are easily impaired when this person becomes emotionally upset, and it shows someone who lacks objectivity and is sentimental and emotional.

When the Head Line is joined to the Heart Line at its beginning, it indicates that the emotions interfere with the thinking ability and demand consideration. In this person, it is likely that the emotional realm will be more important than the mental realm.

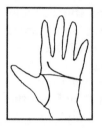

If the Head Line is connected to the Heart Line, the line which is deepest will show which line is most dominant. Traditionally, this is read as selfishness. This person's sentiments constantly overpower reasoning. This marking is often found in the hands of criminals who lose self-control and commit crimes of passion.

When the Head Line is forked at the ending, it reveals a fair-minded person who considers both sides of a situation before coming to a conclusion. This person is inclined to give the benefit of the doubt. An excellent marking for a judge, it shows a person who will weigh all the evidence carefully before drawing conclusions. This kind of fork shows an inventive mind and a bipartisan approach. A forked Head Line is also quite common among lawyers, since this person is likely to "split hairs." This ending for the Head Line shows an analytical mind and a very definite writing talent. In a bad hand, such as one with gnarled fingers, very short nails and coarse skin, the forked Head Line inclines the person to juggle facts and fib.

A three-pronged fork shows an extraordinary mental ability and indicates diversity of interests, adaptability and versatility.

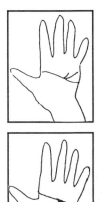

Splits which rise upward from the Head Line indicate aspirations and a desire to rise to a position of prominence in life.

Downward splits show despondency, a lack of mental vigor and severe discouragement.

Head Line Markings

The following is a list of traditional meanings for markings on the Head Line.

Islands

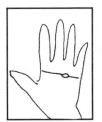

An island on the Head Line shows a period of time when the thoughts were weakened by confusion and indecision. It could signify a mental breakdown that lasted for the duration of time commensurable to the length of the island. Concentration was impossible during this period, and thoughts were plagued by a lack of clarity and an inability to make decisions. This is considered a debilitating marking that is likely to have caused mental imbalance.

If an island is found on the Head Line under the Finger of Apollo, I have found it to be connected with eye weakness. Nearly all the people I have found with this marking wore glasses or admitted a need for them. If this island is also accompanied by an X, the person has had some form of surgery to the eyes. If this X is very red-looking, the surgery was recent. If a dot is present in this area, it indicates an eye infection. The redder the dot, the more recent the problem.

Xs

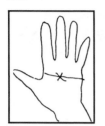

An X is traditionally read as a trauma to the skeletal head through a physical blow. If the X is placed slightly below the Head Line but still touching it, the injury occurred to the neck. This X marking may very well indicate a concussion, but if it is red in appearance, surgery to the head is likely. At the very least, an X indicates a shocking turn of events which devastates the conscious mind. It can also indicate facial surgery.

Squares

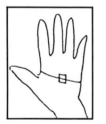

When squares appear on the Head Line they show a period of time where the thoughts were confined to a very specific task. During this time the person was apt to feel constricted, confined by or overwhelmed by commitments, deadlines, and obligations. The mental energy was contained in some way during this period and only surfaced within a prescribed framework. The length of time of this mental containment is proportional to the size of the square. A square may also be read as a repair sign if there are breaks or other unfavorable markings. The square may indicate a period of confinement—such as institutionalization for mental problems or hospitalization for repairs to the skeletal head itself. Check the Head Line's condition prior to the square very carefully before commenting on this feature as it is a relatively rare marking. A square on the Head Line also grants an enhanced ability to organize and concentrate. If it is read in conjunction with mental health problems (which will be verified by other places in the Head Line), the square will indicate the length of the recovery period by its relative size to the rest of the Head Line.

Stars

A star on the Head Line indicates a great shock to the skeletal head. Traditionally, the star on the Head Line is read as a gunshot wound or explosion that causes immense damage and sometimes death. This marking is often found in the hands of suicide victims, especially if the line droops.

A Head Line with a star ending on the Mount of Luna is not a good marking. This warns that the imagination can play tricks and fantasy gets mixed up with reality. Traditionally, this line is read as a suicide marking and is not to be taken lightly whenever it is found. It suggests a violent ending with great damage to the head or complete insanity.

If a star appears on the Head Line, in the area where it crosses the Health Line, it is traditionally read to mean prostate trouble or reproductive trouble in a man's hand. In a woman's hand, it shows difficulty with childbirth or pregnancy.

Grills

When grills are found on the Head Line, they show a person who worries incessantly. It is a sign of tremendous stress. Grills can signify grief or regrets that preoccupied the mind for a duration of time equivalent to the size of the grill.

Bars

When the Head Line is crossed by bars that appear to cut it at their crossing, thinking is impeded and concentration is thwarted. This person will have a tendency to fret. If these bars form a series of X's, they indicate recurrent headaches. If these X's are very deep, migraines are indicated. A single bar that cuts the Head Line indicates an interrupted education or shows circumstances that forced the person to postpone education in some way.

Breaks

Anything that interrupts the Head Line shows interruptions in the thinking process as well. If a break is unaided by Sister Lines or repair signs, a coma or period of complete unconsciousness occurred. If the break has a repair sign, note the condition of the line following the break. This will give a clue as to how well the person recovered.

If the Head Line is broken, look very carefully for repair signs. Squares around the broken areas or Sister Lines which reconnect the Head Line are two repair signs. A break in the Head Line is very significant because it shows a disruption of the concentration. A break here could indicate a devastating trauma that impeded the person's thinking faculties. If the break is accompanied by an X, a severe blow to the head is likely to have been the cause. This kind of marking is traditionally read as a concussion. Breaks indicate outside circumstances that cause a complete change of attitude.

A radical change of environment, such as moving to a foreign country and having to speak a different language may also cause a break in the Head Line, providing there are no other signs of ill health in the hand. This person would have had difficulty learning a new language and would have felt completely cut off from the rest of the environment. Check the Life Line to verify this.

Anything that disrupts the continuity of a line in the hand is a powerful event which greatly changed that person for the duration indicated by the length and depth of the marking.

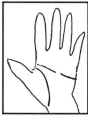 If the Head Line is deep and clear after the break, the person has recovered very well from this trauma, and was able to regain the mental powers which were disrupted by the break.

 If the Head Line wavers after a break it shows that the person never fully regained the power of concentration and clarity of thought. This interpretation will also apply if the line is shallow when it resumes after the break.

—————————— Head Line Checklist ——————————

Test your own Head Line with this checklist of characteristics.

□ Is the line deep or shallow or variable in depth? If it varies, on what mount?

□ Does the line waver in its course through the hand?

□ Does the Head Line have any unfavorable markings? Where, on which mount?

□ Where does the Head Line begin? (Which mount?)

□ Where does the Head Line end? On which mount, under which finger?

□ Is the Head Line connected to the Heart Line?

□ Is the Head Line connected to the Life Line?

□ How does the Head Line in the left hand compare to that on the right?

The Fate Line

The Fate Line or Saturn Line runs vertically up the middle of the palm, starting at the area of the wrist and traveling upward. It ends in the vicinity of the Saturn mount, just below the middle finger. For several reasons, modern palmists refer to this line as the career line rather than the Fate Line as the ancient palmists called it. The concept, fate, is a foreboding one. The term itself suggests effects that are predestined and cannot be altered, thus implying that we must follow what is written in the Fate Line or be contrary to the wishes of the gods.

The modern palmist sees the Fate Line as an index for professional skills. Therefore, it is not advisable to lord over clients wielding the concept of fate as if people have no alternatives. You should observe what your clients do best, and steer them to this purpose along the line of least resistance. It is important to avoid intimidating clients, therefore the term Fate Line should only be used in a metaphorical sense. Today we have the option of creating our own destiny. This option was not always available to clients of days gone by. Let us consider the term fate as describing the place where our creativity will flourish most easily.

It is important to take character into account before giving advice on career matters. Any advice given on the Fate Line should only begin after considering the Life, Heart, and Head Lines, the shape of the palm and length of the fingers. A good Fate Line will begin at the wrist and continue deeply, without any wavering or variance in depth, all the way to the Mount of Saturn. There should be no obstructions to the line such as cross lines, X's, or breaks. The influence of the Fate Line is Saturnian in nature. Duty and responsibility, the two primary features of Saturn, are certainly two of the most important ingredients for a successful career. Saturn also represents the ability for serious study and crystalization of ideas. The following list reviews the proper procedure for collecting information seen in the Fate Line. If you work with this sequence, you will get the most accurate interpretation possible.

1) Note the hand shape. If the present career is not discernible, ask what it is.

2) Note the length of the fingers to assess the measure of patience the person has.

3) Check the Life Line for the degree of vitality and stamina.

4) Examine the Heart Line to understand the emotional orientation.

5) Examine the Head Line to assess the capacity for study and memory.

6) Check the hand and fingers for overall flexibility.

7) Note where the Fate Line begins and ends.

8) Note the character of the Fate Line.

9) Compare the Fate Line of the left hand to that of the right.

When examining the hand shape, keep the preferred profession of the person in mind. You are trying to discern whether the hand shape is appropriate for the chosen profession. Let's consider a conic hand belonging to a person who would like to become a scientist. The conic hand is an advocate of beauty, music, and all forms of art. It is not especially appropriate for a hand shaped like this, with an artistic temperament, to pursue a career in a tedious, exacting profession such as a scientific career. The profession itself may not be suited for the temperament of the individual. The painstaking paperwork and detail would be a bother to the artistic hand. The conic hand would be more suited for an artistic environment, and it is the duty of the palmist to communicate this finding. A hand with a different shape — such as the philosophical hand — would be more appropriate for a career in the sciences, since the natural skepticism and affinity for tedious details would be an asset to the profession.

The finger lengths will disclose the capacity for patience. They offer a clue to the type of work habits a person has, and whether he or she is patient or hasty in methodology. Enthusiasm and perseverance are disclosed by checking the Life Line. A robust and energetic person would be less apt to want a desk job and more interested in outdoor jobs, such as a landscaper or carpenter. Such a person should not seek an occupation that denies an outlet for physical attributes. Examining the Life Line will also reveal the current health status, which is also important when considering an appropriate profession.

When examining the Head Line with the career in mind, note whether the line is strong and deep enough to withstand the stress and other demands required by the chosen profession. Does the Head Line suggest the good memory that would be necessary for someone who chooses to study medicine or law? As a palmist you are training your eye to make these kinds of observations. Your counsel may save your client a great deal of wasted effort when he or she could have been working more effectively at another occupation.

When examining the hand for flexibility, bend it backward from the wrist and test the bending ability of the fingers. This will be a method for measuring the person's enthusiasm as well as the tractability of the mind. Someone with stiff fingers will be out of step in a profession that requires a great deal of flexibility, such as the music business or advertising.

> Remember, the Fate Line is a reflection of the person's drive for achievement in the career world. Because this line is ruled by Saturn, the nature of its influence lends skepticism, caution, and restraint. An analytical ability, serious study, and methodical work habits are added to the disposition if the Fate Line is strong and clear. The Fate Line provides a valuable clue to the type of career that a person will choose. The character of the line, and the line ending are two important reference points not to be overlooked.

Now you are ready to examine the Fate Line itself. The deeper and straighter the Fate Line is, the more important it is to have a traditional career. If the Fate Line is shallow and disconnected looking, the person is not pressed to follow a traditional career pattern, but is more likely to work in many different jobs without serious commitment to any one specialized field.

When the Fate Line starts at the very bottom of the palm, near the wrists, and travels straight up the center of the palm to end on the Mount of Saturn, it is the best kind of Fate Line a person can have. A Fate Line in a hand such as this is referred to by traditional palmists as "a king's hand." It is the mark of a super-achiever who makes steady, unhampered progress, and achieves his or her aims in a scholarly fashion. This person became dedicated and self-confident at a very early age, and allowed nothing to interfere with his or her career goals. Success through personal effort is insured by this kind of Fate Line. Even if the person has no special career intentions, he or she will rise to the top of whatever profession chosen. This kind of Fate Line shows supreme dedication.

When the Fate Line begins high in the hand, it shows a person who was not inclined to choose a career until the late 20s. Early negative conditioning toward career in general may be the reason for this. The person will have to work hard to catch up with peers.

There are two traditional meanings to consider when the Fate Line begins on the Mount of Luna. The first is read as success due to the whim of the public. The imagination, a prominent attribute of Luna, plays an important role in the choice of career, and the person is likely to thrive on applause and recognition.

When the Fate Line starts on the Mount of Luna and continues on to the Mount of Saturn, it is traditionally read as success due to help from the opposite sex. This success is quite likely to be in the realm of the arts, where imagination is a most valuable asset.

Look to see where the Fate Line ends. If it should end on the Mount of Jupiter, you will know that ambition has a powerful influence upon the person, and he or she will be drawn to Jupiterian occupations. This individual will be exuberant, domineering, ambitious, lofty, proud, energetic and fond of challenge. There is a need to organize and to command in order to be at his or her best, and the occupation should include these opportunities. A person who possesses a Fate Line ending on Jupiter is quite likely to find a successful ending for career endeavors due to the beneficial influence that Jupiter adds. Traditionally, this Fate Line is read as representing achievement. When found on the hand of a woman, this marking indicates an ambitious career that reaches its goal. If it is found in combination with a strong, deep Marriage Line, and a deep unbroken Girdle of Venus, a fortunate marriage is indicated— financially as well as sexually. With a very square hand, and straight, pointed fingers, a professional clergyman is likely. Politicians are also inclined to have this ambitious marking.

If the Fate Line ends directly under the Saturn finger, the person is a very serious worker, drawn to Saturnian occupations, such as geology, mathematics, archeology, or any profession where history and serious study are required. The person will be meticulous and methodical, and works slowly and thoroughly to complete tasks. He or she does not lust after success, glory or recognition for achievements. This person is skeptical, philosophical, brooding, restrained, and would not be appropriate in professions where these characteristics would interfere with the work. It is important to point out the strong influences of Saturn in a hand like this, and the occupations that would best accompany the Saturnian talents. This kind of person will be unhappy in the wrong profession. If the Fate Line leans toward one of the other fingers rather than ending exactly in the middle of the Saturn mount, the career is likely to be colored by different planetary characteristics.

If the Fate Line extends to the Mount of Apollo, it is a very favorable marking to find. This ending for the Fate Line indicates a successful career in the arts. The person will have a mastery of acting, painting, music, writing, or any other art form that requires deep study and long-term dedication. The scholarly style of Saturn contributes discipline and seriousness to the brilliance of Apollo, the Sun. This person will find success through hard work and patience. In this hand, wisdom (Saturn) combines with talent (Apollo). The Apollo influence will bring luck as well as talent, but unfortunately, these people are in short supply! The Saturn influence will incline this person to pursue classical arts, such as Shakespearean acting, or the classical music of Beethoven or the texts of lost literature and ancient civilizations.

The Fate Line ending on the Mount of Mercury is a very uncommon marking to find. When finding such a line, the career should be oriented to all things Mercurial. Commerce, buying and selling, communications, the complex world of the stock market and the world of the "fast buck" is where these people will be most at home. If it is a straight, strong-looking Fate Line with a ray-like affect extending downward from the little finger, it signifies people who practice medicine. Nurses, midwives, and doctors nearly always have this marking. These people would also be appropriate for the communications field, where studying and deciphering are needed, or they can work with languages.

If the person has *no* Fate Line it should not alarm you. This person will have to work very hard to create a profession. There may be a struggle to decide on a career and secure it. It will not be easy to fit into a conventional career pattern, so this person will have to make a niche in a nontraditional format.

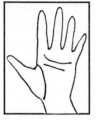

The hand with no Fate Line is not as difficult a hand as one with a broad and shallow-looking Fate Line, or a Fate Line with many cross lines or other lines that indicate obstacles. A self-made millionaire is often found with no Fate Line in one hand and a very deep or unusual looking Fate Line in the other. This is the over-achiever, driven by a fear of poverty and a disdain for the conventional career world. This individual goes out and takes the world by storm, inventing not only a career, but a whole industry to go along with it. Therefore, it is important not to jump to conclusions when finding a hand with either no Fate Line, or a very faint one. Consider the other lines in the hand carefully before venturing an opinion.

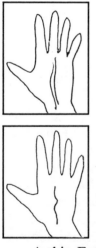

A double Fate Line is traditionally read as increased influence and importance in life or a second career that aids the first. It may also mean a hobby that turns into a career at a later date, or two careers practiced simultaneously. Note where each line begins and ends and on which mounts.

A wavy-looking Fate Line shows uncertainty about the career. Lack of persistence and lack of self-confidence are prominent. One who is carried along by haphazard circumstances and indecisiveness is the owner of this line. The person is plagued with doubt and prefers to work under the guidance of a superior.

A thin Fate Line shows that great exertion will be necessary for the fulfillment of the career aims. This person is easily discouraged, does not have much perseverance on the job, is not driven by a need for achievement, and is likely to have a short fuse. Check the Heart Line to see if the person is overly emotional to confirm this factor. Also check the Life Line to see if it would indicate physical stamina to counter this condition.

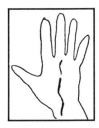

With the Fate Line uneven in depth, the person's career will be unreliable and changeable. This is traditionally read as intermittent prosperity.

A deep and clear Fate Line shows one with a prosperous career that achieves goals, particularly so if there are ascending lines.

When lines ascend upward from the Fate Line, it is a good marking that indicates achievement and recognition in relation to career. The person's career will benefit from offshoots that increase professional status and earning potential. The only problem with this marking is that the person may have too many interests and not enough time to pursue them. Traditionally, these lines are read as promotions.

With descending branches from the Fate Line it signifies that there have been many disappointments in the career and much wasted energy.

When the Fate Line is strong and deep up to the Heart Line and then stops, it indicates misfortune in love which causes one to lose a career. In a weak hand with a bad Heart Line, heart disease can prevent the career from continuing. An emotional event may happen which precludes a career.

A line from the Heart Line that cuts the Fate Line may indicate a physical heart problem that interfered with the career. This may also indicate an emotional block which hampers the career, such as stage-fright or a fear of height.

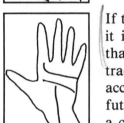

A line extending from the Head Line and cutting the Fate Line indicates difficulties that are the result of an error in judgment.

If the Fate Line stops abruptly at the Head Line, it is traditionally read as an error in judgment that causes a serious setback to career. Another traditional interpretation of this marking is an accident to the head, itself, which prevents a future career. Still another interpretation suggests a conscious decision to end the career abruptly. Check the other lines carefully to determine which interpretation works for the hand you are examining.

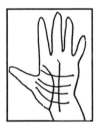

Lines that cross the Fate Line from the Mount of Venus and extend to Luna show family worries that impede the career. They indicate interference to the career by a loved one or family member, or taxing family obligations that alter the career. If the hand is otherwise favorably marked, this line can indicate a family business that becomes this individual's career.

Fate Line Markings

A well-marked Fate Line will include sister lines, squares, ascending lines or triangles.

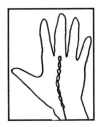

A chained Fate Line tells of difficulties in the career. Many setbacks render the person exasperated with the quest for achievement. This marking shows confusion and a lack of organization. Efforts may be thwarted by a lack of funds. Traditionally, it indicates a lack of career focus and/or a lack of dedication to one goal.

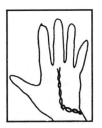

A chained Fate Line beginning on Luna is traditionally read as love for a married man. It also indicates a depletion of the career energy caused by imagination and fantasy. This person may have a talent for writing, but insufficient perseverance to finish projects. This marking shows a lack of staying power and one who is quickly discouraged from career aims. Somehow this person may be undermined by colleagues or insufficiently paid for his or her work.

Islands

An island on the Fate Line indicates a frustrating delay or setback to the career. It shows an event that prevented progress by dividing the energy, and postponing any promotions. Layoffs, company bankruptcy, failed business are all quite likely to be accompanied by this mark. It indicates a serious check to the finances, unless it is countered by a beneficial marking found elsewhere in the hand. An island here may also indicate that the career suffered as a result of a health condition acquired on the job. Be sure to check the other lines to reference this matter.

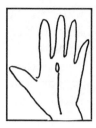

If the Fate Line ends with an island, it indicates financial difficulties in the latter part of life. Finances may be held in check by legal entanglements.

Xs

X's indicate specific events that impede the person's career. These X's represent devastating setbacks that are only overcome if the line continues strongly thereafter. If not, the reverses signified by the X have overcome the person and prevented career success. An X can indicate a shock that happened on the job, such as an accident, or even being shockingly dismissed for no reason. An X would indicate any event that drastically alters the direction of the career.

Grills

A grill on the Fate Line shows worries that affect career. It also indicates a gloomy attitude which permeates the disposition and robs the joy from whatever achievement attained. This person will not be pleasant to work with and will fret and worry over every detail of the job.

Crossbars

Crossbars on the Fate Line signify serious checks to the career. They threaten success and represent impediments. The depth of the crossbars shows the seriousness of their influences.

Breaks

Look for breaks in the Fate Line or any other markings that impede the line's continuity. Certainly, breaks are the most significant markings of all on the Fate Line. They show abrupt changes in the profession and changes in residence. The palmist can then assess at what age the break occurred and the results of that break. Details connected to the break itself will give further information regarding the surrounding circumstances. For example, if the Fate Line is plagued by bars that cut the Fate Line before it breaks, it indicates an outside obstacle that blocked the progress in the chosen profession. Each bar is an annoyance which interfered with promotions, and created setback after setback. The break following the bars indicates that at the time, the person broke with the profession entirely in direct response to these events. If the Fate Line resumes deeply after such a break, it is safe to assume that the person resumed this profession at a later time.

A star on the Fate Line followed by a break would mean a great shock or accident that made it impossible for the person to continue in that line of work. A chance line with an X that extends to the Fate Line and causes a small break in the line would indicate a dismissal from the job which came as an unexpected shock.

Breaks in the Fate Line are read as serious defects. They usually indicate a complete change in career. Also note the character of the line after these breaks to see how well the person recovered. A new outlook usually follows this change, especially if the Fate Line shifts course after the break. Any transition will be easier if the ends of these broken lines overlap.

With breaks in the Fate Line it is essential that both hands be examined carefully to ascertain whether these obstructions are the result of acquired habits, mistakes in calculation, or illness. Also, note carefully how the line resumes to see if the person overcame the obstacles successfully. Check the "sending hand" (the hand the person writes with to send information out), as this will show how the person is likely to handle these obstacles in the future.

Sister Lines

Sister Lines running alongside the Fate Line show aids to the career from outside influences. These lines operate to improve the career. They may also indicate outside interests from the career that contributed to success, such as a lucky break. These markings may also symbolize a hobby practiced in addition to the career. If the outside Sister Line is more prominent than the Fate Line itself, it shows a person whose hobby eventually becomes a career. The location of this Sister Line will give an indication at what age this took place. See fig. 11 on p. 152, which tells how to gauge time from the Fate Line.

When assessing the Fate Line, remember that the Finger and Mount of Saturn are also an important part of the study. A good Fate Line that ends on a defective Saturn Mount will have serious troubles, regardless of how fortunate the ascent to achievement might have been. A defective Finger of Saturn will also detract from the line's potential, and other more important positive markings must be present to compensate for it.

The following markings compensate for a defective Fate Line. They are mentioned in order of importance: a strong Life or Head Line; sister lines; triangles; ascending lines on the Fate Line itself; a strong Line of Apollo; the Fate Line very deeply marked and extending to either the Mount of Jupiter or Apollo.

Fate Line Checklist

Test your own Fate Line with this simple checklist:

□ Is the Fate Line deeply cut in the hand? How does it compare in depth to the rest of the lines in the hand?

□ Where does the Fate Line begin? (Which mount?) Where does it end?

▫ Does it have any outstanding defects? What kind? Is this true in both hands?

▫ Does the Fate Line have any assets, or other lines in the hands which will counter any defects the line may contain?

▫ What is the condition of the Saturn mount and finger? Do they add to or detract from the strength of the Fate Line?

▫ How does the Fate Line of one hand compare to that of the other?

The Minor Lines

In the previous pages we discussed the major lines. These are the Life, Head, Heart, and Fate Lines. There are also a few more lines on the hand which are important, but these lines are not as well-researched and documented by previous palmists as the major lines were. The Minor Lines are: The Mars Line, the Marriage Lines, the Children Lines, and the Health or Mercury Line. In addition to these, there are rings that may encircle a mount which are also considered quite noteworthy. These are: the Ring of Solomon, found encircling the Mount of Jupiter just below the index finger; the Ring of Saturn, found on the mount beneath the Saturn finger; the Ring of Apollo, found beneath the Apollo finger; and the Girdle of Venus, extending in a curving fashion beneath the fingers of Saturn and Apollo. Additional minor lines are the Via Lascium, the racettes, and the travel lines.

Health Line

The final chapter in this study will describe the Via Hepatica. This line is called the Health Line by modern palmists and is of inestimable value when used in conjunction with other lines to examine health and resistance to disease. There are several varieties of Health Lines that are found in the hand and each will give a clue to the stamina and the basic physical temperament of the person. Physical temperament refers to the durability of the constitution, proneness to certain kinds of illnesses, and determination to overcome illnesses.

When examining the Health Line, it is important to keep in mind the overall appearance of the rest of the hand, with an eye to the shape and color of the hand as well as the character of the rest of the lines. For example, if we are looking at a narrow, pale-looking hand with a tangle of hair-like major lines, we palmists already know that the constitution of this person is somewhat fragile and that he or she is susceptible to many nervous afflictions with poor recovery power. To confirm these observations, we look to the Health Line. It is important to remember that the Health Line itself is rarely capable of painting the whole picture. It is always viewed in conjunction with the other major lines as a sort of back-up system for health assessment.

The Health Line is located beneath the little finger, Mercury. It runs vertically and is read from the bottom up. It often begins in the vicinity of the wrist, but is commonly found beginning at the end of the Life Line or in the vicinity of the Fate Line. This can be confusing to the palmist since there are so many lines that converge in the middle of the lower palm. It is hard to separate all the lines and judge them from their individual points of origin. Therefore, the character of the Health Line is far more valuable than any other feature.

If there is no Health Line, there should be no cause for alarm. The traditional interpretation for this is quite simply that the person has never had any serious illnesses and that the constitution is healthy. The hand with no Health Line is usually accompanied by a thick, robust hand with few lines, all of which are deeply marked in the hand and possessing a pink hue. The palmist can safely conclude that this is the hand of a healthy person. This will also be the case if there is a deep, clear and unbroken Health Line extending from the wrist straight up to the little finger. It is quite likely that this person is either an athlete or is interested in health, nutrition and physical exercise.

The Health Line should not have interruptions such as bars, crosslines, breaks, or dots which impede its continuity. These markings will provide information about various illnesses that affect the constitution.

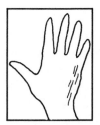

The broad and shallow Health Line is fairly common and indicates a delicate bronchial system. If the line is broken and twisted in addition to the broad and shallow appearance, it would show problems with the bronchial system such as bronchitis, asthma, and allergies. This is especially true if there are grills on the line which form a kind of cross-hatching. These indicate even greater severity of the condition, especially if the grills are located under the Finger of Mercury. The broad and shallow Health Line also indicates a delicate constitution that is highly susceptible to nervous ailments, which deplete the body of vitamins B and C, such as sinus allergies, yeast infections, stress, and improper digestion. These people are high-strung and not partial to crowds, heat, and loud noise.

If the Health Line is broken, look closely to see if there are any sister lines that run alongside the line to mend it. Note also, if there are any hair-like chance lines that run from the break to another part of the hand, as they indicate where the problem originated.

Lines that extend from other major lines and touch the Health Line are valuable markings to consider when attempting to unravel the cause of any major illness. A line that cuts the Life Line and extends to the Health Line, causing a bar or break, is certainly an indication of a major affliction which threatened the very life of the person. Note the condition of the Health Line after the bar or break to see how well the person recovered. If the Health Line looks shallow and wavy, it will indicate that the health was gravely affected and a long period of recovery was required. If the line continues deeply and unbroken, the person made a splendid recovery and the adversity only served to strengthen the constitution. If an X is seen on the Life Line with a chance line running from the X to the Health Line, the person is likely to have been in an accident or had a broken bone causing the health to falter.

A string of deeply marked little X's on the Health Line can indicate a person who is accident-prone. There will be a corresponding string of X's on the Life Line. If there is a string of X's that runs along the Head Line, and also appears to be affecting the Health Line, the person will suffer from migraines, the severity of which can be judged by the depth and redness of these X's.

If there are little dots on the Health Line which look like indentations in the skin, high fevers and infections are likely to be a recurring affliction.

Little bars that cut the Health Line are curious markings, indeed. These would indicate recurring impediments to the health that cause constant interruptions. For example, this might happen to a person who works with toxic paint over a period of years. The respiratory system would have trouble tolerating the paint, the painter would become sick from the exposure, would take time to recover, and would return to work again to face the inevitable consequences. Check the nails for vertical ribbing to see if this problem is indeed affecting the respiratory system. As a palmist, it is your duty to inform your client that this line of work is causing the health to suffer. Suggest a form of work that might be appropriate. One big X on the Health Line is likely to indicate major surgery if the other lines concur. This surgery would have been quite recent if the X is very red in color.

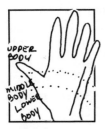

The Health Line is divided into three areas — upper, middle, and lower. Palmists used these divisions to differentiate between the upper, middle, and lower thirds of the body. Using this illustration as a guide, if the Health Line looks twisted, marred, or broken in one of these thirds while straightening and running consistently in the other two, we can surmise that the health problem was confined to one of these three locations. For example, if there are deep indentations that look like dots on the Health Line in the middle third, we can assume that the stomach and intestines are likely to have been inflamed with fever and infection. If the lower third is the area in question, the sexual organs, lower intestine, and legs will be the area affected.

Basically, the Health Line acts as a guide to the health assessments drawn from other areas in the hand. Very little conclusive research has been done on the Health Line when compared with the amount of research that was done for so many centuries on the Life Line, Head Line and Heart Line. As a palmist, it is important to ask questions when observing inconsistencies in the Health Line. Express your observations gently. This is important to remember. Any mistakes made when discussing health may be remembered for a long time to come.

The Girdle of Venus

The Girdle of Venus is located just above the Heart Line and extends in a curving fashion beneath the Finger of Saturn (the middle finger) and Apollo (the ring finger). The Girdle of Venus should begin between the Finger of Jupiter (the index finger) and Saturn (the middle finger), and it should end somewhere in the vicinity between the Finger of Apollo and Mercury (the pinky). See fig. 15 on page 220. It is not uncommon to find this line absent or broken in some hands. Its very presence indicates that the person has a healthy amount of desire for sexual gratification, and is fond of the sexual act.

This line is used as a gauge for assessing sexual compatibility. The deeper the line, the more inclined the person is for sexual activity. Its depth, clarity, and direction should all be taken into account before any conclusions are drawn. It is my opinion that no matter what the line looks like, one should not comment on the Girdle of Venus unless it is of dire necessity. It is certainly interesting to peek into the sexual nature of others, but it can be a dangerous endeavor to comment on what one actually finds there. Sex is a highly personal matter, and a very private matter for most individuals. Therefore, this area should be left alone unless it has

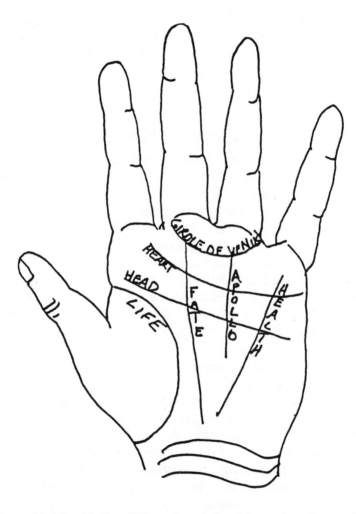

Figure 15. The Girdle of Venus in relationship to the other major lines.

direct bearing on the questions asked by that individual. There are far more important areas to observe in the human hand than the nature of a person's sexuality.

Always remember that the Girdle of Venus is not a major line, and it should only be read to confirm information surmised from the major lines. The Girdle of Venus should be considered a sister line to the Heart Line. Its presence enhances the ability to express and share love in the physical sense. The deeper the line is, the more demonstrative the person will be in love matters. If the Heart Line is weak-looking or shallow in any way, the Girdle of Venus acts as a support line and strengthens any debilities which may be found in the heart, its circulation, or in the person's emotional expression.

It is not uncommon to find this line broken, incomplete looking, or frayed. This would indicate that sexual self-expression was interrupted in some fashion. More often than not, this break in the line shows a break up of a relationship and a decrease in sexual activity.

If the line droops after the break, it shows disappointment from which the person suffered grievously.

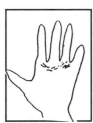

If the line frays after the break, it shows a frazzling of sexual energy and dissipation. The way the line resumes will indicate the way the person is likely to recover from this debility.

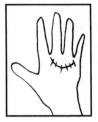

Crossbars on the line tell of obstacles in the love relationship. If the mate were involved in an extramarital affair, it may cause a block to the person's affections. Another obstacle would be an episode which caused an insurmountable rift between the person and the mate. In some cases, this cross line could indicate the death of the sex partner, preventing the person from ever loving again. Look carefully to see if the line which breaks the Girdle of Venus extends to the Heart Line on across the top of the hand and ends on the Marriage Line. If this should occur, the person was devastated by the loss of a mate.

An X on the Girdle of Venus would indicate a shocking circumstance causing a violent collapse of a relationship. Be sure to check the Heart Line and other areas of the hand for confirmation before commenting. Any kind of impediment to the Girdle of Venus suggests a block to sexuality; frigidity, or sexual reluctance is all too often the result. When the line is faint, the person is rather inexperienced in sexual matters, whether married or not. This person is naive and unconcerned with the gratification aspect of personal desire. It is not easy to express sexuality, because this person has never really been encouraged to do so.

When the Girdle of Venus is very deeply cut, it shows just the opposite. This person is highly sexed, and must be given a free rein to express sexually. This individual will need a great deal of sex to be happy. If the Girdle of Venus is the deepest line on the hand, the person will be adamant about getting as much sex as possible, and will border on the obsessive. He or she will play the dominant role in the sex act, and will be very demanding in sexual matters.

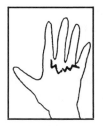

If the Girdle of Venus has a zig-zagging appearance, it is called a tortured line. (The same is true for any line on the hand which zig-zags.) The tortured Girdle of Venus is a very tragic marking, indeed, and sex will be unbearable or traumatic. This person will be torn with doubts about inadequacy and performance, and will constantly feel guilty for any sexual enjoyment he or she may find.

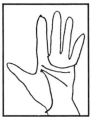

The direction of the Girdle of Venus is also important. If the line extends very tightly under the fingers of Saturn and Apollo, it signifies conservatism in sexual matters.

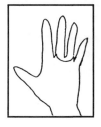

If the Girdle of Venus spreads out across the upper part of the mounts, reaching all the way across the hand, it shows one who is so liberal and outgoing about sexuality that he or she may be considered promiscuous. This person is not inhibited in any way about sexuality and is insatiable in the quest for love and affection. This looseness of attitude can make the person subject to anyone who flatters or entices. This person is also more likely to become exposed to venereal disease than other people.

If the Girdle of Venus remains connected, but droops down to touch the Heart Line, it reveals a very emotional person who has put great stress on the heart due to a disappointing relationship. Compulsive behavior, such as a bout with alcoholism, may follow the failure of a relationship with a person such as this.

The Girdle of Venus which extends properly across the hand, curving gracefully, with no breaks or unfavorable markings belongs to a lucky person indeed. This line shows one who expresses sexuality comfortably and naturally. Uninhibited and sexually active, this person enjoys both the sexual act and the sexual partner.

Remember, none of these findings on the Girdle of Venus are any of your business. You are peeking into the most private and sensitive part of a person's nature, and a haphazard comment here can cause a great deal of sadness. Remember that *no one* forgets the things you tell. Only venture a comment on this area if the person is suffering from depression, or other such matters whose cause stems from the Heart Line, and always make your comment in this area as constructive as possible. Such a person may not be able to recover the love life or the enthusiasm for good health unless properly counseled as to how to love again. No matter what you may see on this line, *always* look to the positive. Remember, when you are discussing the Girdle of Venus, the person's living, beating heart is right there in your hands.

Mars Line

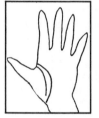

The Line of Mars is the most important of the minor lines as it acts as a sister line to the Life Line and adds strength and protection in regard to physical health. It is located on the Mount of Venus and runs down the mount, parallel to the Life Line. It will strengthen a weak Life Line considerably, and it is called a mark of preservation by traditional palmists. It shows an uncanny luck for avoiding injury, as if the person had a guardian angel looking after health and well-being. Should the person get into an accident, he or she might walk away without a scratch with this Line of Mars in the hand.

Should the health fail for any reason, this person is likely to make a startling recovery. The aid of Mars shows resilience and courage. This line increases stamina, and provides more energy and determination. It can also add the pig-headedness and quarrelsome tendencies of Mars. If these characteristics are already present, they will be doubly accentuated.

Another traditional explanation for the Mars line is that its presence in the hand signals the presence of a male ancestor who serves the person as a guide or guardian. This guardian rouses the person from unconsciousness to flee the burning wreckage, calls to the person in dreams to warn of disasters, and revives the heart very mysteriously when it ceases to beat. Whenever I find the Mars line, I consider it a fortunate marking for both the conscious and subconscious mind. I assume the constitution of the person is stronger than average. This is a very masculine influence, and it will increase the person's stamina and aggression.

Chance Lines

Chance Lines are found in all types of hands and are very confusing for the beginning palmist. What is meant by a Chance Line is any line or lines which are other than the major lines on the hand, the major lines being the Life, Head, Heart, Fate, Saturn, Apollo and Mercury Lines. Sometimes these Chance Lines are faintly marked and wind their way across the hand connecting one major line to another. Or they lead from a major line to a mount. In other cases, the whole hand is a complex tangle of these Chance Lines, giving the effect of a spider's web. In still other cases, the Chance Line leads from one mount to another, cutting through major lines to do so.

It has been my experience that prominent Chance Lines can reveal explicit details about traumas, prison, health setbacks, and personal details of every description. However, it takes a seasoned palmist to follow these spindly lines and interpret them with precision and accuracy. A whole volume could be written on Chance Lines, but enough information is available on the major lines and mounts that scrutiny of the Chance Lines is not entirely necessary. The basic information about the person is already in plain sight without driving yourself crazy trying to read each and every hairlike Chance Line!

A good palmist is working with both the technical skills of hand-reading, and psychic skills that emerge spontaneously as the palmist starts the reading. Although I speak sparingly of the psychic ability necessary if you are going to read a palm, I must acknowledge its presence, which becomes particularly evident when you begin to examine Chance Lines.

A good example of how revealing a Chance Line can be was found in the hands of an ex-convict named Robert, whom I read for one day. First, I saw a square on his Life Line—a square of such size that seven or eight years of confinement were indicated. As I looked further, I saw a deep Chance Line that extended from the ball of the thumb (the Mount of Venus) through the square. It turned sharply upward under the middle finger (the Finger of Saturn = duty, restriction, limitation). Somehow I knew this man had been to prison and I told him so. He admitted that he had been there."It was a woman [noting the Chance Line originating on the Mount of Venus] who put you there, wasn't it?" I asked. He replied, "Yes, lady, I raped her and I did time for it; now go on to something else." I looked up at him, and his eyes were blazing! So — reading Chance Lines can be helpful to reveal greater detail, but it is also sometimes chance-y for the reader to do this!

Marriage Line

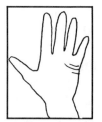

The Marriage Line is a line, or lines, located on the upper part of the percussion, just below the Finger of Mercury. It runs horizontally along the Mercury mount on the side of the hand. There is not much information regarding this line from traditional palmists, and from personal experience I find this line varies too much to make accurate assessments. However, the subject of marriage is one of the most frequently asked questions for a palmist, and it is important to at least have an outline for reading this line.

I always consider the Marriage Line as indicative of relationships, rather than actual formal marriages. Many people have deep lines in this location, but have never actually been married in the legal sense of the word. The line's presence indicates close relationship. Basically, the palmist is looking for a deep, well-marked line that extends toward the Line of Apollo without any breaks, stars, or drooping. This would indicate a long, healthy relationship that grows steadily, and has a positive affect on the person.

If there is more than one Marriage Line — and this is quite often found — it indicates several significant relationships that leave a lasting impression on the life. By reading the area from the bottom up, beginning at the Heart Line, we can judge the approximate age of the person at the time when each relationship occurred.

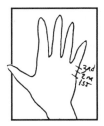

It will help to divide the area into thirds with the eye. Lines that occur on the first third of the area, the bottom third, signify an early relationship between age 15 and 25. The second third of the area represents age 25 to 45, and the final third represents age 45 and on.

If we find a Marriage Line in the first third that is very deep and droops down to touch the Heart Line, we can surmise that the person had a relationship that was very important at a rather young age, and which ended with an overwhelming disappointment.

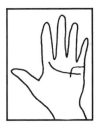

When a Marriage Line actually touches the Heart Line, it is considered very significant, as the heart organ, and the whole emotional structure was touched by this disappointment. The person with this marking is likely to feel discouraged and hurt by this event, and it is the palmist's job to encourage the person to get over this sadness and find the resilience to love again.

If there are several lines in this area and they do not droop, the person had several deep relationships at the age indicated, all of which left a lasting impression and touched him or her very deeply.

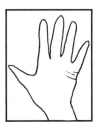

If the person is currently married, and has a rather shallow Marriage Line, we can deduce that the relationship is not an especially profound one, and that the partners keep their distance from one another. Although these two may be legally married, they may have different schedules which prevent them from spending much time together.

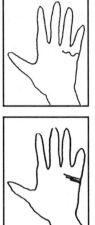

If the Marriage Line wavers, in addition to being shallow, the relationship will be non-committal, inconsistent, and fluctuating in nature.

The deeper the Marriage Line, the deeper are the feelings shared, and the longer lasting the relationship is likely to be. If the line is broken and then resumes its course again in a different direction, it suggests the relationship took the same course, ended, and then resumed again.

If the Marriage Line droops with a star or a cross upon it, there was a shocking end to the relationship, and it is very unlikely to resume again. A star on the Marriage Line is traditionally read as the untimely death of the spouse.

Children Lines

Lines that extend downward from the little finger and cross the Marriage Lines are traditionally read as Children Lines. Be very careful when commenting on these lines as the person may have had miscarriages or abortions which left a line on this area without producing an actual child. Traditionally, these lines are considered male offspring if they are crossing the Marriage Lines vertically and are deeply marked in the hand.

If they cross the Marriage Line in somewhat diagonal fashion, they are read as female offspring. The deeper the line, the older the child. If these lines are very faint, the person shows a potential for that number of offspring, but whether they actually produce them or not, remains to be seen.

These faint lines may also be seen in the hand of a person who has children, but who doesn't have direct contact with them.

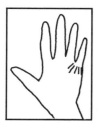 If there is a rayed-affect of lines extending downward from the Finger of Mercury, they are not considered Children Lines at all. This is a special marking known as Medical Stigmata. It indicates a talent for medicine and nursing, and an affiliation with the medical profession. It is quite likely to be found on the hands of doctors and nurses, and will always herald a compassion for the sick, a fondness for children, and a talent for healing and cheering others.

Compatibility

To analyze the compatibility of two individuals, it is important to study the emotional needs portrayed by the Heart Line of each party. People's emotional needs are clearly spelled out by the character, direction of, and markings found on the Heart Line. To properly analyze a hand for compatibility, the palmist is scanning the hand for specific information. The following list suggests areas of life that should be examined.

1) What is the nature of the person's self expression? To answer this question, look to the depth of the Heart Line and to its beginning. With this question in mind, we can assess if someone is shy, outgoing, excitable, fickle, able to talk about emotional matters or not.

2) What kind of intellectual stimulation does this person require? This can be assessed by examining the depth and length of the Heart Line. Check the hands of both partners to see if there is a similarity.

3) Examine the kind of recreation each person prefers and compare the needs of one person to the other. This can be done by examining the depth of all the lines, muscle tone and the flexibility. Check these areas for similarity.

4) Assess the person's professional needs. For example, a person who has gone to law school may not be happy marrying into a family whose occupation is farming, no matter what he or she may say about romantic attractions. It is very important to take the profession of each party into consideration when examining the

hands of two people for compatibility. A person from an academic background may feel deprived if intellectual needs are not met and maintained. The same goes for one who is physically oriented if he or she is matched for a lifetime with someone who prefers intellectual life over the physical.

C H A P T E R 12

How to Read Palms

So, now you're ready to read palms! The first thing to do is to take a look at the demeanor of your client. Is he nervous? Are his eyes darting around as he tries to evade your inquires? Does he stare at the floor, as if he feels guilty or remorseful? Does he look you straight in the eye, brave, honest and inquisitive? Is he flushed, appearing to hide embarrassing secrets, or is he deadly pale, assuming you'll see too much? Are his palms sweating—showing tension or high blood pressure? Is he wringing his hands—denoting that he is worried about something specific? Is he hiding his thumbs, showing anger to the point of violence, or is he concealing his pinkies, showing a liar, a cheat or a sexual deviate—someone who doesn't want you to know about him?

What is the overall hue of the hand? Red shows high blood pressure or aggression. Pink shows good circulation. Dead white denotes low blood pressure and poor stamina. Blue refers to a heart condition or colitis. Spotted indicates a proneness to heatstroke.

What is the general shape of the hand? A broad shape denotes one who is brave, bold and aggressive. A narrow hand belongs to one who is introspective. A pointed hand introduces one who is religious and sometimes scatterbrained. A round hand shows someone cheery and impulsive.

Notice the length of the fingers. Long fingers point to a patient person. Short fingers are found on the hasty and commanding person.

How are the fingers held? Tightly closed fingers belong to the secretive tightwad. Fingers spread widely show a curious and outgoing person. Fingers held with the thumb bending widely outward show someone generous, outgoing and a gambler. Fingers held with the thumb held tightly against the side of the hand indicate someone insecure, secretive, suspicious or cheap.

Notice the muscle tone of the hand. Is it firm, denoting good physical stamina and good circulation or is it flabby, indicating a lazy person or someone with poor stamina?

Are all of these features the same in both hands? Ascertain which hand the person writes with. Is this hand firmer, or unusually different than the other hand? If so, this shows how the client improved on the features bestowed at birth.

Look at the fingernails. Long nails show a patient person. Short nails show a hasty critical person. Ribbed nails indicate lung problems. Brittle nails indicate poor nutrition. Pink nails show good circulation. White nails portend anemia. Yellow nails suggest jaundice, hepatitis, excess nicotine or excess carotene. Blue nails denote a heart condition. Bitten nails indicate stress and impatience. Broad nails show boldness or patience. Narrow nails express a highly strung, suspicious nature. Round nails entail musical talent and a whimsical nature. Flaring nails — either at the top or bottom — show a person who is original and inventive. Nails that bend downward show a willful or domineering person.

Is any one finger more prominent than the others in length, width, posture or knuckle development? This will emphasize the features of that finger. How do these findings compare with the fingers of the other hand?

Do any of the fingers lean noticeably toward the other fingers? If so, they would lend their characteristics to the finger toward which they lean. Is this so in both hands?

Is any one finger joint longer or more pronounced than the others? Assess this using the Three Worlds of Palmistry. Is this so in both hands?

Are the fingers knotty, showing a fussy and skeptical nature, or smooth, indicating a person who is quick and intuitive. Is this true in all fingers or just one? Which one? Is this true in both hands?

Are any of the fingers gnarled or twisted on their axes? If so, this would bring out the worst qualities of the finger in question.

Identify the fingertip shapes. Are they consistent or do they differ with each finger? Is this true with the fingertips on both hands?

What kind of skin texture do you see? Fine texture denotes a love of luxury. Coarse texture indicates a rustic person. Glossy texture shows someone who is spoiled or pampered.

What kind of muscle tone does the overall hand possess? Press down on the mounts and observe how quickly the skin returns to its original position. The muscle tone indicates the state of the person's strength, endurance and recovery powers.

Ascertain the flexibility of the hand by bending the hand backward. Is the hand flexible, denoting mental and physical flexibility, dexterity and agility? Is the hand stiff, showing stubbornness, rigidity and an uncompromising nature? Is the hand overly flexible, indicating one who is easily led?

Now, look at the overall consistency of the lines in the hand. Is there an abundance of lines indicating a worry-wart or someone in poor health? Are there just a few simple, straight-forward, healthy lines?

Are the lines deep, showing someone who is healthy and determined? Or, are the lines shallow, showing someone with a superficial character and poor stamina? Is any one line noticeably deeper—indicating an emphasis of that line's qualities—or is that one line more shallow than the others—showing an absence of the qualities associated with that line? Is this so in both hands? Are any of the lines broken or otherwise unfavorably marked? Which ones?

Now you are ready to make your first detailed observation! Compare this broken or unfavorably marked line with the same line on the other hand. Are these markings prevalent in both hands? Are there any repair signs such as squares or sister lines present in the vicinity of the unfavorably marked lines? Verify your observations by checking to see if there are detrimental markings on only one line or are these markings repeated in the Life Line or other lines.

Are the lines weak-looking—pointing to inconsistent energy? Or are they tangled—indicating someone confused and complex? Are they marred by many crosslines showing impediments either by worry or the need to surmount physical obstacles? Are the lines zig-zagging, indicating torturous circumstances? Are they short, long, or curving? Do the lines begin and end in their appropriate places? Is this so in both hands? What does this tell you? Go on, make a deduction! Which line is deepest? Which line is weakest? What does this tell you? How do you inform the client without inflating or alarming him?

Is any one mount more prominent either by its development, by its red color, by its marking with unfavorable lines, or by deep lines running to it from the major palm lines? Which mount and in what manner? Is this mount colored (red, blue, white, yellow, spotted) differently than the others? Is this mount concave or convex in appearance? Is it marred by cross lines or other unfavorable markings? How does the same mount appear in the other hand? Does the mount in question have favorable markings — such as lines rising to it from a major line? This would add strength from that line's higher qualities. Does it sport triangles showing achievements; stars, showing a potential for fame; sister lines, showing added strength and adaptability? Look at the fingers. Are they stiff or flexible? Is any one finger more flexible, emphasizing the higher qualities of that finger? Which one? Is this true in both hands?

Examine the thumb. Is it short (brusque), or long (patient, a planner) in comparison to the size of the palm? Is the thumb broad, showing a fighter? Narrow — indicating less stamina; waist-shaped — indicating tact; overly thick — argumentative; supple — indicating someone innovative; flexible — an adaptable one; stiff — a pigheaded one? Is the thumb knotty — a planner; or smooth and intuitive? Does it have a red hue indicating someone hostile?

What kind of tip shape does it have? What kind of nail does it have? How far will it bend away from the rest of the palm?

Examine the ball of the thumb. Does it have a pink hue, exposing a healthy sex drive? Firm — allowing good stamina; pale and flabby — warning of someone not sexually inclined? Are these features true in both hands?

Well, there you have it. An ancient system for indexing the human personality — health, resistance to disease, stamina, likes and dislikes, talents, afflictions, and yes, even the love nature. Train your eyes wisely and make your comments with consideration. Remember always that no one forgets what the palm reader has said. Weigh your deductions in the order of the most prominent feature first, then the feature most dominant in both hands. Look at the hands from a distance, first to examine their gestures, overall shape, color, texture, length and width. Examine also, the character of the fingers, their tips and their nails. This sequence will tell you just about everything about the person. As you familiarize yourself with it your assessments will come very rapidly indeed. Above all, be kind and always bear in mind that there's another human on the other end of that hand.

Good Luck, Palmist, and Good Judgment,

Madame Jan La Roux

Appendix A
How to Make a Palm Print

1) Use block printing ink, a block printing roller, and a flat sheet of glass (glass from an old picture frame is suitable).

2) On a flat table, place a thin piece of foam rubber or a folded towel. A stack of clean, white typing paper should be close by.

3) Roll ink onto glass with roller. Use enough ink to spread evenly over the glass, keeping the roller evenly covered. The ink should be sticky and tacky, but not wet or runny.

4) Roll the ink onto a palm covering the entire palm evenly. Do not overlook the little hills and valleys between the fingers.

5) You will probably have to make several prints to obtain one that is crystal clear. Do not smudge the ink.

6) Place the paper over the foam rubber or towel and gently place the palm on the paper. The inked palm will adhere to the paper. Turn the palm over (paper goes with it) and very lightly run the fingers of the other hand over the areas which may not have picked up the ink. This means you are touching the reverse side of the paper. Work slowly, making sure that every square inch has ink, press very lightly so as not to smudge the ink.

7) Peel off the paper slowly and examine the print. The ink should be evenly distributed, not blotched or smudged. The print should read like a topographical map; darker areas are read as the highest peaks, lighter areas being the lowlands. Several prints should be made.

8) See figure 16 on page 238 for a sample of a good clean palm print.

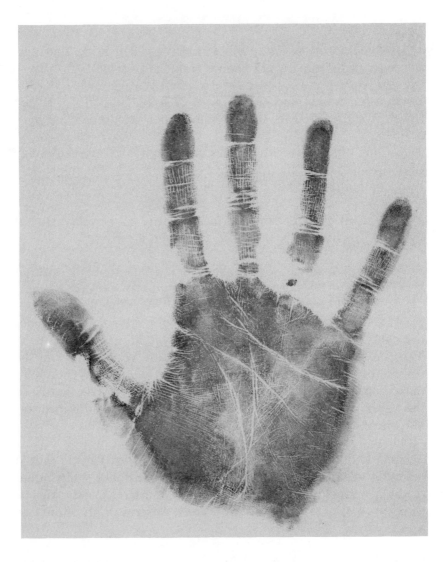

Figure 16. Sample of a completed palm print.

Appendix B
Reading the Palm Prints

Here are several samples of palm prints that might be used to train the eye to scan the palm for clues. It is very important to gauge the shape of a palm and any other predominant features at a glance. We cannot assess the color of the hand from a palm print, but we can learn other things of great significance.

Let us look at these prints and try to ascertain some facts about them. What is the shape of the palm itself? Square, round, broad, spatulate, narrow? Are the fingers long, average, or short? Are there any prominent features — such as one finger leaning noticeably toward any other, or any misshapen fingers? Is the thumb in keeping with the shape and length of the rest of the fingers? Are the lines deeply marked in the hand? Are there many lines or just a few? Does any one area of the hand overshadow the rest?

By answering these questions about a hand, a great deal of information can be obtained. The more detailed observations can be made later. By examining the hand in this preliminary fashion, generalized features of the personality can be identified. For example: square-handed people are analytical. They will be drawn to jobs where this manner of thinking can be put to use and will attempt to apply logic to whatever problems they come upon. A broad hand would tend to rely on physical strength and stamina, and would be more comfortable doing a job where these assets were employed. They will try and resolve problems through hard work and will tend to minimize the more tedious frailties they find present in others. A person with a narrow hand would be rather highly strung and detail-oriented. People with this hand would be more likely to specialize in one field and concentrate their efforts on perfecting details behind the scenes.

This first set of palm prints (fig. 17, 18, on pp. 242 and 243) belongs to me, and I am left-handed. First, note the shape of the palm itself. The overall look of it is fairly square but the left hand is more-so than the right. The fingers are long by comparison to the rest of the hand. The thumb is bending outward. The pinky is rather long and is set apart from the other fingers, stressing the need to communicate. This is particularly noticeable in the left hand, where it appears darker than the other fingers. The Heart Line is somewhat wavy. There is a double Fate Line in both hands, which suggests two professions. The Head Line is forked under Apollo, and tapering slightly downward. There is an island fairly early in the Head Line. The middle finger, Saturn, is very straight in shape with a very square tip. It leans, however, toward the index finger, indicating that the energy of Saturn—reason, logic, and deep study—is expended in a Jupiterian fashion—an outgoing extroverted manner.

The next print (fig. 19 on page 244) is a rare photostat with remarkable clarity. This photostat was made in a completely darkened room. Notice the shape of the palm, itself. Although the muscle tone gives this print a somewhat fuller appearance, I would still classify it as a narrow palm. This would incline the person to be rather specialized in his profession. A diligent researcher with an eye for detail is shown by the long fingers. This person is not afraid to put in long hours on the job (long fingers are a sign of patience). He prefers working alone (the middle finger bends toward the introverted side of the hand). This person greatly values privacy. He has a very deep, sloping Head Line, which suggests a good capacity for memory, strong imagination, but a tendency to suffer from melancholia and a need to get away from it all. He has an abundance of lines on his hand, suggesting a rather complex personality.

His Heart Line is very deep and well defined, curving nicely. This person has a tremendous capacity for love and affection, as well as a good sense of humor. He tends to keep his problems hidden and makes a real effort to face the world with a cheerful disposition. The beginning of this Heart Line is between the index and middle finger, showing a good balance between reason and ambition, rendering this person understanding, loyal, and durable in affairs of the heart. His thumb is waist-shaped, indicating tact. The Mount of Jupiter, the ball under the index finger, is very pronounced, bulging out in a fleshy pad. This shows a strong religious streak, ambition and courage. This is a risk-taker and a great lover of fine foods and wines. His fingertips are rather pointed, showing strong intuition. His pinky is rather square showing diplomacy, and a very organized manner of speaking.

The next hand (fig. 20, page 245) is very distinctive in appearance. Its overall posture suggests alertness and staying power. The equidistant spacing of the fingers suggests reliability and practicality. The fingers shoot from the palm in a straight-up fashion, but still appear rooted firmly to the rest of the hand. This person is independent and outgoing. The Life Line is deep and long, curving widely outward from the ball of the thumb. This shows good stamina, and resistance to illness. The outward curve of the Life Line shows a generous nature which improves itself and expands its horizons with age. The thumb is long and firm in appearance showing patience and perseverance. It bends widely outward from the palm, again showing generosity. The Head Line is long and forked, showing intelligence, a good memory, and a sense of fair play. There are ray-like extensions beneath the pinky, showing an instinct for healing, possible involvement with hospitals and the medical profession and a great love of children. There is a very pronounced Line of Mars running somewhat parallel to the Life Line, which is a further sign of durability and resilience. The general trend of the crosslines and minor lines is upward toward Apollo, the ring finger, and expanding outward toward the other fingers. This shows an artistic bent, a flair for decorating, a love of the beautiful and devotion to it; a patron of the arts.

The next print (fig. 21, page 246) belongs to a talented psychic who is currently engaged in a professional writing career. The prints that follow belong to her children. Notice how square the fingertips are on her index and middle finger. This woman is a real stickler for details and is meticulous about organizing them. She has really consolidated her ideas as shown by the square tips, and is working with a format which she is making a diligent effort to follow. With long fingers, she is patient and skeptical. The very pointed Apollo finger shows that her inspiration comes from very eclectic channels, and that she is inclined to work in a stream of consciousness style of writing once she gets started. Then she will go back later and edit, using the analytical side of her mind. (This is demonstrated by the square tip on the middle finger.)

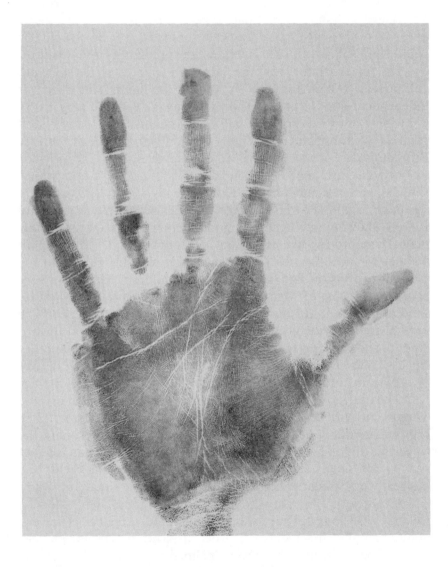

Figure 17. Left-hand palm print belonging to the author. Note the double Fate Line, which suggests two professions.

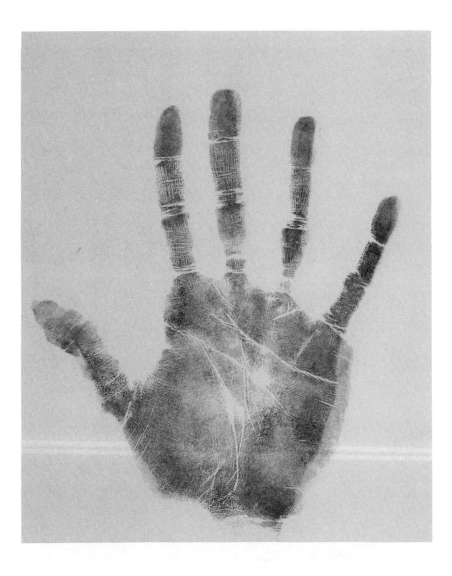

Figure 18. Author's hand. Note how the pinky is long and set apart from the other fingers, stressing the need to communicate. It is also much darker than the other fingers.

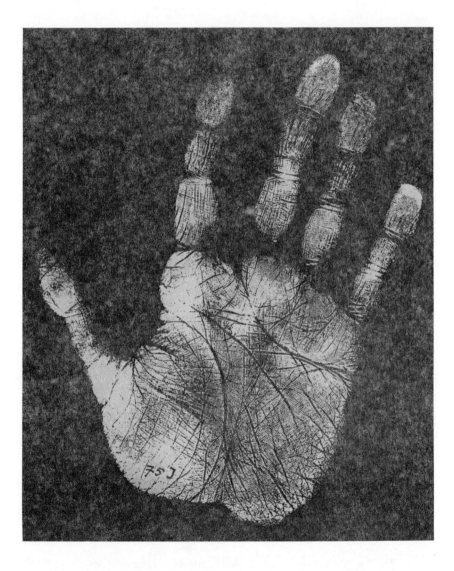

Figure 19. Photostat of a palm. The narrowness of the palm suggests that the person would be specialized in his profession.

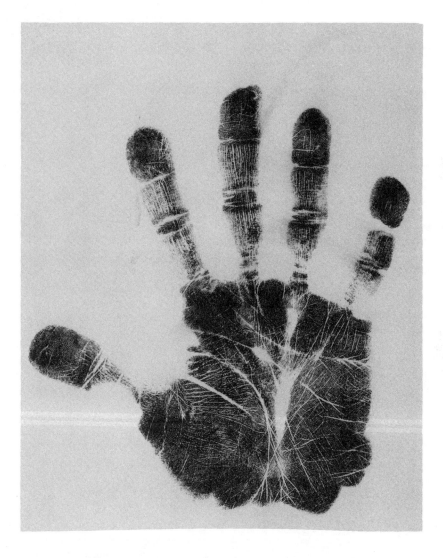

Figure 20. Palm print of an independent, outgoing person.

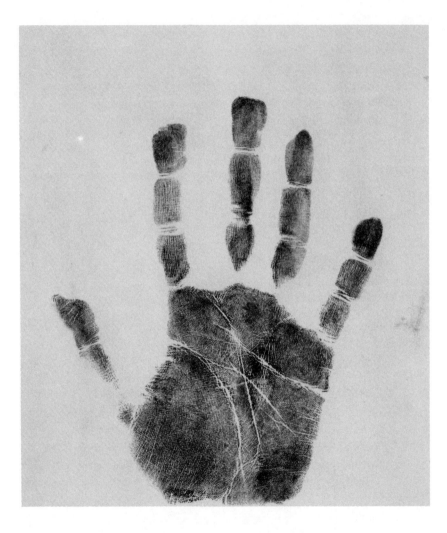

Figure 21. Palm print of a psychic. Her pointed Apollo finger shows that inspiration comes from eclectic channels.

Her Heart Line is chained, suggesting the presence of allergies and a sensitivity to pollution, smoke, or any other irritants. Her Fate Line doubles just above the Head Line suggesting her second career did not begin until after age 30. The Head Line also indicates a big change for the better after age 30 noted by the depth of the line and its upward branch. Also note how the line deepens after the branch. The Head Line wavers and is rather frail in appearance prior to this upward branch. This suggests uncertainty, a period of confusion, and enmeshment in family life (see how the line attaches itself to the Life Line for a long stretch).

The line gets stronger after the upward branch, suggesting a pointed effort to break free from family commitments in order to pursue her own unique way of viewing life. The Life Line deepens and becomes more solid-looking as it ages, suggesting that she will improve health and stamina as she ages. The middle finger is very straight and upright, suggesting a traditional person, a great love of history and a very serious and truthful personality.

The following series of prints (figs. 22 and 23 on pp. 248, 249) were taken of the daughter of a woman who writes fantasy books and who is psychic (see figure 21). Although the hands were smaller six years ago, when the first set was made, the curve of the index finger is unmistakable. The Head Line is noticeably forked and branching downward. There may be a problem with this child because her imagination is so great that it can play tricks on her. She may have trouble distinguishing fact from fantasy as her imagination so engulfs her that she would rather not know. The abundance of lines on the hand shows, once again, a very complex personality, with a great love of detail (long fingers, narrow palm). She has a proclivity for allergies, as shown by the chained Heart Line. Notice how the hand has changed as she matured. Her hand became much more square — more analytical. The pinky bends way out from the hand suggesting a great desire to communicate. Clearly this child has been inspired by the writing abilities of her mother and aspires to write, herself.

She has a lot of ambition as seen by the pronounced area under the index finger, but suffers from self-doubt (the abrupt sloping of the Head Line). The fingertips are all fairly pointed, showing strong intuition with a tendency to be a scatterbrain at times. The fingers separate much more widely in the most recent print. This is a very interesting development. It shows that the

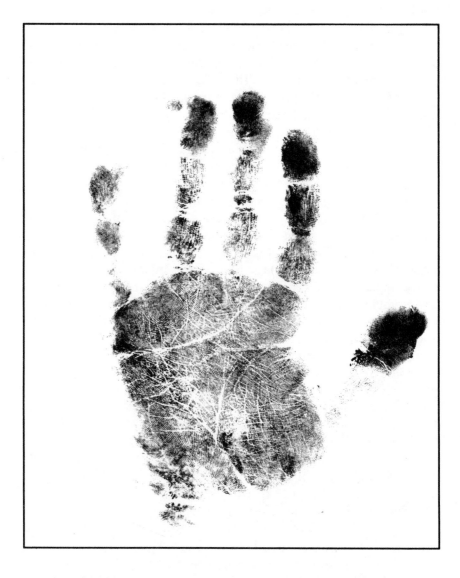

Figure 22. Palm prints of a young girl. Note the narrow palms and long fingers—suggesting a great love of detail. This is the left palm.

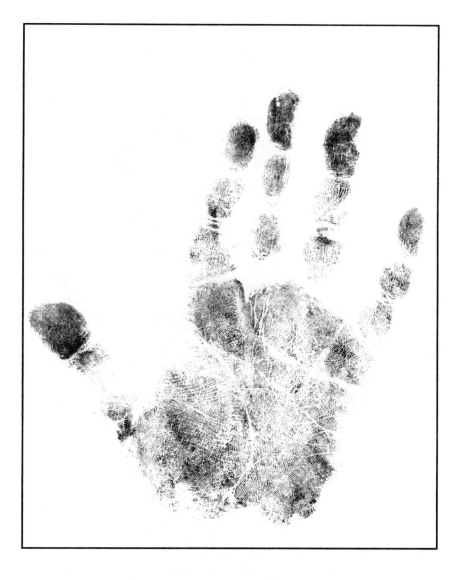

Figure 22 (Continued). This is the right palm.

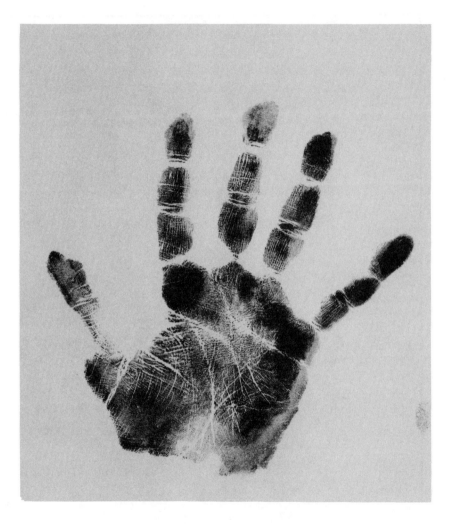

Figure 23. Palm print of the same girl taken six years later. Notice how the fingers separate much more widely than in the earlier print. This shows that the once shy, withdrawn girl has matured and become much more outgoing. Note also the similarity to her mother's hand (figure 21).

child was once very shy and withdrawn, but as she matured she became more outgoing and extroverted. Her self-confidence improved and talent for communication became her greatest asset. Her fingers are also much more pointed in the later print, showing a development of psychic abilities. Notice how long her Apollo finger is. This girl definitely has artistic talent.

Appendix C
Worksheets for Readings

Fill in the boxes with an L for left and an R for right. In the case where a marking is found on both hands, mark the box with an L/R. Use these charts when conducting a reading. The following is a guide to the symbols that I use.

$2\!\!\!/$ = Jupiter

h = Saturn

$\odot$ = Apollo

$\g;$ = Mercury

$\female$ = Venus

$\mathbb{D}$ = Luna

δ = Mars

$\delta-$ = Lower Mars

$\delta+$ = Upper Mars

GV = Girdle of Venus

HAND CHART*

LINE MARKINGS	♃	♄	☉	☿	Fate	Life	Heart	Girdle of Venus	Travel	Health	Head
Sister lines											
Forks											
Tassels											
Rising lines											
Descending lines											
Chains											
Breaks											
Square											
Star											
Crosses											
Dots											
Crossbars											
Triangles											
Islands											
Splits											
Starts high											
Weak											
Broad and shallow											
Overlapping											
Other											

*Fill in L (left) or R (right) or L/R when the markings are found on both hands.

LINES IN RELATION TO HAND TYPES	Psychic	Philosophical	Broad	Narrow	Conic	Spatulate	Square	Small	Large
Few lines, deep and well marked									
Few lines, deep and badly marked (especially with coarse skin)									
Few lines, fine and well marked									
Few lines, fine and badly marked									
Main lines deep other lines superficial									
Main lines and fine lines all equally superficial									
Many lines, all deeply marked									
Many lines, all deeply and badly marked									

TEXTURE (HAND TYPES)*	Psychic	Philosophical	Broad	Narrow	Conic	Spatulate	Square	Small	Large
Smooth									
Coarse									
Calloused									
Fine									
Varying									
Flexible									
Other									

*M = Mount, F = Finger. An example of how to mark this chart is as follows: L ⊙ M = Left Apollo Mount on a conic hand.

DEVELOPED MOUNTS	LEFT								RIGHT							
	♃	♄	☉	☽	♀	♂	GV	Other	♃	♄	☉	☽	♀	♂	GV	Other
Jupiter																
Saturn																
Apollo																
Mercury																

MOUNT MARKINGS	♃	♄	☉	☿	☽	♀	♂	♂+	♂−
Square									
Star									
Cross									
Dot									
Crossbar									
Deficient									
Developed									
Red									
White									
Yellow									
Coarse									
Smooth									
Other									

FINGER SHAPES	LEFT-HAND FINGERS				RIGHT-HAND FINGERS			
	♃	♄	☉	☿	♃	♄	☉	☿
Long								
Very long								
Long and thin								
Long and thick								
Long and spatulate								
Long and square								
Long and smooth								
Long and conic								
Long and two knots								
Long with top knot								
Long with bottom knot								
Long and bent								
Other								

FINGER SHAPES	LEFT-HAND FINGERS				RIGHT-HAND FINGERS			
	♃	♄	☉	☿	♃	♄	☉	☿
Short								
Very short								
Short and thin								
Short and thick								
Short and spatulate								
Short and square								
Short and smooth								
Short and conic								
Short with two knots								
Short with top knot								
Short with bottom knot								
Short and bent								
Other								

MOST DEVELOPED CHARACTERISTICS OF EACH FINGER	LEFT				RIGHT			
	♃	♄	☉	☿	♃	♄	☉	☿
Tip								
Mid								
Lower								
Long								
Thick								
Bent								
Short								
Calloused								
Stiff								
Flexible								
Knots								
Other								

KNOTS WITH FINGER SHAPES	TOP KNOT				BOTTOM KNOT				BOTH KNOTS			
	♃	♄	☉	☿	♃	♄	☉	☿	♃	♄	☉	☿
Square												
Spatulate												
Conic												
Pointed												

FINGERNAILS	LEFT				RIGHT			
	♃	♄	☉	☿	♃	♄	☉	☿
Square								
Spatulate								
Conic								
Pointed								
Short								
Ribbed								
Long								
Broad								
Other								

NAIL CONDITION	LEFT				RIGHT			
	♃	♄	☉	☿	♃	♄	☉	☿
Brittle								
Short								
Long								
White flecks								
Narrow								
Square								
Bulbous								
Bending downward								
Ribbed vertically								
Ribbed horizontally								
Other								

NAIL COLOR	LEFT FINGERS				RIGHT FINGERS			
	♃	♄	☉	☿	♃	♄	☉	☿
White								
Yellow								
Red								
Blue								
Pink								
Other								

FINGERTIP SHAPE	LEFT FINGERS				RIGHT FINGERS			
	♃	♄	☉	☿	♃	♄	☉	☿
Square								
Pointed								
Spatulate								
Conic								
Other								
Most emphasized tip								

TIP PRINTS	LEFT				RIGHT			
	♃	♄	☉	☿	♃	♄	☉	☿
Ulnar								
Radial								
Whorl								
Arch								

RINGS	LEFT (DEFINITION)	RIGHT (DEFINITION)
Ring of Solomon ♃		
Ring of Saturn ♄		
Ring of Apollo ☉		
Marriage Lines ☿		

QUADRANGLE MARS	OBSERVATIONS
Square	
Triangle	
Star	
Dot	
Island	
Red	
Cross	
Narrow	
Cross lines	
Other	

This chart can help organize the information found in the hands. When observing the palm, or palm print, check the appropriate box and list observations in larger boxes. Use ♂+ for "upper Mars" under the index finger. Use ♂- to indicate "lower Mars" under the pinky.

THE LIFE LINE

CHARACTERISTICS	L/R	DEFINITION
Deep		
Shallow		
Broken		
Starting on Mt. of Jupiter		
Starting on Mt. of Mars		
Starting on Mt. of Venus		
Starting with a fork		
Joined to Heart Line		
Other		
ENDINGS	L/R	DEFINITION
Ending on Venus		
Ending on Luna		
Ending on Fate Line		
Forked (where)		
Tassels		
With an X		
With a Star		
Descending Lines		
Other		

THE LIFE LINE

MARKINGS	L/R	LOCATION	DEFINITION
Islands			
Breaks			
Dots			
Cross lines			
Chained			
Splits			
X's			
Descending Lines			
Color			
Other			
No marking			
Line to Mt. of Jupiter			
Line to Head Line			
Line to Heart Line			
Rising Lines			
Triangles			
Squares			
Sister Lines			
Ascending Lines			
Other			

Location Column: These are indicators that show how the markings on the Life Line can be correlated with the mounts: ♃ = Jupiter (under the index finger); ♄ = Saturn (under the middle finger); ☉ = Apollo (under the ring finger); ☿ = Mercury (under the pinky); ♂ = Mars (triangles in the middle of the hand); ♀ = Venus (ball of the thumb); ☽ = Luna (outer side of palm, under pinky).

THE HEAD LINE

CHARACTERISTICS	L/R	DEFINITION
Running straight across hand		
Beginning on Mount of Jupiter		
With branch to Jupiter		
Ending under Mount of Saturn		
Long Head Line		
Drooping toward wrist		
Broken Head Line		
Wavering after a break		
Resuming deep and clear after break		
Drooping toward Mount of Luna		
Head Line connected to Life Line		
Widely separating from Life Line		
Other		

MARKINGS	L/R	LOCATION	DEFINITION
Island on Head Line			
An X on Head Line			
A square on Head Line			
Island under Mount of Apollo			
Grills on Head Line			
Breaks in Head Line			
Ending with a fork			
Bars on Head Line			
Head Line deeper than Heart Line			
Joined to Life Line			
Widely separating from Life Line			
Straight Head Line			
No Head Line			
Head Line joined to Heart Line			
Simian Line			
Head Line placed too low in hand			
Dip in Head Line			
Star on Head Line			

THE HEAD LINE

MARKINGS	L/R	LOCATION	DEFINITION
Star on Head Line at Health Line			
Broad and shallow Head Line			
Begins on Plain of Mars			
Begins under Jupiter finger			
Ends with upturned hook under Mercury			
Ends on Mount of Luna			
Ends with a star on Mount of Luna			
Depth variance on Head Line			
Wavy Head Line			
Chained Head Line			
Head Line with downward splits			
Other			

Location Column: These are indicators that show how the markings on the Head Line can be correlated with the mounts: ♃ = Jupiter (under the index finger); ♄ = Saturn (under the middle finger); ☉ = Apollo (under the ring finger); ☿ = Mercury (under the pinky); ♂ = Mars (triangles in the middle of the hand); ♀ = Venus (ball of the thumb); ☽ = Luna (outer side of palm, under pinky).

THE HEART LINE

CHARACTERISTICS	L/R	DEFINITION
Deep		
Shallow		
Broken		
Broad and Shallow		
Wavy		
Begins joined to Head Line		
Begins between Jupiter & Saturn fingers		
Begins on Mount of Jupiter		
Begins on Mount of Saturn		
Begins on Mount of Venus		
Begins on Mount of Mars		
Begins with Fork to Jupiter and Saturn		
Running straight across hand (non-curving)		
Double Heart Line		
Located high in the hand		
Beginning with an X		
No Heart Line		
Heart Line with no Head Line		
ENDINGS	L/R	DEFINITION
On the Mount of Saturn		
On the Mount of Apollo		
On the Mount of Mercury		
On the Mount of Luna		
On the Mount of Mars		
Ending with fork (note where each part ends)		
Frayed at end		
Other		

THE HEART LINE

MARKINGS	L/R	LOCATION	DEFINITION
Islands			
Dots			
Squares			
Triangles			
With an X			
With grills			
Frayed			
Chained			
With ascending lines			
With descending lines			
With cross lines which cut it			

Location Column: These are indicators that show how the markings on the Head Line can be correlated with the mounts: ♃ = Jupiter (under the index finger); ♄ = Saturn (under the middle finger); ☉ = Apollo (under the ring finger); ☿ = Mercury (under the pinky); ♂ = Mars (triangles in the middle of the hand); ♀ = Venus (ball of the thumb); ☽ = Luna (outer side of palm, under pinky).

THE FATE LINE

CHARACTERISTICS	L/R	DEFINITION
A good Fate Line (starts at wrist, ends on Mount of Saturn)		
Fate Line beginning high in hand		
Beginning of Mount of Luna		
Broad and shallow		
Fate Line with ascending branches		
Descending branches from Fate Line		
With an island		
A broken Fate Line		
A Fate Line with a break and a star		
A Fate Line Ending on Mount of Jupiter		
Ending on Mount of Saturn		
Ending on Mount of Apollo		
Ending on Mount of Mercury		
Starting on Mount of Luna		
A grill on Fate Line		
A wavy Fate Line		
Chained Fate Line		
Chained Fate Line beginning on Luna		
Sister Lines to the Fate Line		
An X on Fate Line		
Line from Head Line cutting Fate Line		
Line from Heart Line cutting Fate Line		
Fate Line ending with island		
Double Fate Line		
Crossbars on Fate Line		
Breaks in Fate Line		
Fate Line uneven in depth		
Fate Line stops at Head Line		
Horizontal Chance Lines cut the Fate Line		
Fate Line stops at Heart Line		
Other		

THE HEALTH LINE OR VIA HEPATICA

CHARACTERISTICS	L/R	DEFINITION
Broad and shallow Health Line		
Broken Health Line with a Sister Line		
Lines extending from Head Line to touch the Health Line		
String of X's on Health Line		
Little bars cutting Health Line		
Divisions of Health Line (upper, middle, lower)		
Other		

Index

accidents, 99, 153, 154
accountants, 34
actors, 44
aggressive, 6, 11, 60, 126, 169
allergies, 98, 175, 180, 181
ambition, 56, 73
analysis, 71
analytical, 40, 120
anemia, 13, 132
animals, 47
apex, 67, 86, 96
Apollo fingers, 50
    crooked, 102
    leans to Mercury finger, 102
    leans to Saturn, 102
    phalanges, 100
    second phalange, 100
    third phalange, 100
Apollo fingertips, 101
Apollo type, 39, 56, 94
Apollonian apex, 96
Apollonian fingernails, 100
Apollonian illnesses, 95
apoplexy, 75
appendicitis, 133
arch, 50
architects, 17
argumentative, 6
arthritis, 11
artistic ability, 31, 35, 43, 97
asthma, 98, 175, 180

bad hands, 11, 80, 85
bars, 200
beautician, 35
belligerent, 6

bile, 14, 86, 147
biological drives, 16
bladder, 107, 133, 134
blood, 166
blood circulation, 13
bone problems, 175
bowel trouble, 133
brash, 6
breaks, 149, 200, 202, 213
bricklayers, 17
broad-mindedness, 7
broken bone, 153
bronchial troubles, 121
bronchitis, 14, 95, 98, 180

career, 2
carpenter, 204
chained lines, 12, 133, 211
Chance Lines, 225, 226
chicken pox, 155
childbirth, 199
Children Lines, 215, 228
circles, 93, 98
circulation, 13, 166, 171, 178, 182, 221
    poor, 132, 134, 169, 170, 182
circulatory system, 94, 179, 180
cold love nature, 55
colitis, 13, 169
color, 1
coma, 200
compassion, 166
compatibility, 226, 227, 228, 229
composers, 129
computer technicians, 109
concentration, 189, 190

concussion, 154
crossbars, 93, 99, 112, 125, 143, 202, 213, 222
cuticle, 29

dancer, 35
dents, 12, 83
depth of lines, 4
depression, 192, 193
diabetes, 132, 133
diagnosticians, 112
digestive disorders, 106, 169, 178
dignity, 73
diplomatic, 63
dominance, 15
dots, 12, 73, 83, 90, 93, 133, 149, 153, 162, 178
draftsman, 31
dreams, 15

ears, 87
emphysema, 14
engineers, 17
explorer, 17
extravagant, 36
extroverted, 15
eyes, 94, 95, 96, 98, 99, 153, 175, 178, 197

Fate Line, 2, 83, 99, 161, 164, 202–215
  breaks, 213
  chained, 211
  crossbars, 212
  descending branches, 209
  double, 208
  grills, 212
  islands, 211, 212
  no, 207, 208
  sister lines, 214
  stars, 213
  wavy, 208
  x's, 212

female organs, 133
fever, 14, 95, 162, 219
fickleness, 173, 192
finger
  crooked, 69, 102
  index, 23, 30, 159, 166, 170, 173, 178
  leaning, 102
  lengths, 23, 33, 203
  little, 23, 166, 216
  middle, 23, 48, 171
  mounts, 67, 68
  of Apollo, 23, 69, 93, 100, 175, 178, 197, 214, 215, 219, 221
  of Jupiter, 23, 77, 80, 93, 219
  of Luna, 135
  of Mercury, 23, 109, 110, 131, 194, 227
  of Mercury, fingertips, 110
  of Saturn, 23, 54, 83, 84, 86, 88, 171, 175, 178, 194, 206, 215, 219
  of Saturn, crooked, 86
  of Saturn, straight, 10
  of Venus, 120
  ring, 23, 30, 50, 69, 93, 153, 175, 178, 219
fingernails, 13, 100, 121, 137
fingers, 16
  bent, 25, 110
  crooked, 86, 109
  flexible, 10, 138
  gnarled, 86
  held together, 30
  inflexible, 86
  knots, 40
  knotty, 19, 34, 41, 42, 71, 107, 120, 135
  knuckles, 40, 71
  lean, 35
  length, 2
  long, 33, 34, 35, 36, 71, 120, 135

separate widely, 30
separation, 26
short, 9, 35, 36, 38, 39, 44,
    70, 127, 133, 136
short, stubby, 11
smooth, 43, 53, 120, 135
stiff, 12
twisted, 25
twisted or gnarled, 12, 68,
    109, 110
fingertip
    flexibility, 23, 25
    prints, 49
    shapes, 23
fingertips, 45, 68, 71, 101, 122
    conic, 31, 35, 37, 43, 46,
        122, 137
    conic and pointed, 42
    Jupiter, 77
    long, 13
    pointed, 35, 37, 48, 111,
        122, 137
    spatulate, 10, 30, 31, 32,
        35, 42, 44, 47, 111, 122,
        138
    square, 13, 30, 31, 32, 34,
        35, 42, 44, 46, 47, 122,
        137
Fissue of Rolando, 141
food service industry, 32
fractures, 154
fraying, 149, 162, 163, 165, 221
frugality, 83

gambling, 47, 109
gastric problems, 87
geology, 19
Girdle of Venus, 2, 215, 219,
    221, 222, 223, 224
    crossbars, 222
    deep, 222
    frayed, 222
    x's, 222
gluttony, 78
good health, 11

gout, 75, 133, 175
grills, 12, 68, 73, 83, 90, 93, 98,
    99, 109, 112, 115, 117, 119,
    125, 133, 144, 199, 212
gunshots, 162

hand gestures, 7
hands
    blue, 12
    broad, 20
    conic, 19, 203
    flabby, 12, 42, 113
    flexibility, 1, 4, 37, 113,
        123, 203, 204
    four quadrants, 14
    good, 9, 10
    good and bad, 8
    hard, 122
    long and narrow, 20
    muscular, 127
    narrow, 17
    oval, 19
    pale, 12
    philosophical, 19
    psychic, 19
    receiving, 3, 4
    red cast, 11, 12
    right and left comparison,
        3
    sending, 3, 4
    spatulate, 17
    square, 17
    stiff, 113, 123
    yellow, 12
Head Line, 2, 39, 45, 73, 75,
    86, 105, 116, 121, 123, 131,
    134, 136, 142, 154, 155,
    157, 164, 174, 188–203,
    204, 210, 214
    bars, 200
    breaks, 200
    broad and shallow, 190
    chained, 192
    deep lines, 10, 189, 190,
        201

dips, 192
droops, 12, 192
forked, 196
good, 54
grills, 199
islands, 197
squares, 198
stars, 199
strong, 10
wavers, 191, 201
x's, 198
healers, 227
health, 5, 115, 143, 155, 163, 185, 186, 187
Health Line, 75, 86, 133, 134, 142, 144, 199, 215, 216, 217
    bars, 218
    broad and shallow, 217
    broken, 217
    divided, 218
    x's, 217, 218
heart, 2, 134, 166, 179
heart condition, 13
heart disease, 95
    open heart surgery, 180
Heart Line, 2, 73, 75, 86, 93, 96, 105, 109, 142, 147, 153, 157, 166, 169, 170, 171, 172, 173, 174, 175, 176, 178, 180, 181, 182, 183, 185, 195, 196, 202, 203, 208, 209, 219, 221, 222, 223, 224, 225, 227, 229
    bars, 181
    breaks, 180
    broken, 83, 91
    chained, 184
    color, 182
    curving, 184
    deep, 170, 183
    descending branches, 184
    droops, 12, 174
    faint, 169
    fraying, 14, 181, 182

    islands, 98
    red, 170
    shallow, 169, 183, 221
    splits, 182
    strong, 10
    triple-pronged fork, 184
    wavy, 184
hemorrhage, 182
hemorrhoids, 169
hepatitis, 14
high blood pressure, 170
horizontal lines, 68
horses, 47
hospital, 153
hypersensitive, 6
hypertension, 107

idealism, 31, 37
illness
    timing, 157, 162
imagination, 15
impetuous, 36, 37
improvisation, 103
impure blood, 75
independence, 189
index finger
    third phalange, 52, 93
indigestion, 75
inner world, 15
insane, 132
insolent, 132
instincts, 15
intellect, 15
intestinal disorders, 133, 219
introversion, 158
intuition, 15, 19
investigation, 71
islands, 83, 93, 133, 149, 161, 178, 197, 211, 212

jaundice, 14
jealous, 171, 195
jewelers, 20
Joint of Apollo, 108

joints, 71, 120
    flexible, 11
    knotty, 38, 47, 120
    stiff, 86
Jupiter finger, 76, 80
    phalanges, 78
    second phalange, 78
    third phalange, 78, 79
Jupiter fingernails, 79
Jupiterian apex, 75
Jupiterian illnesses, 75
Jupiterian type, 39, 56, 74
justice, 73

kidney weaknesses, 107, 132,
    133, 134, 153
kleptomaniacs, 11
Knot of Material Order, 41, 43
Knot of Mental Order, 41, 43
knuckles, 27, 28, 71

lacemakers, 20
landscaper, 204
languages, 107, 108
laziness, 121
leadership, 51, 56
legs, 219
level-headed, 20
Life Line, 2, 5, 73, 133, 142,
    144, 147, 153, 154, 155,
    156, 157, 158, 159, 160,
    161, 162, 164, 174, 194,
    195, 200, 202, 203, 204,
    208, 214, 216, 217, 218,
    219, 224
    breaks, 163
    free of breaks, 10
    wavering, 165
lines, 141, 144, 149
    blue, 147
    character, 143
    breaks in, 5, 12
    deep, 4, 10, 143, 144
    red, 147

shallow, 4, 12, 143
    straight, 144
    tangled, 143
    wavy, 144
    yellow, 147
linguists, 109, 129, 135
logic, 51
low blood pressure, 13
Lunar type, 39, 130, 132, 138
Lunarian fingernails, 137
Lunarian fingertips, 137
Lunarian illnesses, 133
lungs, 94, 96

mapmaker, 31
Marriage Line, 206, 215, 226,
    227, 228
Mars
    lower, aggression, 127
    Plain of, temper, 127
    upper, resistance, 127
Mars Line, 215, 224
Mars type, 39, 56, 125, 128
material world, 16
mathematics, 83
measles, 155
Medical Stigmata, 112, 229
memory, 189
menopause, 161
mental concentration, 2
mental health, 198
mental world, 16, 79, 135
Mercurian apex, 107
Mercurian deformities, 109
Mercurian illnesses, 106
Mercury, 48
Mercury fingers, 50, 107
    length, 108
    phalanges, 108, 109
Mercury Line, 215
Mercury type, 39, 56, 105
mind, 15
minor lines, 215
money, 16, 29
mongoloids, 195

mood swings, 170
moody, 20
Mount of Apollo, 10, 34, 87,
    93, 96, 97, 98, 107, 214
    red, 96
    white, 96
    yellow, 96
Mount of Jupiter, 11, 73, 76,
    147, 159, 171, 193, 206,
    214, 215
    grill, 14
Mount of Luna, 11, 34, 57,
    129, 130, 131, 132, 133,
    134, 136, 138, 160, 193,
    199, 205, 210
    color, 134
    deficient, 130
Mount of Mars, 125, 126, 127,
    159, 172, 193
    deficient, 127
    developed, 127
Mount of Mercury, 105, 111,
    125, 129, 176
    color, 107
    crossbars, 112
    grills, 112
    square on, 111
    star on, 112
    triangle on, 111
Mount of Pluto, 139
Mount of Saturn, 51, 54, 65,
    75, 83, 85, 86, 87, 201,
    205, 206, 214
    concave, 89
    flabby, 83
    red, 87
    white, 87
    yellow, 83, 87
Mount of Venus, 10, 12, 34, 51,
    52, 56, 65, 66, 88, 115,
    116, 158, 160, 172, 210,
    224, 226
    color, 119
    flabby, 122
    red, 115, 119

smooth, 117
mounts, 4, 65, 67, 223
    blue, 21
    flabby and white, 4
    flat, 12
    pink, 21
    red, 21
    well-developed, 11
    yellow, 21
mumps, 155
muscle tone, 1, 10, 138
musicians, 34

nails, 23, 110, 133, 176
    blue, 14
    brittle, 12, 14, 69, 137
    broad, 13, 110, 121, 137
    bulbous, 121
    defective, 69
    fluted, 121, 137
    hard, 122
    narrow, 13, 110, 121
    pink, 70
    red, 13
    short, 137
    square, 13
    white, 13
    yellow, 14, 86
nerves
    pinched, 13

openminded, 123
originality, 10, 31

painter, 35
palm, 15
    clarity, 1
    depth, 1
palm prints, 237
palm shapes, 17
passion, 39, 56, 115, 117
patience, 71
percussion, 15, 125, 127, 130
persistence

lack of, 54
personality, 15
phalange
    first, 28, 51, 113
    lower, 29
    middle, 29
    second, 28, 51
    seocnd, long, 31
    third, 29, 31, 51
    phalanges, 28
    philosophical, 40
    physical world, 16
    pickpockets, 11
    pigheaded, 37, 122
    pinkey, 11, 48, 50
    Plain of Mars, 125, 126, 127
    politician, 193, 206
    practical, 34
    pregnancy, 199
    pride, 73
    psychosomatic illness, 183
    punctual, 34

racettes, 215
radial loops, 50
reading palms, 231, 237
relationships, 226
religion, 73
repair person, 35
reproductive organs, 106
research, 83
residence, 157
respiratory problems, 14, 96, 175
restlessness, 31
rheumatism, 86, 133, 175, 178
Ring of Apollo, 215
Ring of Saturn, 215
Ring of Solomon, 215
rings, 73, 83, 90, 93, 97

salesmen, 109
Saturn, 48

Saturn finger length, 88, 173
Saturn fingertip, 89
Saturn finger phalanges, 89
Saturian apex, 87
Saturnian illnesses, 86, 87, 178
Saturnian type, 39, 56, 84, 85
sculptors, 17, 31
second knots, 42
self-assertion, 170
self-centered, 30
self-control, 116
selfish, 6, 34, 123
sex organs, 219
sexual guilt, 223
sexual nature, 2, 170, 219
Simian Line, 169, 195
sister lines, 149, 154, 165, 173, 181, 200, 214
skin
    coarse, 6
    fine, 6, 87
    pink cast, 10, 11
    red, 127
    texture, 2, 5, 79, 102, 122, 138
smokers, 14, 181
solitude, 19
squares, 73, 83, 93, 97, 111, 149, 153, 179, 198, 200
stamina, 1, 6, 13, 17, 157, 159, 176
    lack of, 126, 181
stars, 73, 93, 97, 125, 133, 162, 199, 213
stingy, 30, 36
stomach, 153, 219
strength of character, 10
strep throat, 155
surgery, 154, 180, 218
suspicious, 33, 34
sympathy, 115

tact, 51
tassels, 162
technician, 35

temper, 126
temperamental, 20
tented arch, 50
texture
    fine, 6
    medium, 6
Three Worlds of Palmistry, 16,
    23, 39, 47, 69, 76, 79, 108,
    133, 189
thumb, 3, 15, 38, 51, 113, 121
    ball of, 51, 88, 164
    broad, 59
    clubbed, 38
    color, 55
    conic tips, 57
    elementary, 59
    flat, 38
    flexible, 10, 54
    good, 52, 126
    knots, 60
    large, 53, 54, 121, 123, 136
    long, with square or spatu-
      late tip, 10
    pink, 54, 55
    pointed tip, 61, 136
    red, 55
    second phalange, 60, 61
    second phalange, coarse,
      62
    second phalange, flat, 62
    second phalange, long, 61
    second phalange, narrow,
      63
    second phalange, short, 62
    second phalange, slender,
      62
    short, 53, 88
    short tip, 38
    small, 19, 54
    spatulate, 11, 58
    square, 88
    square tip, 58, 61, 62
    stiff, 55
    strong, 35
    thin flat tip, 58

    tips, 57, 121
    weak, 52
    well-formed, 11
    white, 55
    yellow, 55
thyroid disorders, 106
tip shape, 29
tooth problems, 175
toxins, 55
travel lines, 215
triangles, 73, 83, 93, 111, 149,
    153, 179
trident, 73, 93, 97

ulnar loop, 49, 50

vainglorious, 74
varicose veins, 13, 169
venereal disease, 117
Venusian fingernails, 121
venusian type, 39, 116, 117,
    118
vertical lines, 68
Via Hepatica, 215
Via Lascium, 215
violence, 6, 11, 59
virus, 14
vitality, 2

watchmaker, 35
water, 131
whorl, 50, 51
will-phalange, 60, 62, 121
willpower, 15, 53, 60, 61, 113,
    121
wisdom, 83
writers, 109, 129

x's, 12, 73, 83, 90, 99, 149, 153,
    154, 155, 179, 180, 197,
    198, 200, 202, 212, 217,
    218, 228, 222
    blue, 180
    red, 180, 186, 197

Nils Vidstrand

Madame La Roux has spent 17 years as a gypsy reader in a caravan. This caravan is an actual living theatre that travels around California. She is currently pursuing a B. A. in literature at the Dominican College in San Rafael, California. La Roux also has other books up her sleeve. Since she works with tarot and astrology in addition to palmistry, she is presently writing *The Fool's Journey*, the story of Parsifal.